University of Limerick

This book is based on a research project commissioned by the Department of Enterprise and Employment and conducted by faculty at the Department of Personnel and Employment Relations, College of Business, University of Limerick.

Department of Personnel and Employment Relations
College of Business
University of Limerick

Irish Studies in Management

Editors:

W.K. Roche
Graduate School of Business
University College Dublin

David Givens
Oak Tree Press

Irish Studies in Management is a new series of texts and research-based monographs covering management and business studies. Published by Oak Tree Press in association with the Graduate School of Business at University College Dublin, the series aims to publish significant contributions to the study of management and business in Ireland, especially where they address issues of major relevance to Irish management in the context of international developments, particularly within the European Union. Mindful that most texts and studies in current use in Irish business education take little direct account of Irish or European conditions, the series seeks to make available to the specialist and general reader works of high quality which comprehend issues and concerns arising from the practice of management and business in Ireland. The series aims to cover subjects ranging from accountancy to marketing, industrial relations/ human resource management, international business, business ethics and economics. Studies of public policy and public affairs of relevance to business and economic life will also be published in the series.

Continuity and Change in Irish Employee Relations

Patrick Gunnigle
Patrick Flood
Michael Morley
Thomas Turner

with

Kieran Foley
Noreen Heraty
Juliet McMahon
Bill Toner

Oak Tree Press
Dublin

in association with
Graduate School of Business
University College Dublin

Oak Tree Press
4 Arran Quay, Dublin 7

© 1994 individual contributors

A catalogue record of this book is
available from the British Library.

ISBN 1-872853-57-9 paperback
ISBN 1-872853-65-X hardback

Cover Design: Robin Hegarty

Printed in Ireland by Betaprint Ltd.

CONTENTS

Chapter 1
CONTINUITY AND CHANGE IN IRISH EMPLOYEE RELATIONS

Chapter 2
EMPLOYEE RELATIONS IN IRELAND:
AN ORGANISATIONAL LEVEL PERSPECTIVE
Patrick Gunnigle, Michael Morley and Thomas Turner

Chapter 3
EMPLOYEE RELATIONS AND HUMAN RESOURCE MANAGEMENT:
SOME RECENT DEVELOPMENTS
Patrick Gunnigle, Michael Morley and Thomas Turner

Chapter 4
THE PERSONNEL/HUMAN RESOURCE FUNCTION
AND EMPLOYEE RELATIONS
Kieran Foley and Patrick Gunnigle

Chapter 5
A REVIEW OF ORGANISATIONAL REWARD PRACTICES
Patrick Gunnigle, Kieran Foley and Michael Morley

Chapter 6
TRENDS AND DEVELOPMENTS IN THE ORGANISATION OF
THE EMPLOYMENT RELATIONSHIP
Noreen Heraty, Michael Morley and Thomas Turner

Chapter 7
TRENDS IN FLEXIBLE WORKING PATTERNS IN IRELAND
Michael Morley and Patrick Gunnigle

Chapter 8
EMPLOYEE RELATIONS IN SMALL FIRMS
Juliet McMahon

Chapter 9
EMPLOYEE RELATIONS IN GREENFIELD SITES
Patrick Gunnigle

Chapter 10
HUMAN RESOURCE STRATEGY AND THE NON-UNION PHENOMENON
Patrick Flood, Bill Toner and Thomas Turner

Chapter 11
CONCLUSIONS

FOREWORD

In the modern economic arena, a world of rapid technological change where competitiveness is of such supreme importance, it is clearly of key significance to identify the factors that either enhance or inhibit performance. Obviously the "people" factor — the relationship between employer and employee — is a critical aspect, worthy of especial analysis. From a policy perspective it is worthwhile to establish how workplace relationships are developing in today's Ireland, how they respond to the modern management and production methods that are characteristic of the new enterprises setting up in business here. There are lessons to be learned, and this report, which represents the completion of the first phase of a study of employee relations practices in Ireland, commissioned by the Department of Enterprise and Employment, and prepared by the University of Limerick's Department of Personnel and Employment Relations, will assist greatly in the learning process.

Ruairi Quinn, TD
Minister for Enterprise and
Employment

ACKNOWLEDGEMENTS

This book represents the culmination of extensive research, analysis and discussion over two years. The views and experiences of many individuals, including many employee relations practitioners, have been incorporated in the text.

A number of people made a particularly significant contribution and we would like to express our appreciation.

Colleagues at the University of Limerick were most helpful. Professor Noel Whelan and Professor Donal Dineen provided particular support and encouragement; Joe Wallace, Gerard Fitzgerald, Bernard Delany, Sarah Moore and Tom Garavan provided valuable comments and direction; Claire McCracken and her colleagues in the Information Technology Department provided data processing assistance and particular thanks to Kaye Downey and Geraldine Flanagan for their administrative and data processing skills.

Various external organisations and individuals provided data and assistance. In particular we would like to thank Professor Aidan Kelly, University College Dublin; Dr Gerry McMahon, College of Commerce, Rathmines; Dr Kathy Monks, Dublin City University; Professor Phil Beaumont, University of Glasgow; Professor Shaun Tyson, Cranfield School of Management; Mr Joe McLoughlin, Department of Enterprise and Employment and Mr Michael McDonnell, Mr Tom Kennedy and Mr Peter Squire of the Institute of Personnel and Development in Ireland.

Staff at the Centre for European Human Resource Management, Cranfield School of Management have been instrumental in pioneering and supporting the Price Waterhouse Cranfield Project on Human Resource Management in Europe and provide invaluable support to our activities at the University of Limerick. We would especially like to thank Professor Chris Brewster, Ariane Hegewisch, Leslie Mayne, Trixi Alberga and Olga Tregaskis for their support and assistance.

We would like to thank staff at the Department of Enterprise and Employment for instigating and co-ordinating this research in a most professional and effective manner. Particular thanks to Mr Pádraig Cullinane, Mr Larry O'Grady, Mr Martin Territt and Mr Damien White, of the Department of Enterprise and Employment. Many thanks also to

Mr Kieran Mulvey and Mr Sean Healy of the Labour Relations Commission whose enthusiasm and support has been most appreciated.

Finally, I would like to thank two people who have been particularly instrumental in bringing this work to fruition. Firstly, to Professor Bill Roche, University College Dublin, who provided both expert editorial advice and tremendous assistance to the research team. Secondly, I would like to single out my colleague, Mike Morley, and express my personal thanks for his enthusiasm and commitment in co-ordinating this project and ensuring its successful completion.

Many thanks to all.

Paddy Gunnigle
Department of Personnel
Employment Relations
College of Business
University of Limerick

LIST OF ABBREVIATIONS

CBI   Confederation of British Industry
CEO   Chief Executive Officer
CSO   Central Statistics Office
ER   Employee Relations
ESB   Electricity Supply Board
EURO   European
FIE   Federation of Irish Employers
GDP   Gross Domestic Product
HQ   Headquarters
HRM   Human Resource Management
IBAR   Irish Business and Administrative Research
IBEC   Irish Business and Employers Confederation
IBM   International Business Machines
ICTU   Irish Congress of Trade Union
IDA   Industrial Development Authority
ILM   Internal Labour Market
IMS   International Manpower Services
IPM   Institute of Personnel Management
IRN   Industrial Relations News
MD   Managing Director
MNC   Multinational Corporation
NESC   National Economic and Social Council
NWA   National Wage Agreement
P/HR   Personnel/Human Resource
PBR   Payment by Results
PCW   Programme for Competitiveness and Work
PESP   Programme for Economic and Social Progress
PNR   Programme for National Recovery
PRP   Performance Related Pay
PWCP   Price Waterhouse Cranfield Project
R&D   Research and Development
T&D   Training and Development
UCD   University College Dublin

LIST OF TABLES

LIST OF FIGURES

Chapter 1

CONTINUITY AND CHANGE IN
IRISH EMPLOYEE RELATIONS

OBJECTIVES

The 1980s was a period of considerable change for Irish firms. The onset of recession lessened the emphasis on some core workforce management activities such as recruitment. Trade union membership fell in the period 1980–87 and industrial unrest also declined significantly over the decade. Concomitantly, many organisations sought to establish a competitive edge through improvements in quality, service and performance. One key source of such improvements has been an increased emphasis on the more optimal utilisation of human resources. However, in Ireland little empirical evidence has been advanced to substantiate whether this emphasis has translated into specific employee relations practices on the shop floor. A recurrent theme in the extant literature is the extent of change in the conduct of employee relations, and this book attempts to contribute to the debate by providing a profile of employee relations practice at company or organisational level in Ireland.

This research was commissioned by the Department of Enterprise and Employment with a view to achieving the following objectives: to develop a general profile of current approaches to employee relations in Irish organisations; to examine the conduct of employee relations in a cross-section of manufacturing companies; and to identify key indicators of employee relations performance and highlight action areas to achieve improvements in employee relations at organisational level.

This book is the product of an extensive literature review and an analysis of systematic data generated by two independent studies, namely the Price Waterhouse Cranfield Study on International Strategic Human Resource Management and a study of employee relations in "Greenfield" sites in Ireland. The Price Waterhouse Cranfield Project on International Strategic Human Resource Management was established in 1989 and is designed to analyse the nature of HRM practice at enterprise level in

1

Europe. The most recent survey, conducted in 1992, involved an analysis of HRM practices in twelve European countries. The project is co-ordinated by Professor Chris Brewster and Ariane Hegewisch at Cranfield School of Management.[1] The Republic of Ireland participated in the Price Waterhouse Cranfield Project for the first time in 1992. The Irish component of the study is located at the Department of Personnel & Employment Relations at the University of Limerick and is co-ordinated by Paddy Gunnigle, Mike Morley and Tom Turner.

The second major data set used in this book draws on a study of employee relations in some 53 recently established Greenfield firms in the manufacturing and internationally traded services sector. This independent study is directed by Paddy Gunnigle at the Department of Personnel & Employment Relations, University of Limerick.

The book divides into three broad generic areas. Firstly, major trends in employee relations and in the personnel function are examined. Secondly, a number of specific issues regarding the role of the personnel function and organisation of the employment relationship are discussed. Thirdly, the book examines employee relations developments in small firms, Greenfield sites and non-union firms.

In Chapter 2 we review the nature of workplace employee relations in Ireland. Firstly, public policy issues are discussed. Systematic data is then provided on trade union membership, trade union density and trade union recognition. Also, key factors influencing union density and union recognition are examined in some detail. Finally, variations in employment practices between public and private sector establishments are discussed.

In Chapter 3 we examine more recent developments in employee relations in Ireland, focusing in particular on the human resource management (HRM) debate and its implications for employee relations practice. The relationships between both union and non-union firms and the use of HRM practices are evaluated and significant variations in employment practices are highlighted.

Chapter 4 concentrates on the personnel/HR function and workplace employee relations. Because of recessionary pressures and the ever increasing complexity facing organisations, it is suggested that there has been a reappraisal of the practice and legitimacy of the personnel/HR function in recent years. Here we examine the role of the personnel/HR

---

[1] For a review of data emanating from the Price Waterhouse Cranfield Project, see Brewster, C. & Hegewisch, A. (eds.), *Policy and Practice in European Human Resource Management*, Routledge, 1994.

function, highlighting its traditional role and how it has developed and changed in recent years. Contemporary models are examined as they provide a basis on which to gauge the impact of the function on workplace employee relations.

In Chapter 5 we review reward practices. Reward practices are considered important because decisions on the reward system have implications not only for the effectiveness of the organisation as a whole, but also for the climate of employee relations within the organisation. Decisions in key areas such as pay and benefits provide important insights into an organisations approach to the management of workplace employee relations. This chapter considers pay determination and collective bargaining in Ireland and examines the legislative and institutional framework for pay negotiations. We examine three particular facets of reward practices in Ireland; the level at which pay is determined for different employee grades, the extent of variable pay and non-money benefits and the use of financial incentives.

Chapter 6 discusses trends and developments in the organisation of the employment relationship. The way in which this employment relationship is organised and managed is seen as an important factor in defining the climate of employee relations in an organisation. Here we examine selected aspects of that employment relationship. Firstly, trends in recruitment and selection and training and development practices are examined. Secondly, the concept of the internal labour market (ILM) is discussed and the factors affecting the presence of ILMs are examined.

Chapter 7 considers recent trends in flexible working patterns. We examine the context for change in Ireland highlighting the labour market changes and sectoral shifts that have occurred in recent years. The extant evidence for the emergence of the planned development of the core/periphery employment model is evaluated. Then we assess the extent to which non-standard contracts of employment are used in Ireland, the degree to which the use of these has changed over the past three years, and finally, the extent to which changes have occurred in the specification of jobs for various employee categories. These are three areas of enquiry that are central to the flexibility debate because, despite some evidence of a growing reliance on non-standard workers, it is not at all clear that employers are deliberately moving into flexible employment for long-term strategic reasons.

In Chapter 8 we examine employee relations in the small firm. In Ireland, there have traditionally been two parallel goals in relation to industrial development: encouragement of overseas industry to establish facilities in Ireland and the development of indigenous industry, much of which is composed of small manufacturing or service units employing less than 100 people. In recent years there has been a growing realisation of the importance of the latter in achieving self-generating growth. Indeed, the Culliton Report emphasises the need for concrete Government policies to provide greater support for indigenous enterprise and to shift away from the reliance on foreign multinationals. However, given this increased awareness of the importance of small firms, it is surprising that very little research has been carried out in this area, especially in the area of employee relations. The purpose of this chapter is to begin to redress the balance by examining the current state of knowledge on employee relations in small firms. We examine managerial styles in the small firm, trade union influence, conflict and conflict resolution, recruitment, training and reward practices in the small firm.

Chapter 9 is based on findings from a recent study of employee relations in Greenfield sites. It has been suggested that organisations locating at Greenfield sites are less constrained by established practice and thus possess greater scope to develop desired employee relations styles. This chapter examines the nature and role of the personnel function in such organisations, the extent and nature of trade union recognition and the incidence of performance related pay. Finally, the issue of communications is discussed.

Chapter 10 focuses on the non-union phenomenon. As late as a decade ago, the non-union company scarcely received a mention in the employee relations literature. It now appears that in the 1990s non-unionism has come out of the closet. It is now not uncommon for the managers of non-union firms to go public about their non-union policies. We examine the debate on union avoidance and organisational competitiveness and evaluate the development of the non-union phenomenon. Finally, Chapter 11 summaries the main findings of the research.

At the outset it is important to clarify what is meant by employee relations, as the term itself is a source of some confusion. The traditional management focus has been on the pluralist concept of industrial relations, encompassing the premise that a basic conflict of interest exists between management and labour and that this conflict can be optimally handled through collective bargaining between employers and trade unions over divisive issues, particularly pay and working conditions. During the 1980s it became evident that although this definition aptly described management/worker relations in many organisations, it did not encapsulate organisations where the focus was more unitarist in perspective. This latter approach placed the emphasis on dealings with the individual employee using various mechanisms such as elaborate communications, career development, quality circles and merit pay. In this book, employee relations are seen in generic terms as incorporating all employer/employee interactions concerning pay, working conditions and related employment matters; the term includes both pluralist and unitarist models.

Survey Data

The sample frame used for the Price Waterhouse Cranfield Project in Ireland was the Business and Finance list of the top 1,000 trading companies and the top 500 non-trading bodies in Ireland. Companies are ranked according to the level of turnover, financial institutions by the size of their assets, and non-trading bodies by the number of employees. A questionnaire addressed to either the personnel manager or chief executive was mailed to 1,180 companies and a total of 269 usable questionnaires were returned, giving a response rate of 22.7 per cent. This response rate can be considered very acceptable for large-scale positivist research of this kind. If one excludes establishments employing less than 50 employees, the size distribution of establishments in the sample is broadly similar to the size distribution in the relevant population as outlined in Table 1.1. While there is a slight bias in the sample towards large establishments, compared with the population, these differences are small and the sample can therefore be considered to be reasonably representative of the overall population.

TABLE 1.1: SIZE DISTRIBUTION OF ESTABLISHMENTS

Size	Sample Frame	Population
51–100	40 (18%)	275 (26%)
101–200	50 (23%)	309 (29%)
201–500	73 (33%)	289 (27%)
501–1000	32 (14%)	100 (9%)
1001+	27 (12%)	87 (8%)
Total	222*(100%)	1,060†(99%)

* Three respondents did not indicate size and 44 companies had less than 50 employees and are not included in this table.

† Of the top 1,500 companies, 440 had less than 50 employees and are excluded from this table.

Source: Price Waterhouse Cranfield Project (Ireland); University of Limerick 1992.

Table 1.2. gives a breakdown of the number of establishments in each industrial sector from the sample.

TABLE 1.2: INDUSTRIAL SECTOR OF RESPONDENTS

Agriculture/Hunting/Forestry/Fishing	9 (3.3%)
Energy/Water	3 (1.1%)
Chemical	20 (7.4%)
Metal Manufacture	37 (13.8%)
Other Manufacturing	64 (23.8%)
Building & Civil Engineering	5 (1.9%)
Retail & Distribution/Hotel & Catering	25 (9.3%)
Transport & Communication	7 (2.6%)
Banking & Finance	14 (5.2%)
Personal Services	3 (1.1%)
Health	20 (7.4%)
Other Services	6 (2.2%)
Education	20 (7.4%)
Local Government	8 (3.0%)
Central Government	7 (2.6%)
Fire/Police	19 (7.1%)

Source: Price Waterhouse Cranfield Project (Ireland); University of Limerick
       1992.

TABLE 1.3: SAMPLE DISTRIBUTION AND REPRESENTATIVENESS*

Industry	Sample	Population
Agri/Hunting/Forestry/Fishing	2.3%	4.0%
Energy/Water	1.4%	0.3%
Chemical Products	8.6%	7.0%
Metal Manufacturing	14.4%	13.1%
Other Manufacturing	26.6%	22.9%
Building & Civil Engineering	1.8%	3.4%
Retail & Distribution/Hotel & Catering	8.6%	11.8%
Transport & Communication	2.7%	3.3%
Banking/Finance/Insurance	4.5%	6.0%
Education	7.7%	7.0%
Rest†	21.4%	21.2%
Total Establishments	222 (100%)	1,060 (100%)

*   Compares the number of establishments in each industry for the sample and
     the population. Establishments with less than 50 employees are excluded.
†   Includes: Personal Domestic/Recreational Services; Health Services; Other
     Services; Local Government; Central Government; Fire/Police.
Source: Price Waterhouse Cranfield Project (Ireland); University of Limerick
       1992.

A comparison of the number of establishments in each industrial sector also reveals a close similarity between the Price Waterhouse Cranfield Project sample and the population, as outlined in Table 1.3.

While origin of ownership is not available from the population data we can, using the census of industrial production (1989), calculate the number of foreign-owned firms in the industrial sector where the vast majority of these firms are located. A total of 893 firms are foreign owned, representing 19 per cent of all firms, 46 per cent are US owned, 43 per cent from EC countries and 11 per cent are owned by other countries. In the sample 31 per cent of establishments are foreign owned. Of these, 51 per cent are US owned, 36 per cent are from EC countries and 12 per cent are from the rest of the world.

TABLE 1.4: PRINCIPAL ACTIVITY BY COUNTRY OF ORIGIN

	Irish	US	European	Japanese	Other	TOTAL
Metal Manufacturing & Engineering:						
* Mechanical Engineering	0	2	4	0	0	6
* Office/Data Processing Machinery	1	10	0	6	1	18
* Motor Parts/Vehicles	0	2	4	0	0	6
Chemical Products	0	1	0	0	0	1
Other Manufacturing						
* Textiles & Clothing	3	0	0	0	0	3
* Printing & Publishing	1	0	0	0	0	1
* Rubber & Plastics	0	1	0	0	0	1
Information/Data Processing	0	5	0	0	0	5
Software	0	6	0	0	0	6
Professional & Other Services	2	0	0	0	0	2
Food & Drink	2	0	0	0	0	2
Transport/Communications Services	2	0	0	0	0	2
TOTAL	11	27	8	6	1	53

Source: Greenfield Site Study, University of Limerick, 1992.

In relation to the Greenfield study, such sites were defined as "locations where an organisation established a new facility in a start-up mode incorporating design of plant". This study was confined to organisations in the manufacturing and internationally-traded services sectors. Also, only organisations which began operations since 1987 and employed more than 100 employees were included in the study.

In total some 53 Greenfield companies were identified which met these criteria. It is worth noting that the incidence of large Greenfield site start-ups in Ireland is relatively small. Furthermore, US companies account for over half the total number of large Greenfield site start-ups in Ireland.

Chapter 2

EMPLOYEE RELATIONS IN IRELAND: AN ORGANISATIONAL LEVEL PERSPECTIVE

Patrick Gunnigle, Michael Morley and Thomas Turner

INTRODUCTION

This chapter reviews the nature of employee relations in Ireland. Firstly, the nature and context of employee relations is briefly sketched. Then, using recent research data from the Price Waterhouse Cranfield Study, we examine trade union membership, trade union density and trade union recognition. Finally, we focus more closely on variations in employment practices between public and private sector establishments.

THE NATURE AND CONTEXT OF EMPLOYEE RELATIONS

At the workplace level, employee relations practice in the great majority of medium and large organisations in Ireland has traditionally been associated with a strong collectivist emphasis (Roche 1990b). In this model, employee relations considerations rarely concerned strategic decision makers, and relations between management and employees were grounded in the pluralist tradition with a primary reliance on adversarial collective bargaining. This pluralist tradition is manifested in high levels of union density, highly developed collective bargaining institutions at establishment level and employee relations as the key concern of the specialist personnel function (Gunnigle and Flood 1990).

As has been the case in the UK, the 1980s in Ireland was a period of considerable change in the environment and practice of employee relations. From an employer perspective, the onset of recession lessened the emphasis on hitherto core workforce management activities such as recruitment and, particularly, employee relations. Trade union membership fell significantly in the period 1980–87 and industrial unrest also declined significantly over the decade (Roche & Larragy 1989). At the

9

same time, many organisations sought to establish competitive advantage through improvements in quality, service and performance. One source of such improvements has been an increased emphasis on the more optimal utilisation of human resources. Consequently, it would appear that there has been greater innovation in employee relations practice, particularly in areas such as work systems, rewards, management–employee communications and employee development.

Public Policy

In terms of Government approaches to employee relations, a number of significant issues emerge. At a general level, Governments have had a largely benign approach to organised labour. The traditional approach of successive Governments to employee relations in Ireland has been grounded in the "voluntarist" tradition. This meant that employers and employees or their representative bodies were largely free to regulate the substantive and procedural terms of their relationship and there was a minimum of intervention from Government or its agencies (Hillery 1989, Breen et al. 1990). This approach was largely an historical legacy of the British voluntarist tradition and endured up to the end of the 1970s. Overall, Governments have been supportive of trade unions and a consensus approach to labour relations.

However, since the early 1980s it would appear that the approaches of British and Irish Governments have taken markedly contrasting directions in the areas of pay and employee relations. In the UK, the Conservative governments have taken progressive steps, both legislative and otherwise, to reduce union power and ensure that wage levels and other employee relations outcomes are determined by market forces. In Ireland, the voluntarist tradition appears to have been considerably diluted in recent years. In contrast to the UK, however, this change has taken the form of a consensus approach to pay and employee relations (Roche 1989). In the period 1970–82 Ireland had a series of National Agreements on pay and related employment issues. These were initially heralded as important vehicles for delivering wage restraint, reduced industrial conflict, low inflation and a new era of co-operation and harmony at the workplace. However, these agreements failed to deliver and the period was characterised by high levels of inflation, wage drift and industrial conflict, reinforcing the traditional adversarial style of employee relations. Central agreements were abandoned by the somewhat disillusioned social partners (particularly employers) and there was a brief return to decentralised bargaining in the 1982–86 period.

In a period of severe fiscal rectitude the Government, with the support of the ICTU and the FIE, revived central agreements through the

Programme for National Recovery (1988–90). This period was character-ised by very moderate wage increases and high GDP growth. Much of the credit for such success has been given to the PNR, although it is plausible to argue that this period would have been characterised by low pay increases and low levels of industrial conflict regardless of whether pay was negotiated centrally or locally. The Programme for Economic and Social Progress (1991–93) provides for average annual pay increases of approximately 3.5 per cent. Recent Governments have been strong advocates of centralised agreements on pay and other aspects of social and economic policy involving negotiations with the main "social part-ners" (viz. employer, trade union and farming federations). In relation to employee relations, the achievement of a high level of national consensus has possibly been the most significant development. This consensus appears to have had an impact at the workplace level with, for example, a considerable reduction in overt conflict. Whether this represents a sig-nificant and enduring shift to a new paradigm of employee relations — that is, from an adversarial to a co-operative style of employee relations — is a question that remains to be answered.

A more established aspect of public policy is the constitutional guarantee of freedom of association. This constitutional guarantee of freedom of association embodied in article 40.6.1. of the Constitution confers on workers the right to form or associate/disassociate with unions or other associations. However, while the Constitution supports the free-dom of workers to organise, there is no statutory or constitutional provision for trade union recognition with a consequence that there is no obligation on employers to recognise or bargain with trade unions. His-torically, this lack of any statutory mechanism for securing trade union recognition did not seem to cause many difficulties as most larger employers seemed happy to recognise and conclude collective agreements with trade unions. However, with the declining membership and power of Irish trade unions, the issue of recognition became contentious in the 1980s with some evidence of increased opposition to unionisation in recent years, particularly among some multinational organisations and indigenous small firms (Gunnigle & Brady 1984, McGovern 1989, Gunnigle 1992a).

A final important aspect of public policy relates to approaches to industrial development. Since the mid-1960s, Government policy has been aimed at actively encouraging direct foreign investment in Ireland. There are now over 950 overseas companies operating in Ireland with a particular focus on the engineering (including electronics) and chemicals sectors. These companies employ some 80,000 employees. The USA and UK have been the major source of overseas investment. Ireland has been the most profitable location for US firms in the EC, achieving an average return on investment of 23 per cent in the period 1982–87, or three times the EC average (US Department of Commerce, 1989). On the employee relations front, it certainly appears that multinational companies (MNCs) have been a source of innovation in management practices, particularly in the application of new personnel approaches and in expanding the role of the specialist personnel/HR function (Gunnigle & Flood 1990). However, it would also seem that MNCs pose particular and unique challenges in the employee relations sphere, specifically in their ability to switch the locus of production quickly, and the recent and increasing trend of union avoidance.

SURVEY FINDINGS ON EMPLOYEE RELATIONS IN IRELAND

The role of trade unions is seen as a key indicator of approaches to, and changes in, employee relations. This aspect incorporates both the extent of union recognition and, where unions are recognised, the nature of management–trade union relations. A particularly important issue concerns trade union recognition and the future role of collective bargaining. This section considers the findings of the Price Waterhouse Cranfield Project on the role and nature of unionisation among Irish organisations. In particular, it considers the issue of trade union density and trade union recognition.

Trade Unions in Ireland

The total number of trade unions in Ireland is some 65 unions catering for a total membership of around 460,000 or 44 per cent of the workforce (see Table 2.1). The period since 1980 has witnessed the most serious decline in trade union density in the post-war period.

Since 1980 trade union membership in Ireland has fallen by almost 10 per cent (Roche & Larragy 1989). However, this decline is principally attributed to macro-economic factors, most notably economic depression, increased levels of unemployment and changes in employment structure, characterised by a decline in traditionally highly unionised sectors (typical employment forms in manufacturing industry and the public sector), and a growth in sectors which have traditionally posed difficulties for union penetration, particularly private services (see Roche and Larragy 1989, 1992; Roche 1992). A study by McGovern (1989) points to increasing opposition to union recognition in the 1980s, suggesting that management approaches to unionisation have either hardened in line with the "anti-union" style or become "more subtle" in attempting to avoid unionisation.

TABLE 2.1: TRADE UNION MEMBERSHIP 1945–90

Year	Membership	Employment Density*	Workforce Density[†]
1945	172,300	27.7	25.4
1960	312,600	49.6	45.4
1975	448,800	59.3	52.3
1980	527,200	61.8	55.2
1981	524,400	61.5	53.5
1982	519,900	60.3	51.4
1983	513,300	61.1	49.7
1984	500,200	60.7	48.2
1985	483,300	59.9	46.6
1986	471,000	58.0	45.0
1987	457,300	56.2	43.1
1988[‡]	470,644	57.1	44.2
1989	458,690	55.6	43.4
1990	462,451	54.6	43.2

*   Employment Density = Trade union membership/civilian employees at work
      x 100
†   Workforce Density = Trade union membership/civilian employee workforce
      x 100
‡   Figures for 1988–90 are estimates and are derived from the annual affiliated
      membership of unions affiliated to the Irish Congress of Trade Unions
Source: Dues Project UCD; Roche 1992.

Trade Union Density
The levels of trade union density in the surveyed companies is high, with almost two thirds of respondent firms reporting that more than 50 per cent of their staff are trade union members (see Table 2.2). Average union density across the companies is approximately 55.9 per cent. This compares closely with a union density of 56.2 per cent for the employed national labour force (i.e. the number of union members as a percentage of the employed labour force).

TABLE 2.2: TRADE UNION DENSITY

Proportion of Employees in Trade Unions	%
0	18.4
1–25%	6.4
26–50%	10.9
51–75%	18.0
76–100%	42.3
Don't Know/Missing	4.1

N=269

Source: Price Waterhouse Cranfield Project (Ireland); University of Limerick
        1992.

A large proportion (60.3 per cent) of the sampled companies have
union levels in excess of 50 per cent of their workforce. The exclusion of
the non-unionised establishments increases union density to 69 per cent.
Given an aggregate union density among the employed labour force of
56.2 per cent, it is not surprising to find a high level of union density in
the top 1,500 trading and non-trading establishments, where concentration of employees is greatest. This is particularly evident in the case of
public-sector establishments which account for 42 per cent of the most
highly unionised establishments, but only 24 per cent of the sample.

FIGURE 2.1: LEVEL OF UNION MEMBERSHIP BY SECTOR

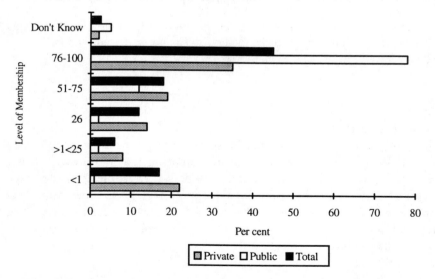

Source: Price Waterhouse Cranfield Project (Ireland); University of Limerick
        1992.

The level of unionisation also appears to be related to the size or number of employees, with large employers more likely to have higher levels of union density. This finding is supported by most of the empirical research on the determinants of unionisation and in the next section we review the salient findings of these studies, as a basis for understanding the results from the Cranfield data.

Factors Affecting Union Density

A number of structural variables have been advanced to account for variations in union membership across industries and single establishments (see Bain and Price 1983, Hirsch and Berger 1984). Variations in union levels are associated with differences in the gender, occupational and industrial composition of potential union membership, particularly differences in employment in the public/private and manufacturing/ services sectors, and variations in industrial structure, such as employment concentration, single or multi-establishment status, product markets and capital intensity.

Size, sector, industry and the proportion of white-collar, part-time and female workers have all figured prominently as significant explanatory variables in the empirical literature on union density (Bain and Price 1983, Bain and Elsheikh 1979, Bain and Elias 1985, Booth 1986, Deery and DeCieri 1991). Drawing from this literature, we can hypothesise that unionisation will vary negatively with the proportion of white-collar and part-time workers in an establishment, positively as size increases, positively in a public sector establishment and positively in specific industries such as manufacturing, transport and utilities. Less prominent but also relevant explanatory variables in the literature are establishment status, product market and capital intensity. Single independent establishments are more likely to have a negative impact on unionisation than establishments which are owned or controlled by a large firm or multinational (Bain and Elsheikh 1980). A single establishment is more likely to relate to its employees in a paternalistic manner in which the terms and conditions of employment are determined in a personal and informal way, rather than by formal rules applied impersonally to all, which facilitates collective organisation. Unionisation, it is argued, is affected by the nature of the market in which the product of the establishment is sold (Bain and Elsheikh 1979), with levels of unionisation being inversely related to the competitiveness of the market. The competitiveness of the product market and the ease or difficulty of unionisation within establishments is essentially related to whether the product market is local as distinct from national, or international. Finally, country of origin may have a significant impact on unionisation at establishment level. In particular, American-owned companies in the Irish electronics industry are reputed to pursue an active strategy of union avoidance (McGovern 1989) or the marginalisation of trade unions through the use of such processes as direct employee communication and the prompt handling of grievances (Gunnigle 1992a). Indeed, Gunnigle (1992a) in a survey of firms established since 1987 found that non unionism was predominantly confined to US-owned firms. We might expect that foreign ownership or at least companies originating in the United States may exert a drag on the level of unionisation.

A statistical analysis of the survey data revealed the following findings in relation to these issues. Being a public sector establishment is more than twice as important as size in influencing union levels in establishments. The proportion of white-collar workers in an establishment has a significant and negative effect on union density, as predicted. Four industrial sectors are positively related to union density, with Traditional Manufacturing having the strongest effect, as perhaps could be expected. Transport and Communications is a traditionally highly unionised sector, while Banking in Ireland is also highly unionised, with the employees in the four largest banks covered by a single trade union. Less anticipated is the relationship between union density and companies in the Agriculture sector. However, the number of establishments in the survey from this sector is low, and there is a possibility of bias in the establishments selected. Equally surprising is the absence of the Services sector, which includes personal services, retail and distribution, catering and hotels, which might be expected to have a significant and negative impact on union levels. The proportion of part-time workers in an establishment appears to have no significant effect on union levels. However, part-time work is positively associated with public sector employment. It may perhaps be the case that unions have been successful in unionising part-time workers, at least in the public sector, where establishments tend to be highly unionised. Finally, what is perhaps most interesting is the absence of any impact on union levels from an establishment's market, status and labour costs. The small size of the Irish economy and its relatively high level of union density in most industries possibly renders these factors negligible as determinants of union density at establishment level.

Trade Union Recognition
Despite some adverse commentaries on the level of trade union recognition and density in Irish organisations, the evidence from the Price

Waterhouse Cranfield (PWC) Survey suggests that union membership in Ireland is quite robust. The PWC survey found that the great majority of Irish organisations surveyed recognised trade unions (see Table 2.3).

TABLE 2.3: TRADE UNION RECOGNITION

Trade Union Recognition	Number of Firms	% of Firms
Yes	207	77
No	57	21
Missing/Don't Know	5	2

N=269
Source: Price Waterhouse Cranfield Project (Ireland); University of Limerick 1992.

TABLE 2.4: UNION STATUS BY INDUSTRY

	Non-union	Union	
Agriculture	37.5%	62.5%	(8)
Non-energy, Minerals	16.7%	83.3%	(18)
Advanced Manufacturing*	43.0%	57.0%	(35)
Other Manufacturing	8.5%	91.5%	(59)
Building & Civil Engineering	33.3%	66.7%	(3)
Distributive Trades	10.0%	90.0%	(20)
Transport & Communications	25.0%	75.0%	(4)
Banking & Finance	81.8%	18 2%	(11)
Professional & Other Services	50.0%	50.0%	(6)
Health & Education	40.0%	· 60.0%	(5)
Fire, Police, Quangos	38.0%	62.0%	(13)
	Number of Missing Observations: 4	(N=182)	

*   Manufacturing is divided into two groups: Metal Manufacturing which mainly covers the electronic and computing industry and which we label as Advanced Manufacturing and Other Manufacturing which refers to all other manufacturing areas and can be labelled as Traditional Manufacturing.
Source: Price Waterhouse Cranfield Project (Ireland); University of Limerick 1992.

A total of 57 companies or 21 per cent of the sampled companies did not recognise a trade union for collective bargaining purposes, while seven of these companies acknowledged the presence of trade union members in their establishments. Since union recognition is not an issue in the public sector, only private sector companies are included in the following analysis. Excluding the companies which either failed to answer the question on union recognition or which cannot be categorised according to sector, there is a total of 183 private sector companies of which 50 — or 28 per cent — did not recognise a trade union. An examination of the distribution of companies not recognising a trade union reveals the prominence of such firms in manufacturing industries.

Given the small number of companies surveyed in most industries, we must be cautious in any interpretation advanced. However, the substantial number in the advanced and traditional manufacturing industries makes generalisation in this area relatively reliable. It would appear that companies in the advanced manufacturing industries are less likely to recognise unions than those in the traditional sector. As already pointed out, much of the literature on union recognition in Ireland has emphasised the propensity of US firms to remain union-free. While Table 2.5 indicates that US firms are less likely to recognise trade unions, the differences are small.

TABLE 2.5: UNION RECOGNITION BY ORIGIN OF COMPANY

	US	Ireland	EC	Rest	TOTAL
Non-union	31.9%	30.6%	21.9%	0	27.6%
Unionised	68.1%	69.4%	78.1%	100%	72.4%
(N)	(47)	(85)	(32)	(10)	(174)
(Number of missing observations: 9)					

Source: Price Waterhouse Cranfield Project (Ireland); University of Limerick 1992.

However, size may be distorting the comparison since the majority of Irish firms which do not recognise trade unions have less than 50 employees, while the majority of non-union US firms have more than 50 employees. The next section examines the literature on the determinants of union recognition and, in the subsequent analysis, controls for variables such as size, allowing a rigorous evaluation of the effect of country of origin on union recognition.

Factors Affecting Union Recognition

In general, the factors which were found to be determinants of inter-establishment variations in the level of union membership are similar to those which account for the presence or absence of union recognition in an establishment (Beaumont and Harris 1989, Bain and Elsheikh 1980). However, Green (1990) distinguishes between the supply of an available union to each workplace and the demand for a union, that is, the decisions of individuals to join. The presence of a union at a workplace acts as a "gateway" enabling employees to join. The determinants of whether there is a recognised union in an establishment, "the determinants of coverage", are viewed as a distinct stage in a two-stage process, the second being the determinants of union membership levels. On the supply side, according to Green (1990), the structural factors associated with the job itself determine whether there is a recognised union available, and on the demand side, individual characteristics also determine whether an employee joins an available union. But, overall, his results (see also Beaumont and Harris 1991) "reaffirmed" the importance of such structural factors as industry, sector, occupation, firm size, gender typing and proportion of part-time workers in determining union status. In Milner and Richard's (1991) survey of firms in the London docklands, size, ownership (negatively if foreign) and age of the establishment (negative if started after 1983) significantly affected the probability of union recognition, while the proportion of women, white-collar workers and part-time workers, sector (service or manufacturing), and single or multi-establishment unit, had no significant effect. Beaumont and Harris (1991), using data from the 1984 workplace survey of private sector firms also found size and age of establishment (for non-manual workers) to be significant, but not ownership. The proportions of part-time workers, women and manual workers were also significant in affecting the probability of union recognition. But in Sproull and Mac Innes' (1987) survey of private sector electronic plants in Scotland, the proportion of females in a workforce did not influence the probability of unions being recognised, even after controlling for part-time workers. Significant variables were size and proportion of part-time workers, while variables which had no significant effect were age of establishment, ownership (UK or foreign), and the proportion of females and employees on staff conditions. Obviously, some variables are more peripheral than others in affecting the probability of union recognition and are more related to the particular focus and level of the data/survey being analysed with contingencies such as region, ownership and proportion of part-time/white-collar and female workers being chiefly a matter for empirical verification, while such factors as size of establishment, sector and industry type are more central, both conceptually and empirically.

A statistical analysis of influences on union recognition revealed the following. Country of origin has no significant impact on union recognition, and while US companies do have a negative impact on unionisation, the coefficient is not significant. Both product market and the single/corporate status of a company are also insignificant and appear to be unrelated to a company's union status. Furthermore, the significant structural variables affecting union recognition are similar to those affecting union density. Thus, increasing size is positively associated with union recognition, and an increasing proportion of white-collar workers in an establishment is negatively associated with union recognition. Finally, the analysis reveals that it is the sector or industry, rather than the country of origin, which has a significant and negative relationship with union recognition.

Practices and Trends in Employee Relations in the Public and Private Sector

One other key question is the extent to which the companies in the public and private sector differ in their use of specific employment practices. According to Cox and Hughes (1989), employee relations in the public sector do not differ to any extent from those in the private sector (Commission on Industrial Relations, 1981). However, while the procedural aspects of employee relations in both sectors may have similarities, it is possible that employment practices may differ considerably, indicating diverging trends. Employee relations may be distinctive in both sectors. There are different imperatives which influence management approaches to employee relations. The most important factor in the public sector influencing managerial strategy is possibly the political contingency or imperative in the form of policy and budgetary constraints. In the private or exposed sector, employment practices are, in the main, directly or indirectly, influenced by market considerations and exigencies. In effect, both of these sectors are subject to very different sets of pressures. The evidence in many western countries regarding public sector employment is that efforts are being made to make the public sector more efficient through the use of private sector techniques and cultures (Ferner 1991). In the Irish public sector this trend is evident in, for example, the attempts to reform public sector pay, the reduced importance of seniority in promotions and the increased use of employee assistance programmes. Thus, convergence rather than divergence would appear to be the prevailing trend. But given the different imperatives operating in both sectors, this convergence may be more superficial than real in the use of specific employment practices. Below, trends in pay and communication practices are compared. There are significant differences in the types of compensation systems, with private sector companies more likely to tie rewards to performance for all occupational levels.

Traditionally, pay/salary in the public sector has been linked to a job/grade, rather than the performance of the job holder. There is some evidence that this is changing, but it is still lagging behind the rate of change in performance related pay (PRP) in the private sector. While the use of variable pay increased in 24 per cent of the public sector companies surveyed (Figure 2.2), it is likely, in the context of the results in Table 2.6, to apply chiefly to managerial grades.

TABLE 2.6: UTILISATION OF PERFORMANCE RELATED PAY SYSTEMS

Group	Public Sector	Private Sector
Management	19%	55%
Professional/Technical	12%	48%
Clerical	3%	37%
Manual	2%	18%

Source: Price Waterhouse Cranfield Project (Ireland); University of Limerick 1992.

FIGURE 2.2: CHANGE IN USE OF VARIABLE PAY

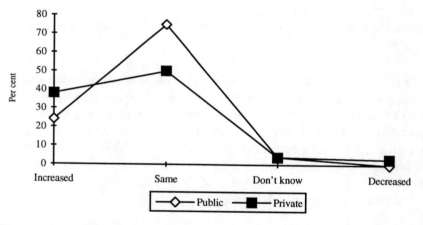

Source: Price Waterhouse Cranfield Project (Ireland); University of Limerick 1992.

Turning to the methods used to communicate with employees, we also find that there are differences, though less pronounced than in the case of PRP. Communication in the public sector is predominantly through the immediate supervisor or/and the established trade union. Apart from workforce meetings, little use is made of alternative methods. In contrast, communication methods in the private sector are more diverse. Even so, leaving aside communication through the immediate supervisor, the trade union structure is still the dominant conduit for communicating with employees in both sectors. However, in the private sector, direct communication with employees through workforce meetings is rated almost as important. In both sectors, direct communication between management and employees is increasing.

TABLE 2.7: MAIN METHODS OF EMPLOYEE/MANAGEMENT COMMUNICATIONS

Mode	Public Sector	Private Sector
Line Management	95% (55)*	99% (171)
Trade Unions/Works Councils	88% (51)	74% (105)
Regular Workforce Meetings	33% (19)	72% (91)
Quality Circles	2% (1)	27% (22)
Suggestion Boxes	14% (8)	36% (30)
Attitude Survey	7% (4)	28% (24)
No Formal Methods	12% (7)	15% (27)

*   Actual numbers in parenthesis.
Source: Price Waterhouse Cranfield Project (Ireland); University of Limerick 1992.

Direct communication with employees, either verbal or written, is increasing more rapidly in the private sector, but there are also increases in direct communication in the public sector. The increased use of PRP and alternative methods of communication in the private sector is paralleled by a greater perceived decrease in the influence of trade unions, with 29 per cent of private sector firms reporting a decrease in union influence. An interesting and unanticipated finding is the perceived stability of trade union influence in both sectors.

TABLE 2.8(a): TRENDS IN EMPLOYEE COMMUNICATIONS (PUBLIC)

Mode	Increased	Decreased	Same
Staff Bodies (inc. unions)	18%	6%	75%
Direct Verbal	44%	0%	56%
Direct Written	32%	2%	65%

Source: Price Waterhouse Cranfield Project (Ireland); University of Limerick 1992.

TABLE 2.8(b): TRENDS IN EMPLOYEE COMMUNICATIONS (PRIVATE)

Mode	Increased	Decreased	Same
Staff Bodies (inc. unions)	21%	20%	60%
Direct Verbal	62%	2%	36%
Direct Written	50%	4%	46%

Source: Price Waterhouse Cranfield Project (Ireland); University of Limerick 1992.

Despite a severe economic recession and the tenuous nature of employment tenure in many private sector firms, 63 per cent of respondents in this sector indicated no change in trade union influence.

TABLE 2.9: CHANGING INFLUENCE OF TRADE UNIONS

Trade Union Influence	Private Sector	Public Sector	TOTAL
Increase	8.0%	2.5%	9.5% (18)
Decrease	29.1%	17.9%	25.8% (49)
Same	62.7%	69.6%	64.7% (123)
TOTAL	100% (134)	100% (56)	100% (190)
		(Number of missing observations: 79)	

Source: Price Waterhouse Cranfield Project (Ireland); University of Limerick 1992.

Overall, the employee relations trends in pay systems and communication practices indicate substantial change in the private sector and a modest change in the public sector. These differences, it can be argued, are a result of the different imperatives confronting public and private sector firms. Competitive pressures, particularly since the removal of the remaining trade barriers in the EC, provide an imperative to adapt and change employment systems in the exposed sector of the economy. In the public sector, the imperative to change employment practices is a function of available resources (budgetary constraints) and political contingencies. From the PWC data, it would appear that market imperatives act as a more powerful mechanism for change in employment practices than do political contingencies.

CONCLUSIONS

The 1980s in Ireland were a period of considerable change resulting in increased innovation in employee relations practice, particularly in areas such as work systems, rewards, management–employee communications and employee development. The thrust of any future change is likely to take the form of the dualist approach associated with neo-pluralism. While assessing union influence is a complex task, largely because influence is, in part, perceptual, the picture emerging from our data does not appear as bleak for trade unions as some commentators have indicated (see Figure 2.3). While 19 per cent of Irish firms felt that trade union influence had decreased in recent years, 52 per cent felt there had been no change and 7 per cent felt that union influence had actually increased.

In general, the survey data seem to indicate that union recognition, density and influence in Irish organisations remain quite robust, with high levels of union recognition and union density permeating most Irish organisations. While the content of employee relations in Ireland is changing, there is a strong impression of continuity. Consequently, it would appear that established employee relations institutions and approaches remain largely intact and will continue to be relevant in the 1990s. Overall, Governments have been supportive of trade unions and a consensus approach to labour relations.

FIGURE 2.3: CHANGE IN TRADE UNION INFLUENCE

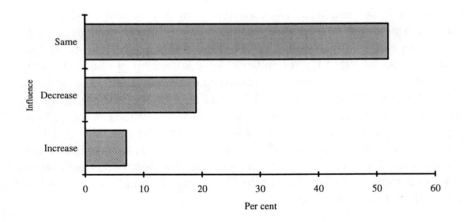

Source: Price Waterhouse Cranfield Project (Ireland); University of Limerick 1992.

The achievement of a high level of national consensus has possibly been one of the most significant developments in employee relations. With respect to trade union density, average union density across the sampled companies is approximately 55.9 per cent, which compares closely with a union density of 56.2 per cent for the employed national labour force, i.e. number of union members as a percentage of the employed labour force. Being a public sector establishment is more than twice as important as size in influencing union levels in establishments. The proportion of white-collar workers in an establishment has a significant and negative impact on union density. Four industrial sectors are positively related to union density, namely, traditional manufacturing; transport and communications; banking; and agriculture. The proportion of part-time workers in an establishment appears to have no significant impact on union levels. An establishment's market, status and labour costs also appear to have no impact on establishment-level union density in Ireland. Union membership remains robust with 77 per cent (207) of the sample recognising a trade union for collective bargaining purposes. Non-unionisation is most common in advanced manufacturing sectors. In relation to those factors which influence union recognition, size (positively), proportion of white-collar workers (negatively), and sector (negatively) emerge as the key factors, while country of origin, product market and company status (corporate/single) appear unrelated to a company's union status. In relation to pay, the private sector is more likely to tie rewards to performance for all occupational levels/grades. Communications in the public sector are predominately through the immediate supervisor and/or the established trade union. Apart from workforce meetings, little use is made of alternative methods. Communications in the private sector are more diverse. While the trade union remains the dominant conduit for communicating, direct communications through workforce meetings are rated almost as important in the private sector. In the next chapter we move into the human resource management debate and examine the extent to which HRM has impacted upon employee relations in Ireland.

Chapter 3

EMPLOYEE RELATIONS AND HUMAN RESOURCE MANAGEMENT: SOME RECENT DEVELOPMENTS

Patrick Gunnigle, Michael Morley and Thomas Turner

INTRODUCTION

An area of particular significance both to researchers and practitioners is the degree to which "tight" HRM-type approaches are being adopted and are replacing the traditional pluralist employee relations model. In Ireland, as elsewhere, it has been argued that competitive pressures, reduced trade union power and new models of management practice have encouraged Irish organisations to adopt more innovative employee relations practices (Flood 1989). However, the nature of change, if any, has remained unclear. It is suggested that much of this confusion seems to stem from the tendency to view HRM as an essentially distinct and homogenous approach, designed to increase employee commitment and performance through the coherent adoption of a combination of "soft" personnel policies. However, research evidence in Ireland and abroad points to the existence of numerous variants of HRM, incorporating different approaches to employee relations, as follows (see Keenoy 1990, Guest 1989, Storey 1992, Gunnigle 1992b):

"Soft" HRM: This approach emphasises the *human resource* aspect of the term "human resource management". This is the most visible form of HRM in Ireland, as practised by companies such as IBM. It is characterised by a resource perspective of employees, incorporating the view that there is an organisational pay-off, in performance terms, from a combination of HRM policies which emphasise consensualism and mutuality of management and employee interests.

Neo-pluralism: This second type of HRM involves moves towards greater consensualism and commitment in unionised companies. It is characterised by what might be termed a "dualist" approach, involving the use of HRM techniques such as direct communications with employees and performance-related pay systems, alongside established collective bargaining procedures. It is indicative of management approaches in a number of Irish organisations such as the Electricity Supply Board (ESB), Aer Rianta and Analog Devices. While possibly less visible and certainly less analysed than "soft HRM", this seems the most common form of HRM in Ireland.

"Hard" HRM: This variant is characterised by the integration of human resource considerations into strategic decision-making to ensure maximum contribution to business performance. The emphasis here is on the *management* aspect of the term "human resource management". In this approach, the organisation's human resources (incorporating not only employees but also subcontracted labour) are seen as similar to any other resource. Thus, human resources should be procured and managed in as cheap and effective a fashion as possible to ensure achievement of the organisations "bottom line" objectives. Examples of this approach are most obvious in the adoption of "atypical" employment forms, particularly the extensive use of subcontracting and temporary/part-time employees in an attempt to improve cost effectiveness while meeting required performance standards.

All of these HRM variants differ from the pluralist model which has traditionally characterised employee relations in the majority of larger organisations in Ireland. While there are obvious differences between these HRM variants, it is significant that the three approaches are all characterised by greater integration of human resource considerations into strategic decision-making and the development of complementary policies to improve human resource utilisation, while the pluralist employee relations model is more reactive in nature.

In evaluating current developments in employee relations in Ireland, there is a danger of confusing prominent examples of "soft" HRM with the widespread pervasiveness of such approaches. Indeed, much of the evidence and support for HRM approaches emanates from the US. However, the context of such developments in the US is considerably different from Ireland and it seems inappropriate simply to extrapolate from the US experience and infer similar trends here. Differences in industrial and employment structure and trade union density are some of the unique factors influencing organisational approaches to employee relations in Ireland.

In this chapter, using data from the Price Waterhouse Cranfield Project, we examine measures of Human Resource Management (HRM) practices, and their relationship with levels of union density in establishments — that is, the extent to which the existence of HRM impacts on union density at establishment level. Furthermore, we analyse variations in employment practices in unionised and non-unionised establishments. Finally, significant differences in organisational approaches to communications are examined.

Trade Unions and HRM Practices

Generally, human resource management (HRM) strategy is aimed at increasing the identification and commitment of the employee to the organisation, and it is sometimes held to be incompatible with the collectivist ethos of unionism (Guest 1989). In a review of American literature on HRM, Beaumont (1992) found that the chief, or at least, most frequently cited components of HRM strategy are: a relatively well-developed internal labour market (in matters of promotion and employee development); flexible work organisations; contingent compensation practices; individual and group participation in task-related decisions; and extensive internal communications arrangements. In this present study, we use the presence of an explicit HRM strategy; employee development (training); contingent compensation practices and communications and flexible work practices to measure the extent of HRM practices in establishments. Unfortunately, no question on employee participation was used in the survey. An explicit HRM strategy is more likely to indicate some level of integration, as well as indicating developed HRM polices and practices. Respondents were asked whether their organisation had a written or unwritten HRM strategy or none at all. Companies with a documented HRM strategy are defined as having a comprehensive strategy. While the existence of an explicit strategy may be a proxy for the components of HRM — rather than a separate factor — it can clarify the interesting question of whether companies which have explicit HRM strategies actually follow through in their employment practices. Employee development is measured by the proportion of salaries and wages currently spent on training. Companies are divided into those which spend greater than or less than 5 per cent on training. Training and development of employees is seen in the HRM literature as an essential component of the flexible firm, improving functional flexibility and also binding the employee to the organisation, particularly where the training is firm-specific (Keep 1992). Although most trade unions encourage the training and development of their members, the relationship between training and union recognition may be negative where training and development are part of a union-substitution strategy. Contingent compensation practices are measured by the presence of performance-related pay schemes and profit-sharing schemes for clerical and/or manual employees, or both. The extent of employee communication with manual and non-manual employees is measured by whether clerical and/or manual employees, or both, are formally briefed on the strategy and financial performance of their company. Flexible work patterns include both functional and numerical flexibility. The increase in, rather than the extent of, functional flexibility is measured here. Respondents were asked to indicate whether jobs had been made wider/more flexible over the past three years for either clerical or manual employees, or both. Numerical flexibility is assessed using the proportion of employees on part-time, temporary or casual and fixed-term contracts of employment. Companies are divided into two categories: those with more than 20 per cent of any one or number of these types of employees in the workforce and those with less.

A statistical analysis of the survey data revealed the following findings in relation to these issues. The existence of profit-sharing schemes and/or performance-related pay is negatively related to the level of unionisation in the establishment. Trade unions are traditionally ambivalent to profit-sharing schemes and often explicitly hostile to performance-linked pay systems. Unions, given their collectivist orientation, aim to standardise wages across workers and prefer such criteria as seniority and the going rate for the job as the determinants of pay levels. Establishments which allocated over 5 per cent of annual salaries on training are also more likely to have a lower level of unionisation. The remaining two measures of HRM practices used in the analysis (communications and flexibility) have no significant relationship to union density in establishments. The existence of a written policy on HRM strategy also has no significant effect on unionisation. Finally, and perhaps somewhat surprisingly, with respect to numerical flexibility, union density does not vary between establishments where more than 20 per cent of the workforce is part-time, temporary/casual or on fixed-term employment contracts. There is no statistical relationship between union density and numerical flexibility, with 60 per cent of establishments which use some form of numerical flexibility having a density level in excess of 76 per cent. However, numerical flexibility is slightly more prevalent in public sector establishments (22 per cent as compared with 16 per cent for private sector organisations).

Union Presence and HRM Practices

Fiorito et al. (1987) argue that HRM practices are often part of attempts by employers either to substitute for, or to avoid, unions. The results of their research support the view that HRM polices affect unionisation. Using a comprehensive index of twelve measures of HRM practices, they conclude that such practices do inhibit unionisation, but that the impact of specific policies varies considerably, with policies in the area of communications and participation having the greatest adverse impact on union-organising success. A relevant hypothesis is, therefore, that the use of HRM practices inhibits union recognition in establishments. On the other hand, Milner and Richards (1991) found a significant positive association between companies which recognised unions and the greater use of employee-involvement techniques such as quality circles, joint consultative committees, suggestion schemes and a regular newsletter. They suggest that recognising a union can facilitate the introduction of employee involvement by providing a ready-made organisational structure, and more importantly, an authority structure among employees which can be utilised to increase the chances of employee involvement techniques succeeding. An alternative — if weaker — hypothesis is, therefore, that unionisation is both compatible with and supportive of the use of HRM practices. Numerical flexibility enables a company to retain a secure, trained and committed core workforce, while coping with uneven demand. It is measured by the proportion of employees on non-standard contracts which are temporary/casual, fixed-term or part-time contracts. Such practices are viewed by trade unions as a central feature of HRM which fragments the workplace, worsening the terms and conditions of employment (Beaumont 1991). A negative relationship can be expected between the extensive use of numerical flexibility and unionisation. Finally, as before, we would expect US companies to have a greater propensity to be non-union.

The following analysis uses the logit technique to examine the effects of HRM practices specifically on union recognition. The variables in the subsequent analysis are similar to the HRM measures used previously. Since union recognition is not an issue for public sector companies, they are excluded.

The results reveal that the nature of payment systems — in this case performance-related pay (PRP) schemes and profit sharing — is the only employment practice which differs significantly in union and non-union firms. There is no significant difference between union and non-union firms in the use of the remaining HRM practices. However, it must be stressed that the measurement of these practices cannot be considered to be empirically extensive or conceptually well developed. For example, functional flexibility broadly refers to the extent to which employees are flexible in the types of work they perform and the range of skills they can use. Our measure of flexibility does not assess the extent of flexibility, but rather whether the perception exists that functional flexibility is increasing or decreasing. Obviously there may be a significant difference in the extent of functional flexibility which our measure fails to establish. Therefore, the conclusion that pay systems are the distinctive factor separating the employment practices of union and non-union firms must be evaluated in the context of the actual measures used. The HRM measures in the Price Waterhouse Cranfield Project do not encompass every aspect of the factor being measured (content validity, for example, may be a problem). However, this is a common problem with empirical studies of HRM practices and partly occurs from the lack of conceptual development in this area. At the same time, there are cogent and convincing reasons for expecting PRP to prevail to a greater extent in non-union firms, reflecting, as we have already noted, a tension between trade union notions of pay and PRP schemes. Moreover, pay practices are more strongly associated with union recognition than size or the proportion of white-collar workers.

EMPLOYMENT PRACTICES AND UNION STATUS

As we have seen, there are no significant differences between union and non-union firms in the use of HRM practices. Nevertheless, there are interesting, if minor, differences. In the following section we compare compensation, communication and work flexibility practices between union and non-union companies.

A significant proportion of companies in the private sector indicated an increase in the use of variable pay as a share of the total reward package offered to employees in both union and non-union companies. Unfortunately, the data does not distinguish between managerial, clerical and manual employees, but it is probable that such increases apply mainly to managerial and professional staff.

TABLE 3.1: UNION STATUS AND UTILISATION OF MERIT PAY AND PROFIT-SHARING SCHEMES

Type	Non-union	Union	TOTAL
Profit Sharing	16% (8)	12% (16)	13% (24)
Merit Pay	60% (30)	53% (69)	55% (99)
Clerical & Manual*	56% (28)	36% (46)	41% (74)

* This measures the combination of performance-related pay schemes and profit-sharing schemes for clerical and manual employees (actual numbers in parenthesis).

Source: Price Waterhouse Cranfield Project (Ireland); University of Limerick 1992.

While the use of profit sharing and performance-related pay for all employees, regardless of union status, is broadly similar, only when clerical and manual employees are included are there substantial differences, with non-union companies making greater use of profit sharing and PRP for lower level employees.

In the area of communications, respondents were asked to indicate whether employees were briefed on company strategy and finances.

TABLE 3.2: UNION STATUS AND PROVISION OF INFORMATION ON BUSINESS STRATEGY TO EMPLOYEES

Grade of Employee	Level of Communications/Briefing on Business Strategy	
	A. Unionised	B. Non-union
Management	91%	96%
Professional/Technical	65%	76%
Clerical	48%	46%
Manual	38%	34%

N = 267

Source: Price Waterhouse Cranfield Project (Ireland); University of Limerick 1992.

TABLE 3.3: UNION STATUS AND PROVISION OF FINANCIAL INFORMATION TO EMPLOYEES

Grade of Employee	Level of Communications/Briefing on Financial Information	
	A. Unionised	B. Non-union
Management	93%	90%
Professional/Technical	60%	62%
Clerical	43%	42%
Manual	35%	28%

N = 267

Source: Price Waterhouse Cranfield Project (Ireland); University of Limerick 1992.

As Tables 3.2 and 3.3 show, there is no significant difference between union and non-union firms with regard to managerial, professional/technical and clerical employees. However, in companies where a union is recognised, manual workers are more likely to be briefed on strategic and financial matters. This reflects, perhaps, the ability of unions to represent the interests of those furthest from the source of such information. In any case, it indicates a significant difference which warrants further research.

Non-union companies have traditionally relied extensively on direct verbal and written communication with their employees. Thus we must be cautious in the interpretation of the large increases in these methods in unionised establishments highlighted in Table 3.4.

TABLE 3.4: UNION STATUS AND TRENDS IN COMMUNICATION

Mode	Non-union				Unionised			
	Increased	Decreased	Same	Total	Increased	Decreased	Same	Total
Staff Bodies (inc. trade unions)	16%	2%	18%	36%	13%	18%	50%	81%
Direct Verbal	46%	2%	46%	94%	62%	2%	28%	92%
Direct Written	30%	2%	44%	76%	45%	4%	35%	84%

The percentages in the table are constructed as a proportion where applicable, of either all union and non-union firms.
Source: Price Waterhouse Cranfield Project (Ireland); University of Limerick 1992.

The trend testifies, particularly, to increasing change in unionised companies with a move towards communication patterns traditionally associated with non-union firms. This indicates, for many firms, a more direct relationship with their employees which includes briefing on strategic and financial matters. Whether this creates a more co-operative climate between management and employees is a moot question and will depend, among other factors, on the nature and extent of the information provided to employees. Post hoc and limited information on strategic and financial affairs is of little use and more often can actually lead to a climate of distrust and calculative behaviour on the part of employees.

Turning to work flexibility, union and non-union firms exhibit similar patterns in the use of numerical flexibility. However, when the trend in specific flexible employment practices is examined, a number of differences emerge (see Tables 3.5 and 3.6).

Sloane and Gaston (1991) separate primary from secondary flexibility and define primary flexibility as non-standard employment contracts where flexibility is built into the job contract. Non-standard employment contracts include part-time work and temporary/casual work. Secondary flexibility refers to such practices as overtime and shift work which can be utilised within the standard employment contract. Union opposition to part-time and casual work encourages the extraction of flexibility from the existing permanent workforce in the form of overtime/shift work and the use of subcontracting and fixed-term contracts. According to this logic, flexibility in unionised firms is more likely to be of a secondary nature, with any subsequent flexibility being sought through subcontracting and fixed-term contracts.

TABLE 3.5: UNION STATUS AND NUMERICAL FLEXIBILITY

	Numerical Flexibility		
	No	Yes	TOTAL
Non-union	86.0%	14.0%	100% (50)
Unionised	82.2%	17.8%	100% (129)
TOTAL	83.2% (149)	16.8% (30)	100% (179)

Number of Missing Observations: 4
Source: Price Waterhouse Cranfield Project (Ireland); University of Limerick 1992.

TABLE 3.6 (a): UNION STATUS AND FLEXIBLE EMPLOYMENT PRACTICES (NON-UNION)

Work Practices	Increase	Decrease	Same	Not Used
Overtime	12%	20%	55%	14%
Part-time Work	22%	4%	26%	61%
Casual Work	45%	9%	28%	15%
Subcontracting	26%	4%	34%	36%
Fixed Contracts	26%	0%	25%	47%

TABLE 3.6 (b): UNION STATUS AND FLEXIBLE EMPLOYMENT PRACTICES (UNION)

Work Practices	Increase	Decrease	Same	Not Used
Overtime	25%	33%	38%	3%
Part-time Work	38%	8%	28%	26%
Casual Work	36%	16%	39%	9%
Subcontracting	34%	5%	29%	30%
Fixed Contracts	37%	4%	31%	28%

Note: Results do not total to 100% because of roundings.
Source: Price Waterhouse Cranfield Project (Ireland); University of Limerick 1992.

The data in Table 3.6 reveal a number of trends. Overtime as a flexibility strategy has increased more in unionised organisations. However, the decrease is also greatest in unionised companies, suggesting perhaps that while they are reliant on it as a means of achieving flexibility, they may be trying to abandon it in favour of other strategies. Part-time work also appears more common in unionised organisations. While casual work has increased more in non-union establishments, the use of fixed-term contracts has grown more in unionised companies.

Significant Change in Employment Practices
Overall, the most notable development arising from the Irish survey data is the increase in direct verbal and written communications with employees. Differences in organisational approaches to communications with employees tend to focus on the nature and content of management–employee communications and the range of mechanisms used to facilitate such communications (see Table 3.7).

TABLE 3.7: COMMUNICATIONS WITH EMPLOYEES

Mode of Communication	Change in Level of Utilisation			
	Increase	Decrease	Same	(N)
Through Representative Staff Bodies e.g. Trade Unions	20.2	16.0	63.8	188
Verbally, Direct to Employees	55.8	1.7	42.6	242
Written, Direct to Employees	44.7	3.7	51.6	219

N = 267
Source: Price Waterhouse Cranfield Project (Ireland); University of Limerick 1992.

It appears from the research evidence that methods of communication employed by organisations and the type of information being communicated to employees have changed in recent years. A number of factors may be used to explain this development, notably:

(i) an increase in quality enhancement initiatives which have facilitated the direct passing on of relevant information on workplace related issues;

(ii) a move towards flatter organisation structures which have facilitated greater and more informative communication at lower levels in the organisation;

(iii) the presence of a more educated workforce — a new kind of person who desires to be involved and informed as much as possible.

In considering the role of trade unions in the communications process, the survey data present quite a stable picture with a majority of organisations reporting little change in the union role. An issue of particular interest here is the degree to which direct communications with employees are being used as a means of circumventing and/or marginalising trade unions in management/employee communications. It is likely that many organisations neither can nor wish suddenly to discontinue to use established collective bargaining fora. Rather, it appears that management–employee communications will increasingly occur through parallel mechanisms.

Turning to the actual content of management/employee communications, the survey data suggest that most Irish firms communicate formally on both business strategy and financial performance with managerial and professional/technical employees (see Table 3.8). However, the level of communications on these issues falls dramatically for clerical and manual grades. The most dramatic contrast arises in the area of communication on financial performance where over 90 per cent of organisations claim to communicate formally on this issue with managerial grades, but only 33 per cent do so with manual grades.

TABLE 3.8: COMMUNICATIONS ON STRATEGY AND FINANCIAL PERFORMANCE

Grade of Employee	Level of Communications/Briefing on	
	A. Strategy	B. Financial Performance
Management	92.5%	90.6%
Professional/Technical	64.4%	57.3%
Clerical	41.6%	39.0%
Manual	36.0%	33.0%

N = 267
Source: Price Waterhouse Cranfield Project (Ireland); University of Limerick 1992.

In general, it seems that the more sophisticated firms tend to use a range of communications mechanisms with particular emphasis on direct communications with individual employees. Such expansive approaches seem to be quite evident in newer organisations but not nearly as widespread in longer established organisations. A study of HRM practices in newly established ("Greenfield") companies (see Chapter 9 for a detailed discussion) confirms this focus on extensive direct communications with individual employees (Gunnigle 1992a). This study suggests that the nature and scope of communications fora are more sophisticated in the great majority of US-owned firms, particularly in the computer/ high technology sector. The more sophisticated firms tend to use a range of communications mechanisms with particular emphasis on direct communications with individual employees. The most common approaches focus on "cascade" mechanisms with briefings for different employee levels augmented by communications through line management, general workforce meetings and other written and oral communications. However, the majority of older established Irish organisations seem to adopt less sophisticated approaches and rely primarily on collective bargaining, basic written communications and normal line management–employee interactions.

CONCLUSIONS

The evidence presented in this chapter does not point to the widespread adoption of HRM approaches. Change in the dominant paradigm of employee relations is more likely to be of a piecemeal nature, with change being gradual, rather than dramatic and involving incremental modification of the adversarial and pluralist model of employee relations. It seems that developments in business strategy and product markets are creating greater organisational awareness of the impact of employee relations issues on organisation performance. In particular, it would appear that employers are increasingly seeking to adopt selected HRM techniques (such as performance-related pay). However, the more widespread adoption of comprehensive HRM approaches would require significant change in the approach of Irish managements, particularly in relation to integrating employee relations considerations into strategic decision making. Thus, it seems more likely that where HRM initiatives are adopted, this will occur alongside, rather than in place of, traditional workforce management approaches, particularly collective bargaining. However, there are indications that some organisations are pursuing more sophisticated approaches, particularly in companies established since 1970, with such approaches ranging from sophisticated, employee-centred HRM policies to "harder" approaches based on low-pay/low-cost strategies. Research evidence in Ireland points to the existence of numerous variants of HRM, incorporating different approaches to employee relations. While there are no significant differences between union and non-union firms in the use of HRM practices, there are interesting, if minor differences in the area of compensation, communication and work flexibility.

Non-union companies make greater use of profit sharing and PRP for lower level employees. In companies where a union is recognised, manual workers are more likely to be briefed on strategic and financial matters, perhaps reflecting the ability of the union to represent the interests of those furthest from the source of such information. There is evidence of change in unionised companies with a move towards communication patterns traditionally associated with non-union firms, which indicates for many firms, a more direct relationship with their employees. With respect to flexibility, union and non-union firms exhibit similar patterns in the use of numerical flexibility, with only minor differences being observed. The impact of contemporary quality initiatives is felt to be significant in the area of management–employee communications and such initiatives have facilitated the passing on directly of relevant information on workplace-related issues. With respect to the content of management/employees communications, the most dramatic contrast arises in the area of communication on financial performance, where over 90 per cent of organisations claim to communicate formally on this issue with managerial grades, but only 33 per cent do so with manual grades.

Chapter 4

THE PERSONNEL/HUMAN RESOURCE FUNCTION AND EMPLOYEE RELATIONS

Kieran Foley and Patrick Gunnigle

INTRODUCTION

A particularly significant aspect of managerial approaches to employee relations concerns the role of the specialist personnel/human resource (P/HR) function. The function, having firmly established itself as a central component in organisational hierarchies by the 1970s, undertook as its key activity the development and administration of employee relations. Practitioners operated in a pluralistic, adversarial environment in which their perceived contribution was largely reactive, dealing with problematic aspects of workforce management.

In recent years there have been some indications of a reorientation of the role of the personnel/HR function (Tyson 1987). With the need to link the functioning of employees explicitly to the strategic direction of the organisation becoming more critical, traditional practices and beliefs have been reappraised in the light of contemporary developments. Aspects of this change would seem to include a broadening of the role of the personnel/HR function to incorporate not only employee relations, but also areas such as employee development, job design and reward systems, greater emphasis on the management of change and greater involvement in developing and implementing business strategy. It is suggested that many organisations are investigating different/more innovative modes of workforce management, the most important being HRM, which Guest (1989) feels is slowly but inevitably replacing personnel management.

THE PERSONNEL/HR FUNCTION IN IRELAND: THE RESEARCH EVIDENCE

Gunnigle and Flood (1990) highlight that the development of a formalised HR function in Ireland is a relatively recent phenomenon with much of the growth occurring in the post-1970s period. Such growth, however, has not been uniform, the precise role of the specialist personnel/HR function varying considerably from company to company depending on various internal and external factors. In attempting to explain variations in the role and status of HRM practitioners, studies by Murray (1984), Shivanath (1986) and Gunnigle (1992) found that company ownership appeared to have a pronounced effect on the role and status of practitioners. The remainder of this chapter considers recent evidence on the effect of ownership and other key variables on the personnel/HR function in Irish organisations, with particular reference to the issue of workplace employee relations. Such evidence will be drawn principally from Shivanath's (1987) survey and the Price Waterhouse Cranfield data. Analysis of the personnel/HR function will be undertaken at four levels:

(i)   presence;
(ii) role of the function;
(iii) activities; and
(iv) characteristics of the department.

Presence of the Personnel Function
Perhaps the most obvious indicator of the status of the personnel/HR function in an organisational context is its existence as a distinct management specialisation, the assumption being that the presence of a specialist department or manager signifies a degree of importance attached to such issues. This indicator was quite favourable in 1986, Shivanath finding that 81 per cent of organisations with more than 100 employees employed personnel/HR specialists, although only 70 per cent had formalised personnel/HR functions. The vast majority of respondent companies to the Price Waterhouse Cranfield Study report the continued enshrinement of formalised personnel/HR departments/managers in their organisational systems. Approximately 62 per cent of respondents report the presence of a personnel/HR practitioner, this proportion increasing to 80 per cent for organisations with in excess of 100 employees and to 87 per cent in those organisations employing greater than 200 employees. Such strong presence offers prima facie evidence of the continuing importance of personnel/HR considerations in respondent organisations and the integral role of personnel/HR functions in interactions with employees. While this result is indicative of the fact that personnel/HR considerations continue to be priorities amongst organisations in Ireland, it is subject to a number of qualifications. As seen above, organisational size,

as measured by number of employees, has a major impact with larger organisations reporting a greater incidence of such departments. While in excess of 75 per cent of organisations with less than 100 employees have no personnel/HR function, this is true in only approximately 6 per cent of organisations with greater than 2,000 employees. The correlation between increasing organisational size and presence is not surprising, given the administration needs of larger organisations and the existence of greater resources to fund such specialist functions. In small organisations such needs are not as great and many of the personnel/HR activities are carried out by other functional managers. Respondents from small organisations indicate that this role is predominantly carried out by the CEO, particularly at board level, where approximately 63 per cent of organisations report this to be the case.

The recognition of a trade union also acts as a determinant of presence, with a greater propensity of organisations which recognise unions to have formalised personnel/HR functions, than of those which do not. As may be seen from Table 4.1 below, just under 44 per cent of the latter have personnel functions/managers. This is relatively surprising, given the more individually based relationships emphasised by many such organisations and the resulting administration needs which this places upon them. In the absence of unions, many organisations have sought to elaborate procedures to enable employees to be dealt with on an individual basis. However, this has not resulted in an increase in the establishment of formalised functions in such organisations.

TABLE 4.1: TRADE UNION RECOGNITION AS A DETERMINANT OF PRESENCE OF PERSONNEL/HR FUNCTION

Personnel/HR Function	Union	Non-union
Yes	66.2% (137)	43.9% (25)
No	32.9% (68)	54.4% (31)
Missing	1.0% (2)	1.8% (1)
	N = 207	N = 57

Source: Price Waterhouse Cranfield Project (Ireland); University of Limerick 1992.

Figure 4.1 demonstrates the impact of ownership on the existence or otherwise of a specialist function. The composition of the Irish industrial structure has traditionally been quite diverse, particularly in light of the penetration of MNCs. While McMahon et al. (1988) feel that MNCs have adapted to accommodate local practices, this has not necessarily resulted in an abandonment of foreign management philosophy, but rather, in the pursuit of such within existing frameworks and customs. Thus, ownership forms an important area of analysis. Japanese and US organisations reported such presence in 100 and 90.4 per cent of cases respectively, as opposed to 78.6 per cent in the case of UK organisations and only 49 per cent of Irish indigenous organisations. While initially the personnel/HR function appeared to have been established firmly as an important subsystem in respondent organisations, such presence is quite polarised, and positively influenced by union recognition and increasing organisational size. Ownership also impacts on presence with all foreign MNCs, with the exception of organisations from Sweden and Switzerland, showing a greater propensity than Irish indigenous organisations to have such functions.

FIGURE 4.1: OWNERSHIP: A DETERMINANT OF PRESENCE

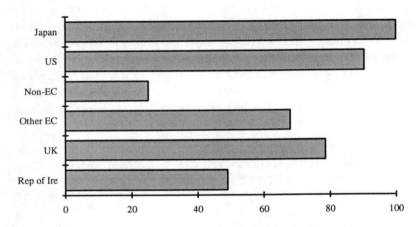

Source: Price Waterhouse Cranfield Project (Ireland); University of Limerick 1992.

It is difficult to generalise on the implications of departmental presence, as an indicator of the role of the personnel/HR function in workplace employee relations, for a number of reasons. First, given the polarisation outlined above, generalisations made without reference to size, ownership and whether or not the organisation recognises unions are unlikely to be valid. Secondly, while presence is the most obvious indicator of the role of the personnel/HR function, it is also the crudest, the assumption being that presence indicates an organisational concern with HR issues. While, indeed, this may be the case, it is not true to say that absence indicates a low priority concern and gives little indication of what role the function is actually entrusted with in the organisation. A second, and perhaps a more enlightening, measure of the role of the function in employee relations may be gleaned by reference to the hierarchical status of the function and of practitioners in respondent organisations.

Role of the Personnel Function

This essentially represents a measure of the level at which the personnel/HR function is operating within the organisation, thus giving an indication of the prevailing attitude towards its contribution to workplace employee relations. It may be understood with reference to two key factors: reporting level; and input into top management decision-making.

Reporting Level

In this instance we are concerned with the reporting level of the top HR practitioner. The top practitioner, as with all functional heads, occupies a powerful position within their department. Reference to their role in the organisation gives an indication of the level at which the function as a whole is operating. In 1986 Personnel/HRM held a prominent position amongst top management with 70 per cent of the respondents reporting to CEO/MD or equivalent and a much smaller 15.2 per cent reporting to a lower level manager.

Shivanath (1986) highlighted a number of factors which influence reporting levels. Ownership has a significant effect in this case with practitioners in both the Irish public and private sectors reporting to one superior in the vast majority of cases (92.9 per cent and 90.0 per cent respectively). European organisations report a greater likelihood for practitioners to have more than one superior and US companies indicate that in more than 50 per cent of cases this is also the situation (see Table 4.2).

TABLE 4.2: OWNERSHIP AS A DETERMINANT OF REPORTING LEVEL

More Than One Superior	Yes	No
Irish Private	10.0%	90.0%
Irish Public	7.1%	92.9%
US	52.9%	47.1%
European	21.1%	78.9%

Source: Shivanath 1986.

Straightforward conclusions, based on these results, should, however, be treated with some caution, as a reason for the lower frequencies cited amongst US and European companies may be more as a result of their multi-establishment structures, rather than a low-level personnel function within the organisation

The sector within which the organisation existed was also found to have an influence on reporting levels. Shivanath found a greater propensity on the part of functions within the services sector, to operate at a more strategic level, possibly as a result of the traditional labour intensity of many of the service industries and the centrality of efficient HR utilisation to overall effectiveness. The general picture provided in 1986 is one of high-level reporting for the vast majority of personnel/HR practitioners and their inclusion amongst top management. The position in relation to further progression up the organisational hierarchy was not as encouraging in 1986, as a significantly smaller percentage is represented at Board and CEO level (9.1 per cent and 3.0 per cent respectively) than was represented at top management level. While the personnel function in 1986 had achieved top management status in the majority of Irish organisations, failure to achieve further progression effectively deprived the function of an arena in which to formulate truly strategic, integrated plans at the highest level.

The Price Waterhouse Cranfield project highlights an encouraging move towards greater representation of top personnel/HR practitioners at board level, with respondent organisations indicating that in almost 30.5 per cent of cases the top personnel/HR practitioner has a place on the board. US companies demonstrate much greater board level participation by top level HR managers (50 per cent) than any other categories. Irish indigenous organisations show a relatively low level of representation, and at 23.2 per cent is quite a deal lower than our EC counterparts, although it is more reflective of the trend amongst UK organisations at 28.6 per cent (see Table 4.3 below). Those organisations which recognise trade unions showed much higher board level participation than those who did not (33.8 per cent and 17.5 per cent respectively).

TABLE 4.3: OWNERSHIP AS A DETERMINANT OF BOARD LEVEL REPRESENTATION

	Rep of Ireland	UK	Other EC Euro	Non-EC Euro	USA	Other	N/A
YES	23.2%	28.6%	41.0%	25.0%	50.0%	37.5%	21.4%

Source: Price Waterhouse Cranfield Project (Ireland); University of Limerick 1992.

It is difficult to generalise about the effect of size on board level participation (Figure 4.2). However, there does appear to be a correlation between increasing organisation size and board level participation. Only 14.3 per cent of respondents in small companies (<100) have personnel/ HR practitioners on the board. This is the case in 66.7 per cent of companies with in excess of 1,000 but less than 2,000 and in 55.6 per cent for organisations with greater than 2,000 employees.

FIGURE 4.2: SIZE AS A DETERMINANT OF BOARD LEVEL REPRESENTATION

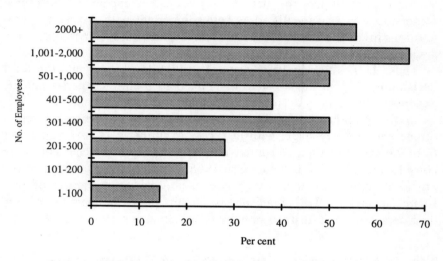

Source: Price Waterhouse Cranfield Project (Ireland); University of Limerick 1992.

HR practitioners in 1992 appeared to enjoy access to the boardroom to a greater degree than they had previously. In theory, this should enable practitioners to ensure that HR considerations are encompassed into any strategy formulation the organisation undertakes. While the above gives primary evidence of a high level of strategic integration of HR considerations, it fails to identify the actual nature of the activity at this level. This information may be ascertained by reference to a second factor; the input of personnel/HR practitioners into top level decision-making.

Input into Top Management Decision-Making
Given the high level of representation at the higher echelons of Irish organisations among the survey respondents, one would expect them to

have a large impact on decisions taken at this level. This indeed would appear to be the case, with Shivanath (1986) identifying a minimum participation rate in a wide range of issues of 70 per cent at early stages. However, the high participation rates cited relate to issues deemed to be directly within the realms of personnel/HRM. Shivanath highlighted a number of factors determining the level of involvement in decision-making. With respect to sector, Shivanath identified that in a number of issues personnel/HR specialists in the public sector were more likely to be involved at an earlier stage than their manufacturing counterparts. This result is predictable given the advanced reporting level witnessed amongst practitioners in the public sector. Company/establishment ownership was also identified as being important with American organisations involving their practitioners earlier than European companies in a wide range of issues.

Thus, the position in 1986 was one of high-level input into top level decision-making in areas ostensibly linked to traditional personnel/HR expertise, with greatly decreased participation in areas outside this.

In the present study, organisations involve their personnel practitioners at an early stage, with in excess of 56 per cent involved either from the outset or on a consultative basis and only 8 per cent not being consulted at all. As was the case in 1986, the ultimate ownership of the organisation has an impact on the decision-making discretion of personnel specialists. US organisations remain more inclined to involve their personnel specialists in strategy formulation at early stages.

TABLE 4.4: HR PARTICIPATION IN STRATEGY FORMULATION

At What Level is HR/Personnel Involved in Corporate Strategy Development?	%
From the Outset	38.3
Consultative	18.2
Implementation	8.6
Not Consulted	7.8

Source: Price Waterhouse Cranfield Project (Ireland); University of Limerick 1992.

As may be seen from Table 4.5 below, almost 70 per cent of US organisations used such practitioners at either the outset or in a consultative capacity, as opposed to 63.7 per cent of European organisations. Practitioners in Irish indigenous companies fare relatively poorly with just over 50 per cent of practitioners involved at advanced levels.

Personnel/HR specialists in UK-owned organisations fare a little better with 42.9 per cent consulted at the outset as opposed to 36.8 per cent in the case of Irish organisations.

TABLE 4.5: OWNERSHIP AS A DETERMINANT OF PARTICIPATION IN STRATEGY FORMULATION

	Rep. of Ireland (%)	UK (%)	Other EC Euro (%)	Non-EC Euro (%)	USA (%)	Other (%)	N/A (%)
From the Outset	36.8	42.9	45.5	—	42.3	25.0	42.9
Consultative	16.1	14.3	18.2	—	26.9	25.0	14.3
Implementation	5.8	14.3	9.1	50.0	9.6	12.5	14.3
Not Consulted	7.1	7.1	9.1	25.0	9.6	12.5	—
Missing	34.2	21.4	18.2	25.0	11.5	25.0	28.6

Source: Price Waterhouse Cranfield Project (Ireland); University of Limerick 1992.

Trade union recognition also influences participation, with practitioners in organisations which do not recognise unions less likely to be consulted at the outset and more likely not to be consulted at all than their counterparts in unionised organisations. While over 40 per cent of specialists in unionised environments are consulted at the outset, this is true in only approximately 30 per cent of non-unionised organisations. 22.8 per cent of managers in such environments are only involved in reactive implementation or not at all, as opposed to approximately 15 per cent of managers where unions are recognised.

TABLE 4.6: TRADE UNION RECOGNITION AS A DETERMINANT OF PARTICIPATION IN STRATEGY FORMULATION

	Union	**Non-union**	**Missing**
From the Outset	40.1%	31.6%	40.0%
Consultative	18.8%	17.5%	—
Implementation	7.7%	10.5%	20.0%
Not Consulted	6.8%	12.3%	—
Missing	26.6%	28.1%	40.0%

Source: Price Waterhouse Cranfield Project (Ireland); University of Limerick 1992.

Sector does not appear to impact greatly on the role of the personnel/ HR practitioner in the development of corporate strategy. As may be seen from Figure 4.3 below, in excess of 75 per cent of respondent organisations, in both sectors, involve their practitioners at advanced stages.

FIGURE 4.3: HR FUNCTION PARTICIPATION IN STRATEGY FORMULATION

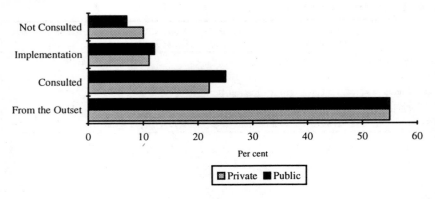

Source: Price Waterhouse Cranfield Project (Ireland); University of Limerick 1992.

The size of the organisation influences personnel/HR involvement in corporate strategy development, with specialists in large organisations more likely to be involved in strategy formulation. In the current survey, 55.6 per cent of practitioners in organisations with in excess of 2,000 employees reported having an input into corporate strategy at the initiation stage, whereas in small companies (under 100 employees) only 36.9 per cent of specialists indicated such involvement. 15.4 per cent of practitioners in small companies were either involved in implementation or were not involved. In the case of large companies, in no instance did the practitioner indicate such low-level participation.

In recent years there have been changes in line management's participation in decision-making on personnel matters. Changes, however, in decision-making patterns have not been homogeneous across organisations. In 1986 the task which took the majority of the HR specialists' time and effort was employee relations. The current survey highlights a large number of organisations reporting an increase in the participation of line managers in this area.

This increase has been particularly significant amongst line managers in organisations where unions are recognised. Thirty per cent of these organisations indicate an increase in line participation with under 3.5 per cent citing a decrease. Line managers in such organisations are no longer willing to leave the resolution of such problems to personnel specialists, but increasingly attempts are being made to solve such problems at the lowest level possible. Organisations are putting procedures in place emphasising the role of line managers and their instrumentality in ensuring employee relations harmony by solving problems as they occur. Such encroachment into traditional HR/personnel practices represents both a challenge to and an opportunity for the HR function. It removes one source of the function's expert power and thus has the potential to undermine the legitimacy of the function within the organisational context. The increasing participation of line management may however provide an opportunity for more proactive pursuits and a further move away from the stereotypical fire-fighting role.

TABLE 4.7: CHANGES IN LINE MANAGEMENT PARTICIPATION IN DECISION MAKING

	Increased	Decreased	Same
Pay & Benefits	13.4%	3.7%	77.7%
Recruitment	24.5%	5.2%	65.4%
Training. & Development.	34.9%	5.2%	55.4%
Industrial Relations	27.9%	4.1%	61.7%
Health/Safety	46.5%	3.3%	45.7%
Workforce Increase/Decrease	19.3%	2.2%	72.5%

Source: Price Waterhouse Cranfield Project (Ireland); University of Limerick 1992.

The increase in line management participation in decision-making has not been as dramatic amongst non-unionised organisations (see Appendix 1, Table 4A). This may not necessarily be indicative of a lack of emphasis on the possible contribution of line managers, but rather the fact that such managers have traditionally had an instrumental role in the pursuit of good employee relations within such organisations.

Increased line management participation also appears to be positively correlated with organisational size. Larger organisations, with the exception of those with between 1,001 and 2,000 employees, show significant increases in the use of line managers in employee relations and no respondent organisation with in excess of 400 employees reports any decrease. The relatively low increase in the smaller organisations may be indicative of the hands on management necessary in such organisations, rather than of a lack of commitment to including line managers in the administration of employee relations.

In small organisations managers' tasks encompass a wide range of areas which need not necessarily be considered within the scope of their particular expertise. This is especially true in relation to personnel activities and the propensity of such organisations to have no formalised personnel/HR function. In such organisations, line managers will almost inevitably be involved in employee relations, and thus the smaller increase may be as a result of the high level of participation rather than declining commitment. All organisations of various nationalities showed an increase in the use of line managers in employee relations, with the exception of Sweden and Switzerland.

TABLE 4.8: OWNERSHIP AS A DETERMINANT OF THE ROLE OF LINE MANAGERS IN EMPLOYEE RELATIONS

	Rep. of Ireland (%)	UK (%)	Other EC Euro (%)	Non-EC Euro (%)	USA (%)	Other (%)	N/A (%)
Increased	27.1	14.3	45.5	—	28.8	37.5	21.4
Same	60.0	78.6	45.5	100.0	65.4	50.0	71.4
Decreased	3.9	7.1	9.1	—	1.9	12.5	—
Missing	9.0	—	—	—	3.8	—	7.1

Source: Price Waterhouse Cranfield Project (Ireland); University of Limerick 1992.

Overall therefore, evidence from the Price Waterhouse Cranfield data in relation to the decision-making discretion of personnel/HR specialists seems to paint a tentatively favourable picture with a trend towards higher strategic integration of the personnel/HR function, a move towards greater board level participation and a potentially greater impact on the strategic direction of the organisation. The move towards a more proactive stance for personnel/HR specialists is coupled with an increasing role for line managers in some of the more reactive and fire-fighting pursuits traditionally associated with personnel/HRM.

Activities of Personnel/HR Function
Thus far, we have examined the presence of formalised departments in respondent organisations and also the level of strategic integration such departments enjoy. What is of concern here, however, is the actual activities undertaken by managers or departments. In 1986 the majority of respondents' time was taken up with the process of collective bargaining, reflecting the link of the personnel/HR function with employee relations concerns. This employee relations emphasis reflects a traditional reliance

on collectivist dealings with employees via trade unions and collective bargaining as the predominant model of personnel practice in most public sector and larger private indigenous organisations. Personnel/HR practitioners in 1986 felt that on the whole they were engaged in activities in which they ought to be involved (Table 4.9).

TABLE 4.9: PERSONNEL SPECIALIST ACTIVITIES

	Rank Time Spent on	Rank Time Should Be Spent on
Industrial Relations	1	1
General Mgt. & Administration	2	3
Training & Development	3	2
Recruitment & Selection	4	5
Pay & Conditions	5	7

Source: Shivanath 1986.

Evidence from this survey also rejects the stereotypical image of personnel/HR practitioners as fire-fighters. A large number of respondents felt a greater percentage of their time was spent on proactive rather than reactive pursuits. Thus, while practitioners in 1986 were involved in the realms of industrial relations, this did not limit their contribution exclusively to day-to-day concerns.

As has previously been noted, the level of input of the personnel function into various activities has been changing in recent times. The present survey, however, brings to light a number of fundamental shifts in emphasis of the personnel/HR function. Traditionally, the key concern of the functions, both in terms of specialist perceptions and the actual time spent, was the administration of employee relations practices. The Price Waterhouse Cranfield data highlights a declining perception of the absolute importance of employee relations issues and increasing concentration on training issues.

TABLE 4.10: PERSONNEL OBJECTIVES IN TERMS OF IMPORTANCE OVER NEXT THREE YEARS

(1)	Training & Development
(2)	Efficiency/Productivity
(3&4)	Quality/Employee Relations
(5)	Health & Safety Environment

Source: Price Waterhouse Cranfield Project (Ireland); University of Limerick 1992.

This perception of a decline in the importance of employee relations may be explained by reference to a number of factors. Here the return to centralised bargaining is of some significance. Unions in Ireland have traditionally concerned themselves with a relatively narrow focus of negotiation, often limited to pay and conditions, while de-emphasising broader social issues. The move towards more individualised relations and also centralised bargaining in the form of the current PCW has removed a key area of negotiation and confrontation from the level of the firm. Economic recession and a shift in the balance of power is also significant. The inability of unions to gain large pay increases in the face of economic recession has served to undermine their credibility in the eyes of employees, a problem which has been exacerbated by the reassertion of management prerogative in many Irish organisations. With the exception of a small number of high-profile conflicts, the restriction of industrial action due to the perceived need to maintain job security has resulted in the possible muting of employee relations conflict and its subsequent declining importance at the level of the firm.

Characteristics of the Personnel Function and the Personnel Specialist

The final determinant of the impact of the personnel/HR function on workplace employee relations which is of concern here is the characteristics of the function. Up to this point the characteristics of the individuals that form the personnel function have not been considered and as such it has been viewed as an entity which varied across organisations in terms of levels of strategic integration and activities carried out. In the succeeding paragraphs therefore, a general profile of personnel functions and managers shall be outlined. This may be subcategorised into two areas:

(i)   General characteristics;
(ii) Profile of those involved in the operation of the function.

General Characteristics

The most important single characteristic is size as it gives not only prima facie evidence of the importance of personnel concerns within the organisation, but also the load of activities carried out by personnel. While size is important, perhaps a more meaningful statistic is the ratio of practitioners to employees. In this respect, Shivanath (1986) found that ownership (whether US, European or Irish indigenous), sector (whether public or private) and company status (whether headquarters or division) all have an impact on the ratio of personnel staff to employees.

Irish private sector companies reported a ratio of 1:117, while

European- and American-owned companies reported much lower ratios (1:74 and 1:65 respectively), which may indicate a greater concern with personnel/HR issues among European and US companies. While Irish private companies reported very large ratios, the converse is true of public sector establishments which reflects the traditional high administrative staff numbers seen in such organisations.

While the above represent key determinants, they are not the only ones. The size of organisation, the company philosophy, the level of unionisation and location of functions also have an influence. Overall, the average size of the personnel function of respondents to the current survey is relatively small with 84 per cent of organisations having departments consisting of fewer than eleven employees and only 5.7 per cent having in excess of 25 employees.

Practitioner Profile
The typical profile of a practitioner in 1986 was male, 41 years of age, of Irish nationality holding at least a diploma, possibly in personnel, but not likely to be a member of the IPM. The practitioner reported to the CEO/MD, had three or more direct subordinates and had ten years' experience when entering the profession from a technical background. The current survey portrays the respondents as a highly educated group of practitioners. More than 64 per cent have been educated to primary degree level, are more likely to have a degree in business studies than any other discipline, and have at least five years' experience. The size of the organisation does not appear to have an identifiable impact on the experience of top practitioners, although small organisations reported a smaller proportion of practitioners with more than five years' experience (35 per cent). Ownership (Figure 4.4) has a significant impact here, with Irish indigenous organisations indicating a greater incidence of top managers with less than five years' experience. The top practitioner is more likely to have originated from either a non-personnel specialism in the respondent organisation or from a personnel specialism outside the organisation. This generalisation becomes less valid as organisational size increases with such organisations tending to hire professionals with proven expertise in the field.

The sector in which a practitioner is employed (see Appendix 1, Table 4C) is a strong indicator of the practitioner's level of experience, with private sector organisations having a much greater percentage of practitioners with more than five years' experience than was evident for public sector organisations.

FIGURE 4.4: EXPERIENCE OF PERSONNEL/HR PRACTITIONERS

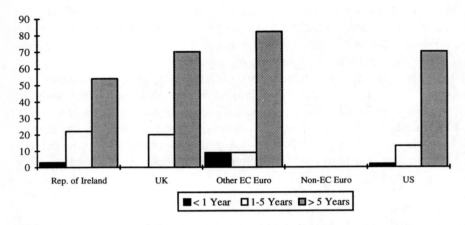

Source: Price Waterhouse Cranfield Project (Ireland); University of Limerick
1992.

Personnel practitioners, as was the case in 1986, represent a highly qualified cohort of managers in terms of academic and job-related achievements. The myth of the personnel manger as being a role for displaced and no longer effective managers has been dispelled by this and other research. Personnel/HR managers at the front line in their organisations are sufficiently qualified to ensure that personnel/HR issues are dealt with effectively and are sufficiently educated and experienced to ensure that human resources are put to effective use.

CONCLUSIONS

The impact of the personnel function on workplace employee relations in recent times has been one of continuity and change. Continuity is evident in that the personnel/HR function remains inexorably entwined in the employee relations of the vast majority of respondent organisations, as previous surveys had indicated. Change has occurred not only in the role which such functions undertake, but also the level at which they act within the organisation. The 1980s, the 1990s and almost certainly the decades beyond, will be, as Charles Handy (1991) terms them, an "age of unreason", in which the only stable presence in an organisational context is likely to be the existence of turbulence and change. The personnel function, as is the case with all functions, has been forced to re-evaluate its contribution to organisational effectiveness in light of worsening economic conditions.

The current research indicates that such re-evaluation has reshaped the face of HR in Ireland and the impact of formalised personnel/HR functions on employee/employer interactions at the level of the organisation. The change has not been homogenous across organisations, however, and generalisations made without reference to trade union recognition and ultimate ownership are of dubious validity and serve to veil much of what the Price Waterhouse Cranfield data has to tell us.

Unlike Shivanath's 1986 survey and the more recent work of Monks, this project provides evidence of a trend towards greater strategic integration of personnel/HR practitioners into the highest echelons of respondent organisations. Presence on the boards of organisations and the prominent role of such practitioners in strategy formulation not only indicates high-level functioning, but also active participation by HR specialists at this level. Unfortunately, however, the enhancement of the impact of the personnel/HR role is not universal, with US MNCs and organisations recognising trade unions showing greater tendencies to incorporate HR concerns at the very highest level. The personnel/HR function at this level has the potential to alter, fundamentally, the face of employee relations at the level of the firm through its participation in decision-making at the highest level. Such findings substantiate Tyson's assertion that recessionary pressures will cause the organisation to tend to the extremes of his typology. While the above outlines a move towards changemaker/architect roles for HR/personnel, such changes are concentrated amongst predominantly foreign multinational companies. While such organisations represent an important component of the industrial structure of the Irish economy, they do, however, represent a minority, important and influential though it might be. The evidence from indigenous Irish organisations is less hopeful and represents a more constrained role for personnel/HRM.

Personnel Practitioners in Indigenous Industry
— the Role Undermined?

Perhaps the most surprising finding arising from the current survey is the large percentage of Irish indigenous respondents who report the absence of formalised HR departments and managers. Less than 50 per cent of Irish-owned organisations in the sample have a formalised function, as opposed to almost 80 per cent among UK-owned organisations. Where a formalised presence does exist, practitioners in such organisations are much less likely to be involved in strategy formulation at advanced levels.

While recent evidence (Monks 1992) indicates that practitioners in Irish organisations are highly skilled — a fact substantiated by the present survey in terms of the level of academic achievement noted — the current survey seems to indicate an increasing polarisation in the role of personnel/HR practitioners in Ireland. Such a shift appears to be from the custodian of procedures either to an increasingly clerical or to a more strategic role. While the present project does not attempt to herald the arrival of HR practitioners to either role, it does, however, attempt to chronicle the first steps of Irish organisations in adopting such models. The personnel function in Ireland is neither predominantly strategic nor predominantly operational. The data, however, does indicate the beginning of a possible polarisation towards one or other of these typologies.

The personnel/HR function in 1992 remains a central component of respondents' organisational hierarchies. Such presence was found to be positively correlated with increasing organisational size and trade union recognition. US- and Japanese-owned establishments exhibited the greatest tendency to have set up such functions. Foreign multinational organisations on the whole showed a greater propensity to have such functions than did Irish indigenous organisations. Sectoral analysis failed to identify any significant differences between public and private organisations. The personnel/HR function is relatively well represented on the boards of respondent organisations. Increasing organisational size, trade union recognition and US ownership appear to be determinants not only of board level representation, but also of the formulation of corporate strategy. Line managers are, almost universally, adopting a more central role in the administration of employee relations in respondent organisations. Larger organisations, particularly those functioning in a unionised environment are typically calling upon their line managers to take ownership for employee relations and traditional personnel activities. Respondents from organisations of all nationalities, report an increase in the role of line managers in traditional employee relations matters. Employee relations is no longer viewed by practitioners as the central personnel/HR activity. Such pursuits have been relegated as training and development, and efficiency becomes the critical issues facing practitioners. Potential explanations for such shifts include the return to centralised bargaining, the economic recession and a shift in the balance of power.

Practitioners, as was the case in 1986, are a highly educated and experienced group. In excess of 60 per cent have been educated to primary degree level, which, in all probability, is likely to be a business-related qualification. Non-unionised organisations indicate the greatest proportion of formally qualified practitioners and also those with the least personnel experience, particularly when compared with private sector organisations in general. The practitioner is likely to have been recruited from either a non-personnel specialism within the organisation or from a personnel specialism outside. Larger organisations, however, tended to recruit practitioners with proven ability in the field.

Chapter 5

A REVIEW OF ORGANISATIONAL REWARD PRACTICES

Patrick Gunnigle, Kieran Foley and Michael Morley

INTRODUCTION

An organisation's reward system is a powerful indicator of its philosophy and reflects the corporate approach to human resources. Decisions made on such systems will impact on a number of areas, not least among them employee relations, supervisory style and employee motivation. The particular package offered will be determined by a variety of factors related to the organisation, the general business environment and the workforce. It will consider the relative emphasis on extrinsic versus intrinsic rewards, the role of pay, whether it is contingent upon individual performance and the system's compatibility with the organisation's business goals. As with other aspects of personnel/HR management, the corporate approach to compensation should complement the organisation's strategic business goals, personnel philosophy and other personnel activities.

The design and implementation of an effective reward system have proven difficult tasks for many organisations. Such difficulties have manifested themselves in the myriad of forms now in common use in Ireland (Table 5.1 below), as organisations strive to develop a system which is instrumental in achieving employee relations objectives. Evidence from 1980 indicates that flat-rate-only schemes represent the key pay system for both direct and indirect employees, although often coupled with a performance-related element.

Beer (1985) suggests that many employee grievances and criticisms of reward systems actually mask more fundamental employee relations problems. Because extrinsic rewards are a tangible outcome of an employee's relationship with an organisation, they are an obvious target for discontent with the employment relationship. Dissatisfaction with elements of this relationship — such as the supervisory style or opportunities for personal development — may manifest themselves in dissatisfaction with aspects of the reward system. Consequently, organisations experiencing problems with their reward systems should examine decisions taken on other personnel policy issues, such as selection, employee relations or work design, rather than making piecemeal changes to the compensation package.

TABLE 5.1: UTILISATION OF PAYMENT SYSTEMS IN IRELAND

Payment System	Utilisation	Direct Manual Employees Only	Indirect Employees Only*
Flat Rate Only	70.5%	53.4%	66.3%
Flat Rate + Individual PBR	15.3%	27.4%	6.2%
Flat Rate + Group PBR	8.6%	12.0%	15.8%
Flat Rate + Company PBR	2.6%	3.9%	6.0%
Piecework	3.0%	3.3%	0.2%

* Figures here do not add up to 100 % because remaining percentage — 5.5 per cent — used some form of "lieu bonus" for indirect employees.

Source: Mooney, P. *An Inquiry into wage payment systems in Ireland* ESRI/ European Foundation for the improvement of Living and Working Conditions, 1980.

Another potential problem concerns suggestions that pay should be contingent on individual performance. Support for contingent payment systems is based on the concept that it is fair and logical to reward individual employees differentially, based on some measure of performance. While this principle is rarely a source of contention, problems may arise in attempting to develop reliable and acceptable mechanisms for evaluating employee performance. These include the limited criteria used (e.g. work study), inconsistency of application (e.g. performance appraisal), or bias/inequity in employee evaluations. A more fundamental issue may be resentment towards the exercise of managerial control via performance measurement and reward distribution, which is inherent in many "reward-for-performance" approaches.

In addition to the choice of payment system, a further important consideration for organisations is that of establishing basic pay levels for various jobs. This often involves *external comparisons* with pay levels in other organisations. Comparable pay rates influence an organisation's ability to attract and retain employees. Suitable comparable organisations should be chosen in order to maintain pay competitiveness while keeping wage costs at reasonable levels. Pay levels are also influenced by factors in the broader business environment, particularly:

(i)   economic climate;

(ii)   labour market;

(iii) centralised incomes policy; and

(iv)   trade unions.

FRINGE BENEFITS

In general, fringe benefits (both statutory and voluntary) are estimated to constitute an additional 25–30 per cent on top of basic weekly pay, for manual grades. For clerical, administrative and managerial categories, a figure of 15–35 per cent should be added. However, the percentage add-on is primarily related to the level of fringe benefits voluntarily agreed at company level, particularly items such as company cars, pensions, health/insurance cover, and sickness benefit, and can, therefore, vary considerably between organisations.

Statutory Fringe Benefits

Perhaps the most widely applicable benefit available to employees under statute is an entitlement to a minimum of 15 days' annual leave. Legislation has further increased this entitlement by providing for nine public holidays per annum. It must be realised, however, that the great majority of organisations provide entitlements greater than the statutory minimum, varying from 18 to 23 days with the average being 20 days per annum. Female employees, where pregnant, are also protected by statute and are entitled to a minimum period of 14 weeks' unpaid maternity leave in accordance with the terms of the Maternity Protection of Employees Act (1981) and the Worker Protection (Regular Part-time Employees) Act (1991). Such employees are also entitled to unpaid time off for antenatal and postnatal care. Employees on maternity leave are paid an allowance under the terms of the Social Welfare legislation.

While there are no statutory requirements for the provision of canteen facilities, the Safety in Industry Act (1980) requires that "where more than five people are employed, there must be adequate provision for boiling water and taking meals". In practice, the majority of larger organisations provide some form of canteen facilities. These may be subsidised by up to half the cost of meals, often with tea and coffee facilities also being provided at subsidised rates.

Voluntary Fringe Benefits

Voluntary fringe benefits refer to an ever-expanding group of facilities provided by an employer, the terms of which are set by unilateral decision or in negotiation with employees and their representatives. The most widely applicable schemes are pension plans and those schemes relating to employee health. Pension schemes in this context refer to those pensions provided by the organisation and governed by the Pensions Act (1990). Most larger organisations have such schemes. A 1988 survey of 579 organisations conducted by the Federation of Irish Employers found that 79 per cent of companies had a pension scheme for all or some employees. The majority of these schemes are contributory with the normal rate of employee contribution at 5 per cent of annual earnings.

While there is no legal obligation on organisations to provide sick-pay or health insurance cover for employees, many organisations do undertake such schemes. A 1990 survey carried out by the Federation of Irish Employers found that of the 515 companies questioned, 351 (68 per cent) had sick pay schemes for full-time manual workers, and 424 (82 per cent) had schemes for white-collar grades. Also, over 75 per cent of private sector companies have VHI schemes in operation for employees. The FIE estimates that over half of the white-collar schemes and one third of the manual grade schemes incorporate an employer contribution to the cost of such schemes.

Other widely used benefits include the provision of company cars for particular grades of employee, managerial incentive schemes and additional payments bonuses (e.g. Christmas bonuses). In an effort to ensure that qualified and skilled individuals remain in the workforce, a number of organisations are adopting childcare facilities. Such schemes are limited to a small number of Irish organisations and currently there are about 50 state-financed crèches sponsored by local health boards, mostly for families with special needs. There are four in Dublin, provided by state-sponsored companies and approximately ten in third-level educational institutions.

SURVEY FINDINGS ON REWARD PRACTICES IN IRELAND

Level of Pay Determination
Wage determination in Ireland has, in the post-war period, oscillated between enterprise and national level, usually based on adversarial negotiations. Prior to the 1980s, pay settlements could be categorised as zero sum, often in cognisance of bottom-line organisational functioning and forged by the negotiating parties "splitting the difference". Deteriorating economic circumstances in the form of increasing Debt/GNP ratios, unemployment and ever increasing redundancies introduced a new realism into employer–employee relationships which was to transcend all facets of organisational activities, not least among them, pay bargaining. Increasingly, it became clear that conflict originating from class-based

dialogues was becoming outmoded and unsustainable (Parker 1988). Viability and economic performance became the key criteria shaping pay, as spurious productivity and anomaly bargaining were committed firmly to history. Despite this realism, however, economic circumstances continued to worsen, and by 1987 a watershed had been reached. Action which incorporated pay restraint in both public and private sectors was viewed as a prerequisite to economic recovery and was to change fundamentally the face of pay bargaining in Ireland.

As can be seen from Table 5.2, pay determination is not homogenous in the Irish context, with a wide range of mechanisms being pursued at various levels, ranging from individual to national determination. The range of determination levels noted below may be rationalised in terms of a number of key developments in Ireland in recent times.

TABLE 5.2: LEVEL OF PAY DETERMINATION

	Managerial	Professional/ Technical	Clerical	Manual
National/Industry-wide Collective Bargaining	31.6	37.5	52.4	62.8
Regional Collective Bargaining	0.0	1.1	4.5	5.9
Company/Division etc.	28.6	24.9	26.0	18.6
Establishment/Site	12.3	14.1	13.8	11.9
Individual	45.0	32.0	20.1	7.1

Source: Price Waterhouse Cranfield Project (Ireland); University of Limerick 1992.

The Return to Centralised Bargaining — PNR/PESP
A budget deficit in the current account of £144 million and the particularly grave situation in relation to the public finances (of which public sector pay was a key contributory component) caused the NESC to comment that "continuation of current policies [was] not a viable option", thus once more pushing the issue of "national" pay determination centre stage. The Programme For National Recovery, formulated and agreed by the Government and the social partners, was published in October 1987 and provided for relatively modest increases for employees. Traditionally, employer and employee organisations in Ireland, because of their fragmented nature, have found it difficult to achieve conformity among their affiliated members. However, the PNR was adhered to with amazing consistency. The relatively high union density amongst manual/clerical workers resulted in the majority of workers at

these levels (62.8 per cent and 52.4 per cent respectively) having their pay determined at national level.

The Breakdown of Regional and Industry Bargaining

The extremely low level of regional bargaining, as evidenced in Table 5.2 above, may perhaps be understood with reference to traditional bargaining practices. Roche (1989) highlights that during the 1960s there were 60 industry-bargaining groups which covered the country. During the period of NWAs, many of these groupings fell into disuse and were disbanded, and they failed to be rekindled during the decentralised bargaining period of 1982–87. The return to centralised bargaining in 1987 has further inhibited the revival of this form of bargaining.

The Move to Individualism

In recent years a key change in the employer–employee relationship has been the increased emphasis on individualism. Individuals at upper levels in the organisational hierarchy have traditionally received individual pay packages, reflecting their predominantly non-union status and their perceived ability to impact directly on organisational performance. This procedure is still very much in evidence with 45.1 per cent of current respondents having their pay determined on an individual basis. The low figure for manual categories is indicative of the difficulty in disaggregating this category's contribution and relating it to bottom-line performance. Overall, in the Irish context, economic and managerial factors, coupled with the strength of the trade union movement, have shaped the face of pay bargaining carried out at all levels. In the European context, there has been a trend towards national determination for manual categories and, as one moves up the hierarchy, pay determination tends to become more individualised.

VARIABLE PAY/NON-PAY BENEFITS

Ireland, has witnessed an increase in variable pay in recent times (Table 5.3 below). Such pay systems have the advantage of allowing employees to share periods of success. However, in periods of poor performance, increases are drastically reduced. This problem is likely to limit the growth of such schemes, as variable pay may be unsuitable for employees paying mortgages and other fixed-sum repayments where stability of income is the overriding concern.

While there has been a substantial increase in the use of variable pay in both the public and private sectors in the past three years (23.6 per cent and 36.6 per cent respectively), Table 5.4 also reveals the extent of stability that pertains, with 72.7 per cent of public organisations and 54.3 per cent of private organisations suggesting that there was no change in the use of variable pay in this period.

TABLE 5.3: CHANGE IN USE OF (1) VARIABLE PAY; (2) NON-PAY BENEFITS

	Increased	Decreased	Same
Variable Pay	31.6%	3.7%	56.2%
Non-money Benefits	20.8%	1.5%	65.8%

Source: Price Waterhouse Cranfield Project (Ireland); University of Limerick 1992.

TABLE 5.4: CHANGE IN USE OF VARIABLE PAY BY SECTOR

	Private	Public
Increase	36.6% (64)*	23.6% (13)
Decrease	4.6% (8)	0.0%
No Change	54.3% (95)	72.7% (40)
Don't Know	4.6% (8)	3.6% (2)

* Actual numbers in parenthesis.
Source: Price Waterhouse Cranfield Project (Ireland); University of Limerick 1992.

The picture in relation to non-money benefits is one of stability with 65.3 per cent and 96 per cent of private and public sector respondents respectively indicating no change (see Appendix 1, Table 5A). Where change has occurred it has been confined largely to the private sector with 28 per cent of respondents indicating increases in its use and only 1.8 per cent reporting a decrease.

We also tested for the influence of unionisation or non-unionisation on both variable pay and non-money benefits (Table 5.5 below).

The presence of a union was not found to have a significant impact on the organisations' propensity to utilise variable pay. In relation to non-money benefits, however, union presence has a significant impact (see Appendix 1, Table 5B), with non-unionised organisations more than twice as likely to have witnessed an increase in the use of non-money benefits in the past three years as organisations with a union presence.

TABLE 5.5: CHANGE IN USE OF VARIABLE PAY IN UNIONISED AND NON-UNIONISED ORGANISATIONS

	Unionised	Non-unionised
Increased	32.5% (65)*	35.8% (19)
Decreased	3.5% (7)	5.7% (3)
No Change	59.5% (119)	56.6% (30)
Don't Know	4.5% (9)	1.9% (1)

* Actual numbers in parenthesis.
Source: Price Waterhouse Cranfield Project (Ireland); University of Limerick 1992.

Finally, we tested for the influence of company origin on the use of variable pay and non-money benefits. There appears to be no substantial difference between Irish, UK- and US-owned organisations in relation to the increase in variable pay. However, the decrease in the use of variable pay that has occurred in Irish organisations is slightly less than in their UK and US counterparts. Ownership had a greater impact on the use of non-money benefits (see Appendix 1, Table 5C), with the increase in UK- and US-owned establishments (35.7 and 31.3 per cent respectively) being almost twice that in indigenous establishments (15.6 per cent).

In the face of increasing competition and worsening economic conditions, respondent organisations to the Price Waterhouse Cranfield Project appear to be increasingly turning away from traditional remuneration systems in an effort to improve employee motivation within the constraints of static or shrinking budgets. The current research points to an increase in the utilisation of both variable pay and non-money benefits. Such an increase, however, has not been universal. While sector, trade union recognition and ownership do not seem to have an impact on the take-up of variable pay, the position in relation to non-money benefits is somewhat different. Privately owned organisations, particularly those of US and UK origin, were far more likely to have such schemes in operation than were public and indigenous companies. Recognition of a trade union was also found to have an impact, with those organisations not recognising unions reporting a much greater tendency to include a non-money element in the remuneration package.

USE OF INCENTIVE SCHEMES

The use of incentives is not a new phenomenon, with Payment By Results schemes having formed a significant part of the traditional remuneration package in many organisations. However, the applicability of pay-related incentive schemes across a wide range of organisational contexts is difficult to generalise on, largely because the empirical evidence to support the notion that money is a motivator is far from conclusive. Indeed, failure of such schemes, in some instances, to fulfil their potential has been attributed to a flawed theoretical base (Pearse 1987) which, in many cases, serves to undermine effectiveness by demotivating employees (Sargeant 1990, Deci 1982). Notwithstanding these reservations, incentive schemes seem to be experiencing increased popularity in many Irish organisations (Table 5.6).

TABLE 5.6: USE OF INCENTIVE SCHEMES

	Managerial	Professional/Technical	Clerical	Manual
Employee Share Options	20.4%	11.9%	8.2%	7.8%
Profit Sharing	15.2%	11.5%	10.0%	8.9%
Group Bonus Scheme	13.0%	11.5%	9.7%	12.6%
Individual Bonus/ Commission	30.1%	22.2%	13.8%	11.5%
Merit/Performance- Related Pay	46.1%	39.0%	28.6%	13.4%

Source: Price Waterhouse Cranfield Project (Ireland); University of Limerick 1992.

Incentive Schemes may be categorised along two continuums, namely, Wide/Narrow Applicability and High/Low Visibility.

FIGURE 5.1: APPLICABILITY AND VISIBILITY AS CRITERIA FOR EXPLORING INCENTIVE SCHEMES

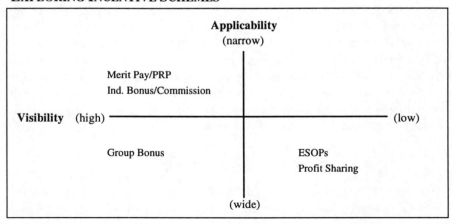

Wide/Narrow Applicability

This classification refers to the broadness or narrowness of the criterion on which reward allocation decisions are made. A widely applicable incentive is one in which rewards are distributed on the basis of performance which encompasses the efforts of a wide range of stakeholders — for example, company/divisional performance. Narrowly applicable incentives are those which use micro measures of performance (i.e. individual) for allocating rewards.

High/Low Visibility

Visibility refers to the explicitness of the link between an individual's performance and the resulting rewards. High visibility has the advantage of generating an obvious and visible link between the individual's/ group's effectiveness and their receipt of financial rewards. It thus represents a potentially strong motivator. Profit sharing and employee share options are not financial incentives per se and are thus not highly visible for the majority of employees. They strive to reinforce the culture of effectiveness and high performance within organisations, rather than to enhance job performance at the level of the individual/group.

HIGHLY VISIBLE/NARROWLY APPLICABLE INCENTIVES

These types of incentives have the potential to be strong motivators in that they are explicitly linked to the individual's own appraised job performance. Individual effort has the greatest impact on individual performance and this forms the criterion for reward allocation. Two such schemes fall within this classification, namely, Merit/Performance Related Pay and Individual Bonus Commission.

Merit/Performance Related Pay (PRP)

McBeath & Rands (1989) define Performance-Related Pay (PRP) "as an intention to pay distinctly more to reward highly effective job performance than you are willing to pay for good solid performance", the objective of which should be to develop a productive, efficient, effective organisation (Hoevemeyer 1989).

Ireland has, in recent years, seen a number of shifts in the application of financial incentives as a cure for low productivity. This change has been from a preoccupation with the productivity bargaining of the 1960s, measured day work in the 1970s (Exorbitant levels of taxation in the 1970s, according to Clarke (1989), rendered bonuses and merit rewards ineffectual as a cure for low productivity), to PRP in the 1980s (Grafton

1988). As the operating environment became ever more complex during the 1980s, organisations turned increasingly to performance appraisal and merit pay (Randell 1989).

As highlighted in Table 5.6, over 46 per cent of respondent organisations operate Merit/PRP Schemes for managerial employees. This figure decreases quite rapidly as one descends the hierarchy, with less than 14 per cent of organisations providing such schemes for manual employees. The established practice of differentiating between manual and managerial employees in the application of such schemes is thus still very much in evidence. It may be rationalised in a number of ways. As previously mentioned, the difficulty of isolating the impact of the individual's performance at the lower echelons of the organisation has resulted in Merit/PRP usage being largely confined to managerial levels. This problem has been overcome in many organisations, in recent times, by assessing individuals within the confines of their particular task or job.

Perhaps a second and more compelling explanation is the opposition of trade unions which often prefer collective increases achieved through management–union negotiation. As can be seen from Figure 5.2 below, this appears to be very much the case with significantly more non-unionised organisations operating such schemes. At all levels non-unionised organisations have a greater incidence of Merit/PRP, the difference being more clearly marked at the lower levels of the organisation.

FIGURE 5.2: MERIT PAY/PRP IN UNION/NON-UNION ORGANISATIONS

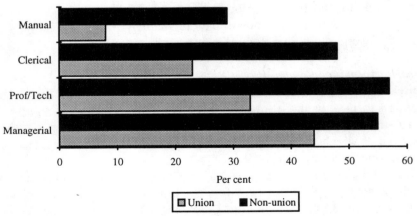

Source: Price Waterhouse Cranfield Project (Ireland); University of Limerick 1992.

The large difference noted above between clerical/manual in union-ised/non-unionised environments may be understood by reference to traditional patterns of unionisation in Irish organisations. Even in estab-lishments which recognised unions, much of the membership was con-centrated amongst the lower levels of the organisation, with proportion-ately fewer union members as one proceeded up the hierarchy. In such environments a substantial proportion of employees, particularly at managerial and professional/technical levels, are subject to a relationship with their employer which was individual in nature and encompassed pay determination on an individual basis, often involving Merit Pay/PRP. Thus, non-unionised employees in both types of organisation, particu-larly at upper management level, are often subject to similar employee–employer relationships. Any union opposition, therefore, is likely to have a greater impact on manual/clerical grades, because of the higher con-centration of union members at these levels.

One of the fundamental influences on an establishment's use of this incentive is ultimate ownership. There is evidence of increasing interest in Ireland in recent times in Merit/PRP. It seems, however, to be largely confined to foreign organisations. While 8.4 per cent of indigenous re-spondents offer such schemes for manual employees, this is exceedingly low compared with UK- and US-owned organisations which adopted PRP schemes for such categories in excess of 21 per cent of cases.

The diversity of practices observed above may be due to the deep penetration of foreign MNCs into Irish industrial structures. MNCs often reflect practices in operation in their country of ultimate ownership, rather than practices in comparable firms in Irish industry. This is par-ticularly true in the case of US multinationals, where successive research has repeatedly emphasised the prevalence of linking pay to a measure of performance, often via performance appraisal practices (Hay Associates 1975, Locker & Teel 1977, Eichel & Bender 1984). The perceived im-portance of PRP amongst US organisations is maintained in their sub-sidiary plants in the Irish context (Table 5.7 below), with almost 80 percent of managerial levels qualifying for PRP/Merit Pay and relatively high levels for all other categories. In Britain, in recent years, there has been a change in emphasis in relation to performance management tech-niques. Much of the effort traditionally was directed at assessing future labour requirements and labour training needs (Gill 1977). However, as Britain was increasingly feeling the grips of economic recession, empha-sis began to change to one which concentrated on organisational survival and assessment of current performance (Long 1986). Such emphasis has resulted in a large growth in PRP as a method of improving performance, with almost 86 per cent of British multinationals providing schemes for

managerial categories, and in excess of 50 per cent of respondents
operating them for professional/technical and clerical categories.

**TABLE 5.7: THE RELATIONSHIP BETWEEN OWNERSHIP AND THE
INCIDENCE OF MERIT/PERFORMANCE RELATED PAY**

	Rep. of Ireland	UK	Other EC Europe	Non-EC	USA	Other	N/A
Managerial	29.0%	85.7%	72.7%	25.0%	78.8%	50.0%	35.7%
Prof./Technical	23.2%	57.1%	63.6%	50.0%	76.9%	25.0%	21.4%
Clerical	12.3%	50.0%	54.5%	50.0%	63.5%	12.5%	21.4%
Manual	8.4%	21.4%	13.6%	50.0%	21.2%	37.5%	7.1%
	N=155	N=14	N=14	N=4	N=52	N=8	N=14

Source: Price Waterhouse Cranfield Project (Ireland); University of Limerick
1992.

We also tested for the influence of sector on the use of Merit/PRP. Its
use is largely confined to private sector organisations which report much
greater take-up of such schemes at all levels of employees. While almost
20 per cent of respondents in the private sector indicate the operation of
such schemes for manual grades, this is true in less than 2 per cent of
public sector organisations.

**TABLE 5.8: USE OF MERIT/PERFORMANCE RELATED PAY FOR
DIFFERENT GRADES IN THE PUBLIC/PRIVATE SECTOR**

	Private	Public
Managerial	54.6% (100)	19.0% (11)
Professional/Technical	48.1% (88)	12.1% (7)
Clerical	36.6% (67)	3.4% (2)
Manual	18.0% (33)	1.7% (1)
	N=183	N=58

Source: Price Waterhouse Cranfield Project (Ireland); University of Limerick
1992.

A correlation was also noted between grade of employee and Merit/
PRP. The higher the grade of employee, the more likely they are to be on
a merit system, in both the private and public sector.

Evidence from the Price Waterhouse Cranfield Project suggests that

Merit/PRP is the most commonly used financial incentive practised in organisations in Ireland in recent times. Its use is not homogenous, however, across, or within organisations. A general observation is that these incentives are largely confined to managerial grades. The key determining factors on the use of such schemes in the Irish context appear to be the following:

(i) The non-recognition of unions seems, for many organisations, a prerequisite for the use of such schemes.

(ii) Ultimate ownership is also correlated closely with the use of such schemes. US organisations on the whole offer a relatively high level of coverage to all levels of employees, Irish indigenous industry, however, demonstrates a relative reluctance to make use of Merit/PRP.

(iii) Private sector respondents indicate a far greater tendency to adopt such schemes than organisations in the public sector.

Individual Bonus/Commission
While it may be seen above that the use of merit /PRP has in recent years enjoyed an upsurge in popularity, such payments do, however, suffer from a number of potential deficiencies.

Irreversibility
Once an increase is given to employees it becomes installed as a component of basic pay and is therefore difficult to withdraw if an employee does not perform up to the required standard. Since, therefore, such amounts are no longer at risk, their ability to motivate is greatly reduced, if not undermined — a problem greatly exacerbated by the fact that most organisations deliver merit increases through salary schemes (Lawler 1988).

Link with Inflation
A related problem to the one outlined above is the fact that many PRP/ Merit schemes are either explicitly or latently linked to inflation and cost of living increases. While this is a quite reasonable situation it does have the potential to undermine the effectiveness, and potentially the use of, PRP/Merit schemes.

The individual bonus scheme corrects some of these deficiencies. Since it is provided separate from normal salary administration, it does not become encompassed within base pay. Lawler (1988) feels that a bonus system should put all variable pay at risk so the incentive is always there to motivate performance, thus ensuring retention of the best staff.

Since the incentive is rewarded separately from salary, the entire bonus will be motivational rather than being just one component of an overall salary increase.

Despite the obvious advantages of bonus schemes, they remain a relatively under-utilised incentive tool in respondent organisations with only 30.1 per cent of respondent organisations having a scheme in operation for managerial employees and a smaller 11.5 per cent having such schemes for manual categories. As was the case with Merit/PRP, the size of the organisation does not appear to be a key factor in determining the use of this form of incentive (see Appendix 1, Table 5D).

In the case of Individual Bonus/Commission, trade union recognition was also not seen to have a marked influence. Just over 12 per cent of organisations in which unions are recognised allocate individual bonuses for managerial and manual employees, as opposed to 10.5 per cent for those categories in organisations which do not. This finding seems to substantiate Grafton's assertion that schemes which operate merit increases, in addition to general salary awards, are less likely to cause employee opposition, as they operate as a discretionary element which does not cut across the collective bargaining role of the trade union. While the numbers of organisations adopting such schemes is relatively low, this appears to be as a result of management discretion and other financial constraints, rather than union opposition.

Ultimate ownership, however, was seen to have a significant influence. In UK- and US-owned organisations individual bonuses formed a significant component of manual grades remuneration packages, with 85.7 per cent and 78.8 per cent of organisations having schemes in place for these categories. The usage of this scheme, however, was predominantly confined to such levels, with relatively low incidences for professional/technical, clerical and managerial grades in UK organisations. American organisations also reported reduced popularity for this incentive among clerical and professional/technical grades, although it did appear to form a part of managerial remuneration in a significant proportion of respondent companies (Fig. 5.3).

Sectoral influences are also in evidence here. Again, as was the case with merit/performance-related pay, private organisations are far more likely to have a bonus/commission system in operation (Table 5.9 below). Also in private organisations, the higher the grade of employee, the more likely they are to be on a individual bonus/commission scheme. Interestingly, this is not borne out in the results for the public sector, with manual grades as likely to be on bonus/commission as managerial grades in this sector.

FIGURE 5.3: USE OF INDIVIDUAL BONUS/COMMISSION BY OWNERSHIP

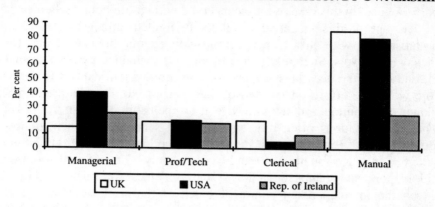

Source: Price Waterhouse Cranfield Project (Ireland); University of Limerick 1992.

TABLE 5.9: USE OF INDIVIDUAL BONUS/COMMISSION FOR DIFFERENT GRADES IN PUBLIC/PRIVATE SECTOR

	Private	Public
Managerial	39.9% (73)	5.2% (3)
Professional/Technical	29.5% (54)	1.7% (1)
Clerical	16.4% (30)	5.2% (3)
Manual	14.8% (27)	5.2% (3)
	N=183	N=58

Source: Price Waterhouse Cranfield Project (Ireland); University of Limerick 1992.

Overall therefore, individual incentive schemes would appear to be getting increasingly common as part of remuneration packages for individuals at all levels of organisations in Ireland.

HIGHLY VISIBLE/WIDELY APPLICABLE INCENTIVES

This type of incentive seeks to allocate rewards on the basis of group performance. It is highly visible because rewards are usually based on small group performance and thus there is an explicit link between performance and reward. Such rewards are wide in applicability as they seek to determine the individual's incentive by reference to the performance of a group of individuals rather than linking them to individual effort and performance. In this case, we are concerned with group bonus schemes.

The use of this incentive is relatively limited amongst respondent organisations, with only 13 per cent providing group bonus schemes for managerial levels. Such a low take-up may be explained by the fact that individual differences in managers jobs are quite significant, it is therefore worth the effort, on the part of management, to measure their individual contribution and relate pay to it (Appelbaum & Shappiro 1991) Thus, organisations often rely on individual schemes for such grades. However, what is a little more surprising is the low level of group bonus schemes in place for manual employees. In only 12.6 per cent of cases did respondent organisations have such schemes for manual grades. Given the interdependent nature of much of the work at manual and clerical grades, it would appear that this was an ideal situation for the use of team-based schemes. This, however, does not seem to be the case.

The size of the organisation, as can be seen from Table 5.10 below, does not appear to be clearly linked with the existence of such schemes within respondent organisations, although there does appear to be a trend, particularly amongst larger organisations, to use such schemes as a basis for allocating rewards to manual employees. This may represent not only a desire on the part of these organisations to promote teamwork and efficiency amongst its employees, but may also be a function of the prohibitive costs of assessing employees on an individual basis and allocating rewards at this level. A further significant finding was that in no company having in excess of 300 employees were group bonus schemes in operation for professional/technical grades. This may be as a result of the opportunity for experts in these companies, given the greater resources available to them, to pursue their specialism to a greater degree (than may be possible in a small organisation) and thus increase the differentiation between themselves and other specialists.

TABLE 5.10: RELATIONSHIP BETWEEN ORGANISATION SIZE AND THE INCIDENCE OF GROUP BONUS SCHEMES

	1-100	101-200	201-300	301-400	401-500	501-1,000	1,001-2,000	2,000+
Managerial	8.3%	14.0%	14.3%	15.0%	16.7%	25.0%	—	11.1%
Prof./Tech.	9.5%	20.0%	42.9%	—	—	—	—	—
Clerical	4.8%	14.0%	17.1%	15.0%	5.6%	12.5%	11.1%	—
Manual	6.0%	12.0%	17.1%	10.0%	16.7%	15.6%	22.2%	27.8%

Source: Price Waterhouse Cranfield Project (Ireland); University of Limerick 1992.

Trade union recognition was seen to have a slight impact at all levels of respondent organisations. Organisations that did not recognise unions recorded greater use for managerial, professional/technical and clerical workers (17.5 per cent, 14.0 per cent and 10.5 per cent for managerial, professional/technical and clerical workers respectively in non-unionised organisations, as opposed to 12.1 per cent, 11.1 per cent and 9.7 per cent in unionised).

Given the traditional suspicion of unions towards incentives schemes, group bonus schemes hold two potential advantages; firstly, since they are provided as a bonus they do not cut across the role of unions; and secondly, they are provided across broad ranges of employees and, as such, the potential for managerial nepotism is reduced. Thus such schemes may receive a less hostile reception from union members, a view substantiated by the level of respondents reporting such schemes for manual employees (that is, 14 per cent). The lower figure of 8.8 per cent may be rationalised by a recognition that non-unionised organisations often pursue competitive advantage by emphasising individual rather than group/collective relations. As was the case with individual incentives, ownership of respondent organisations had an impact on the presence of group bonus schemes.

FIGURE 5.4: USE OF GROUP BONUS SCHEMES BY COUNTRY OF ORIGIN

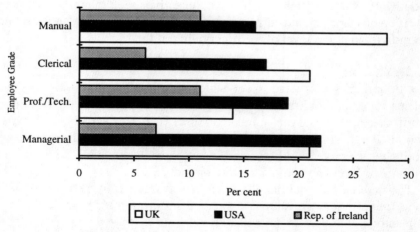

Source: Price Waterhouse Cranfield Project (Ireland); University of Limerick 1992.

US multinationals again indicated a relatively high incidence of this type of incentive with in excess of 23 per cent of organisations having such schemes for managerial employees and just over 15 per cent having this scheme for manual categories. In British companies, the trend is somewhat different with a greater majority of organisations having such schemes for manual employees than were in existence for managerial levels (28.6 per cent and 21.4 per cent respectively). Irish indigenous industry, once again, illustrated a reluctance to adopt such schemes with only 8.4 per cent of companies having group bonus for managerial grades. A surprising fact was the failure of organisations with Japanese origin to operate schemes in any instances, for any employee levels. This is surprising, as Ost (1990) illustrates that one of the triggers to the adoption of team-based schemes was the perceived pre-eminence of Japanese firms and the centrality of workers in production decisions.

The final category we are interested in is those incentives which are widely applicable and low in visibility.

WIDELY APPLICABLE/LOW VISIBILITY INCENTIVES

These incentives are perhaps the furthest removed from the functioning of the individual's job. The criterion for deciding on reward allocation is not usually the individual's own job performance or that of a small group, but rather, a more macro measure of performance.(e.g. company, division, corporate). Thus, the link between the individual's performance and reward is not explicit and, as such, incentives seek to create a climate of efficiency and enhanced performance, rather than trying to motivate the individual at the level of the functioning of their job.

Profit Sharing

Profit sharing is a scheme under which employees, in addition to their normal remuneration, receive a proportion of the profits of the business. Profit sharing may take a number of forms and it is largely at the discretion of the employer and employees to decide to what measure of profit the incentive should be tied, what percentage should be allocated and how it should be administered to employees.

The take up has traditionally been low in Ireland. In a study in 1988, Long found that organisations expressed little interest in profit sharing, with only a minority of organisations having approved schemes. Organisations which opposed profit sharing feared a loss of privacy and control over how the organisation was run. There was also a misconception that tax concessions were only available to publicly quoted companies.

As was seen from Table 5.6 above, the use of profit-related pay in

Ireland is still relatively restricted, with less than 12 per cent of organisations having schemes to share profits with professional/technical, clerical and manual categories, and only just above 15 per cent for managerial employees. Roots (1988) feels that when organisations confine their profit-sharing schemes to directors, then these schemes may be viewed as performance related, as at these levels such individuals have the ability to influence organisational profitability. Thus, while for the vast majority of employees profit sharing is low on visibility, this may not be the case for managers at the upper levels of the organisational hierarchy.

It is difficult to generalise about the effect of size on the take-up of profit sharing (see Appendix 1, Table 5E). It is clear, however that all organisations irrespective of number of employees use profit sharing at least equally, for managerial employees as other grades. There also appears to be a marked decline in the use of profit sharing for organisations in excess of 1,000 employees. Organisations of this magnitude show a decline at all levels ranging from managerial to manual grades.

The recognition of unions also influences the presence of profit sharing in respondent organisations (see Appendix 1, Table 5F). At all employee grades, non-recognition correlates with a higher level of utilisation of this incentive, the difference decreasing as one descends the hierarchy (from 6.9 per cent in the case of managerial grades to 1.8 per cent for manual). The opposition of unions to profit-sharing schemes is understandable from an ideological perspective given that it represents a threat to the legitimacy of their role as employee representatives. This occurs because one of the key underlying philosophies of profit sharing is its attempt to foster a mutuality of interests amongst organisational interest groups. However, in practice, the opposition of unions to such schemes is not universal for a number of reasons. Firstly, the enhanced employee involvement in the production process which results from such schemes is a step towards workplace democracy. Secondly, improved productivity will enhance long-term profitability and thus job security. Finally, such schemes represents an opportunity to increase wages.

This appears to be the approach adopted in Irish organisations. Therefore, in the areas where one would expect high union density (manual and clerical grades), the divergence between unionised and non-unionised organisations is relatively minor.

As has been the established pattern in relation to the previous incentives, US MNCs appear to have quite a high take-up. With respect to UK organisations, the case is somewhat different in that, although there is a relatively high take-up of such schemes, there is no differentiation between the various employee grades, with organisations reporting equal usage, at 21.4 per cent for all levels. Irish indigenous industry, as has been the case with all incentives thus far, shows a relative reluctance to adopt this incentive, with only 2.6 per cent of respondents having schemes for manual categories. This rises to only 9.7 per cent for managerial grades.

TABLE 5.11: THE RELATIONSHIP BETWEEN OWNERSHIP AND THE INCIDENCE OF PROFIT-SHARING SCHEMES

	Republic of Ireland.	UK	Other EC Europe	Non-EC Europe	USA	Other
Managerial	9.7%	21.4%	27.3%	25%	28.8%	12.5%
Prof./Tech.	5.2%	21.4%	22.7%	—	26.9%	12.5%
Clerical	3.9%	21.4%	18.2%	—	25.0%	12.5%
Manual	2.6%	21.4%	13.6%	—	25.0%	12.5%
	N = 155	N = 14	N = 14	N = 4	N = 52	N = 8

Source: Price Waterhouse Cranfield Project (Ireland); University of Limerick 1992.

Overall, profit sharing has not achieved a high level of popularity in Ireland. The most significant influences are: firstly, whether or not the organisation is unionised; and secondly, the place of ultimate ownership of the organisation.

Employee Share Ownership
Interest in Ireland in employee share ownership schemes has traditionally been relatively low (Long 1988). The growth, small though it has been, is rooted in the Finance Acts of 1982–84 which were driven by Governmental commitment to "ensuring the success and efficiency of Irish industry and the prosperity and security of Irish workers for the future" by developing employee shareholding. These Acts sought to provide tax relief for the adoption of share-ownership schemes. However, employers and employees were under no obligation to adopt such schemes, and tax concessions only applied to approved schemes. The Irish Productivity Centre (1986) felt that "the relevant acts do not provide a rigid model for the advancement of employee shareholding, but rather a framework of corporate and individual incentives within required guidelines".

In 1992, the Government amended the approved profit-sharing scheme provisions contained in the Finance Acts, reducing the ceiling on the value of shares from £5,000 to £2,000 which may be appropriated in any one year to an individual under an approved scheme.

The present research supports Long's (1988) survey in that the take-up has remained low with only schemes applicable to managerial levels in 20.4 per cent of respondent organisations and a much smaller 7.8 per cent of companies reporting such schemes for manual grades (see Appendix 1, Table 5G). Size of the organisation does not appear to have an identifiable impact on the existence of such schemes.

Trade union recognition, however, has a significant impact, with those organisations which do not formally recognise a collective presence, in the form of a union, much more likely to have such schemes in place. The divergence between unionised and non-unionised decreases quite rapidly as one descends the hierarchy from managerial to manual grades. Thus, union opposition to such schemes may not be as universal as has been traditionally supposed.

TABLE 5.12: EMPLOYEE SHARE SCHEMES IN UNIONISED AND NON-UNIONISED ORGANISATIONS

	Unionised	Non-unionised
Managerial	17.4%	31.6%
Professional/Technical	8.7%	24.6%
Clerical	7.7%	10.5%
Manual	7.2%	10.5%

N = 207   N = 57

Source: Price Waterhouse Cranfield Project (Ireland); University of Limerick 1992.

Ownership of the respondent organisation is also a determining factor with the data suggesting that organisations of US origin are more likely to provide such schemes. As can be seen from Table 5.13, 38.5 per cent of US organisations offer such schemes for managerial levels as opposed to only 28.6 per cent of UK and 16.1 per cent of Irish indigenous firms. The difference is even more marked at lower levels. While 17.3 per cent and 14.3 per cent of US and UK organisations respectively operate such schemes for manual employees, this is true in only 4.5 per cent of Irish firms.

TABLE 5.13: RELATIONSHIP BETWEEN OWNERSHIP AND INCIDENCE OF EMPLOYEE SHARE SCHEMES

	Rep. of Ireland	UK	Other EC Europe	Non-EC Europe	USA	Other	N/A
Managerial	16.1%	28.6%	22.7%	—	38.5%	—	7.1%
Prof./Tech.	7.7%	7.1%	9.1%	—	30.8%	—	7.1%
Clerical	5.2%	14.3%	9.1%	—	17.3%	—	7.1%
Manual	4.5%	14.3%	9.1%	—	17.3%	—	7.1%
	N = 14	N = 155	N = 14	N = 4	N = 52	N = 8	N = 14

Source: Price Waterhouse Cranfield Project (Ireland); University of Limerick 1992.

CONCLUSIONS

The utility of using pay to promote performance has been a subject of debate for many years with empirical and theoretical support for both sides of the argument. Notwithstanding the reservations expressed, however, pay and benefits are increasingly becoming areas of extreme importance in attempts to increase the effectiveness of the organisation.

The data from the Price Waterhouse Cranfield Project illustrates that pay determination for most non-managerial employees is conducted at national level, principally under the terms and conditions of the Programme for Economic and Social Progress.

Rewards for managerial employees are predominantly, as has traditionally been the case, determined at the level of the individual, although almost 30 per cent of respondent organisations indicated that national determination is the method by which such categories had their pay determined.

For many respondent organisations, pay, for a large proportion of their employees, was determined outside the level of the firm. This, however, did not mean that such organisations were of necessity taking a reactive role in pay determination. Respondents indicated a tendency towards attempting to link the fortunes of the individual worker more closely, through reward mechanisms, to those of the firm. This project also provided evidence of an increase in interest in the use of non-money benefits to promote the achievement of the strategic aims of the organisation without accelerating wage/salary costs.

In conjunction with the increased use of variable pay, respondent organisations indicated an increased interest in the use of financial incentives. Such incentives varied not only on the basis of the criterion on which they were to base reward allocation, but also on the aims they were trying to fulfil. Merit/Performance-related Pay represented the most commonly used incentive amongst organisations in Ireland. While Merit/PRP has become quite popular in recent times, other incentives have not witnessed anything like the resurgence witnessed in respect of this incentive. Consequently, the utilisation of other schemes remains relatively low.

While incentive use in Ireland is quite low, this is subject to the qualification that take-up was correlated quite closely to ultimate owner-ship of the respondent organisation. US organisations were far more likely to utilise incentives than others, particularly Irish indigenous orga-nisations which indicated low take-up across a wide range of incentives.

National/industry-wide collective bargaining represents the predomi-nant mechanism by which pay is determined for professional/technical, clerical and manual employees. Managerial employees in the main, how-ever, are subject to individual pay determination. Variable pay packages have, in the last three years, increased in popularity in almost a third of respondent organisations. While both public and private sector have experienced such an increase, it is particularly noticeable amongst the latter. Ownership and unionisation had no significant impact on the propensity of respondent organisations to use variable pay. Non-money benefits have likewise seen an increase in popularity, although it is prin-cipally confined to private sector organisations. The presence of a trade union correlated negatively with an increase in such benefits, non-unionised organisations showing a much greater tendency to have in-creased their use than unionised respondents. Indigenous respondents were much less likely to use non-money benefits than UK or US multi-nationals. Merit/PRP incentives represent the most commonly utilised incentive across all grades in respondent organisations. These were most popular amongst non-unionised and private sector respondents. Irish indigenous organisations showed a small take-up of such incentives, while their use in UK and US multinationals was much greater. Size was not found to be a significant determining factor. Individual bonus/com-mission was again more popular amongst private sector than public sec-tor respondents. Size and trade union recognition were not significant influencing factors. Evidence suggests that group bonus schemes are relatively under-utilised in the Irish context, with take-up remaining quite low. As appears to be the established pattern, private sector and foreign multinational respondents report a greater propensity to adopt group bonus schemes than public sector or indigenous organisations. Size and unionisation were not found to be significant determining factors. In general terms, the use of profit-sharing schemes remains quite low. Such use appears to be correlated to the non-recognition of unions and to the foreign ownership of respondent organisations.

Chapter 6

TRENDS AND DEVELOPMENTS IN THE ORGANISATION OF THE EMPLOYMENT RELATIONSHIP

Noreen Heraty, Michael Morley and Thomas Turner

INTRODUCTION

The way in which the employment relationship is organised and managed is an important factor in defining the climate of employee relations in a firm (Osterman 1982) and is the focus of much of the recent literature on human resource management with its emphasis on flexibility, the recruitment and selection of employees committed to the goals of the organisation and the training and development of those employees (Atkinson 1984, Storey 1989). This chapter examines selected aspects of the employment relationship. Firstly, trends in recruitment and selection are analysed. Secondly, recent trends in training and development practices are examined. Finally, the structure and prevalence of internal labour markets (ILM) are explored using proxies from the Price Waterhouse Cranfield Project.

TRENDS IN RECRUITMENT AND SELECTION PRACTICES

Since human resources are an integral component of corporate success, decisions relating to the recruitment and selection process are vital management decisions (Gunnigle & Flood 1990; McMahon 1988). Effective recruitment and selection procedures are a prerequisite to the development of an effective workforce, and consequently the costs of ineffective recruitment and selection can be formidable, both in financial and human terms (Plumbley 1985). Lewis (1984) argues that even in the days of fewer vacancies and many applications, the importance of effective recruitment and selection should not be forgotten because shrinking organisations have less capacity to cope with selection errors.

The key choice in relation to recruitment is whether to recruit internally or externally. There are advantages and disadvantages associated with both and the choice largely depends on the position being filled. Smith, Gregg & Robertson (1989) suggest that the benefits of recruiting internally from current employees are that it is good personnel practice, there is a reduction of induction time and the costs and uncertainties of recruiting from outside are reduced. However, there are also drawbacks as it limits the potential range of candidates from the wider labour market and may lead to employee frustration, should employees feel that they have been overlooked for promotion (Gunnigle & Flood 1990). Gunnigle (1992) feels that the apparent desire among some Irish organisations to focus on the internal labour market may be linked to "soft" HRM practices such as career planning and counselling and employee development in place there.

The subsequent selection decision is key and despite the fact that the decision is one of the most important decisions taken in any organisation, McMahon (1988) suggests that this has not provided the impetus for the personnel function to insist upon the most sophisticated and objective selection techniques.

The Price Waterhouse Cranfield Project collected information on a number of key areas: Firstly, the survey investigated where primary responsibility lies for major policy decisions on recruitment and selection. Secondly, we examined whether line management responsibility for recruitment and selection had changed over the last three years. Thirdly, respondents were asked how vacant positions were filled and which methods were used in selection. Finally, the issue of gender in recruitment is also given some coverage.

Responsibility for Policy Decisions on Recruitment and Selection

The survey data indicates that in a majority of cases recruitment and selection will be completed through a combination of the specialist HR function and line management involvement.

TABLE 6.1: RESPONSIBILITY FOR RECRUITMENT AND SELECTION

Line Management Responsibility	25%
Line Management with HR Department	23%
HR Department with Line Management	32%
HR Department	13%

N = 248

Source: Price Waterhouse Cranfield Project (Ireland); University of Limerick 1992.

Conversely, only in 13 per cent of cases did the HR function have sole responsibility in this area. However, it is noteworthy that among 25 per cent of respondent organisations, it is line management alone that takes sole responsibility for recruitment and selection, which may be indicative of some decentralisation in this area. As Storey (1992) highlights, one of the trends associated with HRM in recent times is the transition towards a less hands-on approach by the specialist HR function, and a subsequent increasing devolvement of at least some HR activities to line managers. Furthermore, in the Irish context, Gunnigle & Flood (1990) suggest that the recession has led to a greater devolution of personnel activities to line managers. In relation to changes in recruitment and selection practices which have occurred over the last three years, 25 per cent of respondents suggest that line management responsibility for recruitment and selection has increased, while only 5 per cent suggest it has decreased. However, organisational size does have some influence here, with larger organisations witnessing lower line management involvement in recruitment and selection matters. Consequently, the decentralisation in smaller organisations may be as a result of a poorly developed and resourced specialist department/function.

Recruitment Methods
Respondents were asked to indicate how they filled vacant positions for different categories of employees.

TABLE 6.2: RECRUITMENT METHODS

	Managerial	Prof./Tech.	Clerical	Manual
From among Current Employees	53.0%	35.0%	46.0%	29.0%
Advertise Internally	42.0%	39.0%	57.0%	41.0%
Advertise Externally	65.0%	69.0%	46.0%	36.0%
Word of Mouth	9.0%	12.0%	22.0%	37.0%
Recruitment Agencies	41.0%	42.0%	28.0%	6.0%
Search/Selection Consultants	35.0%	24.0%	1.0%	0.5%
Job Centres	0.4%	1.0%	15.0%	26.0%
Apprentices	—	9.0%	4.0%	15.0%

N=269
Source: Price Waterhouse Cranfield Project (Ireland); University of Limerick 1992.

A number of points can be made about the results. Firstly, the survey data suggests that organisations, when filling managerial and/or professional/technical vacancies favour external advertising, above all other methods — 65 per cent of respondents advertise managerial posts externally, while 69 per cent advertise externally for professional/technical employees. Secondly, internal advertising is favoured most for the recruitment of personnel at clerical and/or manual levels. At these levels it is often cheaper and quicker to avail of this recruitment method as the necessary expertise may already be present in the organisation. Thirdly, as might be expected, the use of recruitment agents and search and selection consultants is mainly confined to the recruitment of managerial and professional/technical posts. One of the key influencing factors here is the cost associated with engaging consultants, and consequently they are often restricted to posts where the necessary skills are in short supply.

Organisational size does appear to influence the recruitment methods utilised, in particular for managerial positions and to a lesser extent for professional/technical positions. However, as mentioned earlier, this does not seem to be the case for manual grades. The picture emerging from the data is that larger organisations make more use of internal labour markets when recruiting more senior staff. Thus 60 per cent of organisations employing more than 200 employees recruit managerial staff from current employees. That figure drops to 46 per cent for organisations with less than 200 employees. As already mentioned, the desire among some organisations to focus on the internal labour market may be linked to the practice of "soft" HRM which is often found in large multinational subsidiaries, hence the relationship with size (Appendix 1, Table 6A).

In relation to smaller organisations, the data seems to indicate that they focus on the external labour market utilising external advertising. This may be indicative of the fact that the expertise required to fill such senior positions may not exist in smaller organisations, hence the need to focus on the external labour market. Furthermore, Watson et al. (1990) suggest that recruitment agencies are popular among smaller organisations as the specialist personnel function is often under-resourced and such agencies can relieve the administrative burden on the department.

Differences also arise with respect to the recruitment methods utilised most frequently, depending on the country of origin of the organisation. The most substantial difference occurs between Irish-owned organisations and their US and EC counterparts with the Irish-owned appearing to make less use of the internal labour market in the recruitment process, across employee categories.

Clearly, this is again consistent with the idea that the multinationals operating in Ireland make greater use of "soft" HRM approaches than do Irish indigenous organisations. These organisations are known to practice career planning and place a strong emphasis on communication and information sharing and as a consequence are more likely to rely on the internal labour market for recruitment purposes. Maintaining a robust corporate culture, shared by all employees is a central aim of these organisations. Such maintenance is aided by relying on the internal labour market.

TABLE 6.3: RECRUITMENT METHODS AND ORGANISATIONAL COUNTRY OF ORIGIN

Recruitment Method	Managerial (%)			Prof./Tech. (%)			Clerical (%)			Manual (%)		
	Irish	US	EC	Irish	US	EC	Irish	US	EC	Irish	US	EC
Recruit from among Current Employees	47	59	77	31	47	38	37	61	74	23	45	40
Advertise Internally	38	49	49	32	55	46	49	71	77	34	55	57

N = 164 54 38　164 54 38　164 54 38　164 54 38

Source: Price Waterhouse Cranfield Project (Ireland); University of Limerick 1992.

Selection Methods

The data emanating from the PWCP in relation to selection methods which are regularly used by Irish organisations seems to confirm the view that, in general, relatively little use is being made of what are classified as the sophisticated methods of selection. The application form, the interview panel and the reference are the most commonly used methods, while methods such as biodata, testing, assessment centres and group selection methods are still used in a minority of cases.

TABLE 6.4: SELECTION METHODS

Application Forms	86%
Interview Panel	85%
Biodata	5%
Psychometric Testing	19%
Graphology	1%
References	88%
Aptitude Test	31%
Assessment Centre	5%
Group Selection Methods	7%

N = 269
Source: Price Waterhouse Cranfield Project (Ireland); University of Limerick 1992.

However, a higher percentage of large organisations do appear to use the more sophisticated techniques (see Appendix 1, Table 6B). Thus, while only 8 per cent of organisations employing less than 200 employees use psychometric testing as a selection tool, 29 per cent of organisations employing more than 200 employees use this method. Similarly, in relation to aptitude tests, 41 per cent of organisations employing more than 200 employees use such tests, while only 22 per cent of organisations employing less than 200 employees use these tests. There are no substantial differences between large and small organisations and their use of the three most common mechanisms of selection, namely, application forms, interview panels and reference checks.

Gender in Recruitment
The labour force participation rate among females in Ireland is much lower than the EC average. While the Irish female participation rate is approximately 30 per cent, the EC average is 40 per cent. Consequently it is worth examining the issue of gender and recruitment. There are a number of key reasons why the female participation rate has traditionally been low. Firstly, marriage bars existed in the public sector in Ireland up until the enactment of the Civil Service(Employment of Married Women) Bill in 1973. Secondly, Drew (1987) suggests that working time today is geared to the participation of workers who do not share domestic duties and child-rearing responsibilities, and who, on entering the labour market, can remain without voluntary interruption until retirement. Thirdly, research (Breen & Hannan 1987) suggests that there are marked differences in the kind of education received by boys and girls, which appears closely related to perceived adult and labour market roles. Fourthly, in Ireland there is a recognised lack of childcare facilities or any monetary support for those who need to use crèches (Callan & Farrell 1991).

In relation to the present survey, only 24 per cent of respondents reported that they monitor the number of women in the workforce with regard to recruitment either in response to skill shortages, demographic changes or equal opportunities. An even smaller proportion, 18 per cent of respondents, had specifically targeted women in their recruitment process.

Trade union recognition appears to have some influence here with some differences occurring between the targeting of women in unionised and non-unionised organisations. Thus, while a large percentage of organisations do not target women, of those which do, a higher percentage are unionised organisations.

Sectoral differences are not seen to have any influence here, with only minor differences occurring between the public and the private sector.

TABLE 6.5: WOMEN TARGETED IN RECRUITMENT BY UNION RECOGNITION

	Women Targeted	
Recognition	Yes	No
No	13%	87%
Yes	22%	81%

N (Unionised) = 181

N (Non-unionised) = 54

Source: Price Waterhouse Cranfield Project (Ireland); University of Limerick 1992.

Overall therefore, the picture emerging with respect to the way in which organisations approach the recruitment and selection process is relatively unsurprising, particularly given the loose nature of the Irish labour market. There is a readily accessible pool of qualified young people available to fill vacant positions, and organisations thus have little difficulty in attracting candidates. The results reveal the continuing popularity of the application form, the interview and the reference as selection methods with only small numbers of organisations utilising more sophisticated techniques such as biodata and psychometric testing. Finally, in relation to gender in recruitment, the results reveal that a relatively small number of organisations specifically target women in the recruitment process.

However, this may well change in the future when the use of non-standard employment increases and the labour market tightens.

TRENDS IN TRAINING AND DEVELOPMENT PRACTICES

In recent times the academic literature has witnessed a resurgent interest in training and development, with much of this literature focusing on the strategic development of human resources as a means of increasing the effectiveness of organisations (see Beer et al. 1984; Brinkerhoff 1988; Buckley & Caple 1990; Cook & Ferris 1988). Much of this interest has perhaps been instigated by the popularisation of Porter's (1980; 1990) notion of competitive advantage, and the emergence of the "excellent" literature proposed by, among others, Ouchi (1981), Peters & Waterman (1982) and Pettigrew et al. (1988). This notion of excellence has, according to Pettigrew, been expanded into an analysis of the management of human resources more generally, and linked to the business strategy in the belief that human resources represent a critical means of achieving competitiveness.

Similarly, a number of factors external to the organisation are in no small way responsible for this increased interest in training and development. These include the pervasive spread of new technologies (Walton 1985), increasing competition on a global scale pushing for greater flexibility (Barrow & Loughlin 1992), and the emergence of skills gaps in certain industries (Collins & Sinclair 1991). The extent to which external pressures will facilitate training and development in the organisation is, according to Pettigrew et al. (1988), largely dependent on the availability of the requisite skills in the external labour market. Where these skills exist externally, the organisation may decide to recruit rather than develop its internal labour market. However, as external markets become more complex and competitive, more and more organisations are recognising the value of enskilling their own employees. To this end, the quality of the internal labour market is continuously upgraded and maintained through high quality recruitment, selection, promotion, career development, multi-skilling and flexibility.

Here we examine the nature of training and development practices in Ireland using the data from the Price Waterhouse Cranfield Project. In particular we examine organisational spending on training and development and where policy decisions for training are taken; particular incidents of training are highlighted and methods used by organisations to analyse and monitor training effectiveness are discussed; finally attention is drawn to organisations' perceptions of future training and development requirements.

Training and Development Expenditure

Respondents to the survey were asked to indicate the proportion of their company's annual salaries and wages budget that was being spent on training. Just under 70 per cent indicated some approximate figure, of which the highest frequency, 27 per cent, was spent in the 0.51–1.00 per cent of the budget on training. Clearly, the result must be treated with some caution since respondents were asked to give an approximate figure of expenditure within set brackets. Indeed Fox (1987) argues that problems of this nature continually arise in drawing up statistics on training and development since different organisations have different perceptions of what training actually is, and since many organisations rely on informal methods of training it becomes difficult to quantify the costs of same. In order to estimate the possible degree to which training was perceived as an important investment, organisations were asked whether the money spent on training for managerial, professional/technical, clerical and manual grades (allowing for inflation) had increased, remained the same or decreased over the previous three years.

The results reveal that the money spent on training per category of employee has increased over the past three years, with slightly higher percentages being recorded for managerial and professional/technical employees. This trend is broadly similar for both public and private sector respondents, and union and non-union organisations. However, organisational size was seen to have some influence here (see Appendix 1, Table 6C for the frequency of increases per employment category for differing organisation sizes).

Spending on training has generally increased over the past three years across all organisation sizes. Larger organisations report higher frequency increases than do the smaller organisations, and this increased spending is more likely to have occurred in the managerial/professional employee categories. However, it is interesting to note that the highest frequencies of increased spending are not recorded in the largest organisations, as might be expected, but occur in the 301–400 and 401–500 organisation size groupings. An explanation might well be that such increased spending on training is largely dependent on the environmental factors influencing particular organisations or industries, and is not dependent on organisation size.

FIGURE 6.1: CHANGE IN EXPENDITURE ON T&D OVER LAST THREE YEARS

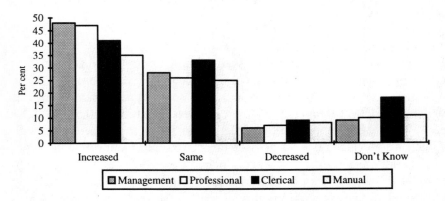

Source: Price Waterhouse Cranfield Project (Ireland); University of Limerick 1992.

Training and Development Practices

A further area of inquiry in the PWC survey was concerned with identifying the amount of training received by all employee categories (Table 6.6).

TABLE 6.6: NUMBER OF DAYS' TRAINING RECEIVED

	< 1 day	1–3	3–5	5–10	10+	Don't Know	TOTAL
Mgt.	4%	23%	36%	32%	4%	31%	253
Prof.	3%	27%	32%	30%	9%	33%	244
Clerical	19%	47%	22%	11%	1%	32%	252
Manual	14%	40%	20%	26%	3%	33%	217

Source: Price Waterhouse Cranfield Project (Ireland); University of Limerick 1992.

The table reveals that the number of days' training received by categories of employees tends to decrease as one moves down the organisation hierarchy. This is indeed interesting, particularly in light of the Galvin report (1988) which found that Irish organisations did not appear either to value management development or devote significant resources to developing their managerial employees. It would appear from the table that managerial employees tend to receive 3–5 days' (36 per cent) and 5–10 days' (32 per cent) training per year. When cross tabulated with organisation sector, it was found that managerial level employees in the private sector were more likely to receive at least 5 days' training per year than were employees in the public sector (29.4 per cent as against 17.2 per cent). Trade union recognition was not significant. Similarly, professional/technical categories in the private sector were found to receive 5–10 days' training (26.1 per cent), while public sector employees in the same category received 3–5 days' (17.3 per cent). Training trends were broadly similar for clerical and manual positions in both sectors. Cross tabulations with organisation size appear to uphold existing results. However, managerial employees in organisations employing less than 100 employees tend to receive 1–3 days' training, significantly less than managerial employees in larger organisations who invariably receive 5–10 days'.

It is worth questioning the wisdom of targeting greater levels of training at the higher level employees in an organisation, since the latter invariably represent the smallest proportion of the total workforce. Given the push for greater flexibility and multi-skilling, one would perhaps expect a greater emphasis on training requirements at the lower level employee categories. Respondents were further asked to identify particular areas in which at least one third of their managers had received training in the previous three years. Table 6.7 below presents the results.

TABLE 6.7: EVIDENCE OF MANAGEMENT DEVELOPMENT

Staff Communication	50.9% (137)*
Motivation	49.1% (132)
Team Building	41.6% (112)
Delegation	39.0% (105)
Performance Appraisal	34.6% (93)
Foreign Language	15.0% (41)

*   Actual number of firms in parenthesis.
Source: Price Waterhouse Cranfield Project (Ireland); University of Limerick
        1992.

Training in communications appears to be the most popular management development activity in the organisations surveyed. When this was
cross tabulated with union recognition, it emerged that managers in
unionised organisations were more likely to have received training in this
area than were managers in non-union organisations (54.6 per cent as
against 38.6 per cent). These findings serve to augment earlier findings in
Chapter 2 which suggested a large increase in direct verbal and written
communications. Larger organisations were found to have delivered a
broader range of management development initiatives than were smaller
organisations, particularly in the areas of team building, motivation and
delegation — the largest organisations surveyed were twice as likely to
provide training in these areas as were the smallest organisations
(delegation — 61.1 per cent as against 29.8 per cent; motivation — 66.7
per cent as against 32.1 per cent; team building — 55.6 per cent as
against 29.8 per cent). Cross tabulations with organisation sector did not
reveal significant differences except in the area of performance appraisal
training where managers in private sector organisations were more likely
to have received training in this area than were their public sector
counterparts (38.8 per cent as against 24.1 per cent).

Analysis and Monitoring of Training and Development
The analysis of employees' training needs is a necessary prerequisite for
effective training and development practice (Donnelly 1987, Buckley &
Caple 1990). However, just 63 per cent of respondents to the present
survey indicated that they analyse the training needs of their employees.
This is indeed surprising, particularly in light of the overall reported
increase in spending on training and development, and begs the question

as to how effective the end result actually is. Analysis of training needs was found to differ significantly with organisation size where larger organisations were found to be much more likely to analyse training needs than were smaller organisations (see Appendix 1, Table 6D).

Sector and trade union recognition were also found to influence the extent to which training needs were analysed. Over two thirds — 69 per cent — of the private sector organisations surveyed analyse the training needs of their employees while 53 per cent of the public sector organisations surveyed do likewise (see Appendix 1, Table 6E). One plausible conclusion may be that training is, in some way, more strategic in the private sector since it allows for skills gaps to be detected and for training to be more proactive and long-term oriented. The results also lead one to question the rationale for providing training without first assessing where training is needed, yet almost half of those surveyed in the public sector appear to do so. The table also appears to indicate that unionised organisations are more likely to analyse training needs (68.1 per cent) than are non-unionised organisations (52.6 per cent).

Respondents were further asked whether they monitored the effectiveness of their training. While 67.3 per cent indicated they did, 23.4 per cent did not and a further 1.9 per cent did not know. Interestingly, when cross tabulated with union recognition, unionised organisations were more likely to monitor the effectiveness of their training than were non-unionised organisations (71 per cent as against 59 per cent). Large organisations were also found to be more likely to monitor the effectiveness of their training.

A combination of techniques is used by respondent organisations to monitor training effectiveness, which range from very informal mechanisms such as feedback from line managers and trainees, to more quantifiable methods such as tests or formal evaluation after training. Table 6.8 below presents the data on the techniques used by organisations to monitor the effectiveness of training.

The findings indicate that respondent organisations tend to place a large emphasis on informal mechanisms of evaluation, and are much less likely to use more structured mechanisms such as formal evaluation after training or tests. This is indicative of training and development in general where the difficulty arises in determining the "valued added" of training at the bottom line, hence the reluctance to apply "hard" evaluation criteria that may not reflect the intangible benefit of the intervention.

Cross tabulations with organisation sector reveal a consistency with the use of informal or "soft" evaluation criteria, but private companies were found to be more likely to use tests than were the public sector organisations (15.3 per cent as against 5.2 per cent). However, in cross tabulations with organisation size, the most significant disparities occurred in relation to the use of informal feedback, both from line managers and from trainees. Of organisations employing less than 100 employees, 46 per cent monitor effectiveness by informal feedback from line managers, while 83.3 per cent of organisations employing 2,001+ employees utilise same. Similar results emerge for use of informal feedback from trainees (44 per cent as against 77.5 per cent respectively) — thus, increasing usage of this mechanism corresponds with increasing organisation size.

TABLE 6.8: TECHNIQUES USED TO MONITOR TRAINING EFFECTIVENESS

	Use	**Do Not Use**
Informal Feedback From Line Management	98.8% (164)*	1.2 % (2)
Informal Feedback From Trainees	97.5% (155)	2.5% (1)
Formal Evaluation Immediately After Training	76.6% (89)	23.3% (27)
Formal Evaluation Some Months After Training	49.4 % (42)	50.6% (43)
Tests	47.4 % (37)	52.6% (41)

*   Actual number of firms in parenthesis.
Source: Price Waterhouse Cranfield Project (Ireland); University of Limerick 1992.

Overall, therefore, there has been a general increase in spending on training and development over the past three years for all employee categories, and rather than such increases being related to organisational size, they may well be largely determined by the environmental factors influencing the organisation. With respect to responsibility for training and development policy decisions, line management involvement appears to be high. In relation to training and development practices, the data reveals that the number of days' training received tends to decrease as one moves down the organisational hierarchy. Staff communication training emerges as the area in which most managers have been developed in the past three years. Finally, in relation to the analysis and monitoring of training activities, it was found that larger organisations are more likely to analyse training needs and monitor training effectiveness than are their smaller counterparts.

INTERNAL LABOUR MARKETS AND EMPLOYMENT SYSTEMS

A number of distinct employment systems with different sets of rules applying to white-collar workers, craftsmen and unskilled workers can exist in one firm (Kerr 1954, Edwards 1979, Osterman 1987). There is also a wide variation even across firms in similar industries and between similar industries in different countries (Marsden 1990). An employment system refers to the rules which govern the employment relationship. These can be grouped into four distinct areas, the rules relating to the way tasks are grouped and classified into jobs, the rules covering the deployment of labour with regard to promotions, transfers and recruitment, the rules governing compensation and the rules covering security of employment, in particular layoffs (Osterman 1987). The organisation of employment systems determines the way jobs are classified and graded, the availability of career ladders, the nature of compensation and the rules governing job security and layoffs. A key concern of management and employees is the regulation and control of the rules and procedures governing these substantive aspects of the employment relationship. The closure of these rules and procedures from any direct relationship with changes in the external labour market and their institutionalisation over time separates the labour market in a firm from the external labour market, creating an internal labour market.

Doeringer and Piore (1971) define an internal labour market (ILM) as an administrative unit such as a manufacturing firm where the pricing and allocation of labour are governed by a set of administrative rules and procedures and not only by the economic forces of the external labour market. It is the allocation of labour, according to Pfeffry and Cohen (1984), which has received most attention in the literature on employment relationships. One of the essential features of ILMs is promotions from within the firm and only a limited number of ports of entry into the firm. While there is no direct data on promotions in the Price Waterhouse Cranfield Project, respondents were asked to indicate whether jobs were advertised internally for managers, professionals, clerical and manual staff. Respondents were also asked whether current positions were filled internally from among their employees. Table 6.9 shows the percentage of firms which advertise and recruit internally for vacant positions.

It can be argued that both of these measures are a reasonable proxy for the internal allocation of labour. Not surprisingly the majority of firms tend to fill senior managerial positions with internal candidates.

TABLE 6.9: INTERNAL ADVERTISING AND RECRUITMENT FROM CURRENT EMPLOYEES FOR VACANT POSITIONS

	% of Firms			
Process	**Managers**	**Professional**	**Clerical**	**Manual**
From Current Employees	52%	35%	45%	29%
Internal Advertising*	41%	38%	57%	41%

* In most firms it is unlikely that internal advertising is used to fill senior managerial and professional positions although the positions are filled internally.
Source: Price Waterhouse Cranfield Project (Ireland); University of Limerick 1992.

While 52 per cent of firms recruited 30 per cent or less of their senior managers externally, only 29 per cent indicated that 60 per cent or more were recruited externally. However, internal recruitment of managers appears to be lower than that reported elsewhere, where firms filled as much as 90 per cent of higher level positions from internal candidates (Mace 1979, Osterman 1984). A significant and interesting difference emerges in the pattern of internal recruitment in public and private sector firms with 40 per cent of public sector firms compared with 26 per cent of private firms recruiting over 60 per cent externally. We can find no available explanation for such a finding which runs counter to expected patterns and requires further, more focused research. A more central indicator of the extent of ILMs regarding the allocation of labour is the degree to which positions are filled internally by manual workers since traditionally career ladders and internal mobility are a feature of clerical work. However, the filling of positions internally from manual grades is not necessarily an indicator that there is a hierarchy of positions or established career paths available to manual workers. Internal appointments are often filled from a pool of casual/part-time workers and it would be inaccurate to represent this process as a form of career mobility through internal promotion. Furthermore, the actual number of positions advertised and available to manual workers may be few in number, a factor which the PWCP data cannot measure. Even so, the process of advertising and the filling of positions internally is insulated from the external labour market and can be considered a measure of an ILM. In the following analysis we focus on the incidence of internal advertising rather than the filling of current positions for manual workers. There is a difference between the two measures, with 41 per cent of the sampled firms advertising positions internally to be filled from manual workers, while 30 per cent report that they actually fill vacant positions from among their manual workforce. Internal advertising is regarded as a more inclusive measure of the existence of an ILM and is therefore the preferred measure since companies who use internal advertising are essentially providing existing employees with the first opportunity to fill positions before resorting to the external labour market.

FIGURE 6.2: PROPORTION OF SENIOR MANAGERS RECRUITED EXTERNALLY

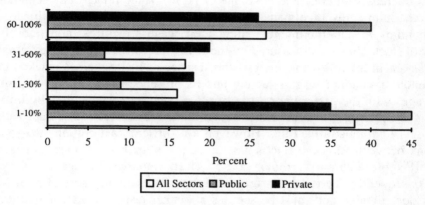

Source: Price Waterhouse Cranfield Project (Ireland); University of Limerick 1992.

The second aspect of ILMs is the internal pricing of labour, usually through mechanisms like job evaluation and wage surveys to establish the going wage rate in comparable companies (see Doeringer and Piore 1971). The defining characteristic of wage setting in an ILM is that it is based on principles such as fairness, cost of living and expectations concerning the economic return for investments in education and professional qualifications, rather than external market processes. Standard wages are attached to jobs and it appears that internal wage structures in most firms are quite rigid. Indeed, research indicates that firms are capable of continuing for substantial periods with wages that are higher than are needed to recruit a given workforce (Brown 1989, Osterman 1984). The rigidity of wage structures would appear to be confirmed by the PWCP survey where only 13 per cent of firms deviated from standard wages for manual workers by using performance-related wage schemes, 29 per cent in the case of clerical workers, 39 per cent with professionals and 46 per cent for managers. In contrast, wages which are free to fluctuate according to external market forces will move relatively quickly upwards or downwards in reaction to swings in the business cycle and its resultant local effects on product markets and the supply of labour. Dual labour theory argues that the labour market is segmented into primary jobs, which have all the characteristics associated with developed internal labour markets, including standard wages, usually to be found in the core area of the economy and secondary jobs, having few benefits and experiencing high exposure to market forces, existing on the periphery of the core economy (Gordon et al. 1982). There are signs as witnessed by the increased interest and coverage of performance related pay schemes in the human resource management literature that some firms in the core economy are attempting to realign their wage structures more closely with fluctuations, as measured by the firms' performance, in the external market. In the following analysis the absence of PRP schemes is taken to denote a standard wage structure and its presence as an attempt to link wages with the performance of a firm's product or service, thereby linking the pricing of labour with external market processes rather than with a set of administrative rules. However, it is difficult to ascertain the exact link between PRP and fluctuations in a firm's market and in most cases PRP represents only a minor portion of an employee's wage or salary. Consequently, the reliability and validity of PRP as a measure of an ILM is questionable and must be seen as a weaker test than that of internal advertising. Allowing for this caveat, the absence of PRP schemes for clerical and especially manual workers is used to indicate the internal administration and setting of wages and salaries.

Factors Affecting the Presence of ILMs
The factors related to the presence or absence of an ILM are divided into structural factors and strategic human resource factors. The structural factors include sector (public or private), size, presence of a trade union, union membership levels and industry type. Generally the features of an ILM are most typically associated with employment systems in government organisations since these organisations require a high degree of social legitimation (Tolbert and Zucker 1983) and need to be seen as "good employers". Thus, developed ILMs are more likely to be found in public sector employment's than elsewhere (Pfeffry and Cohen 1984). Size is considered an important element in the development of ILMs. Goldberg (1980) argues that the development of ILMs is historically related to the growth in firm size along with an increasing productive capacity. The firm's ability to monitor the work processes declined as firm size increased and led to a need for firms to establish an elaborate governance structure for employees. Conversely, small establishments are unlikely to have an ILM as the number of promotional opportunities

is related to establishment size and there is little choice for employers other than to recruit from the external labour market (Granovetter 1984).

Union recognition and the level of union membership can be expected to have a positive effect on the presence of an ILM for manual workers. According to Jacoby (1984), the development of ILMs for industrial workers in the United States was not a managerial innovation but was imposed from below. What emerged from the union struggle was an ILM whose features represented a compromise between employer and employees, with an emphasis on seniority as a guiding principle in the allocation of labour and strict job classifications tied to standard wages — a combination which Edwards (1979) referred to as the "compromise model", a form of employment relations similar to the dominant pluralist and liberal paradigm prevalent in Irish employee relations since 1946 (see for example the Report of the Commission on Industrial Relations (1981), and Roche's (1992) discussion of liberal theory). The effect of union recognition and union membership levels on the presence of ILMs for white-collar workers is less clear. Historically, employers have been inclined to insulate their white-collar employees from the external labour market through the provision of implicit employment guarantees, internal career ladders and a variety of non-monetary benefits such as pensions and medical care. Edwards (1979) views this "employer model" of control as a tactic used to fractionate the workforce and prevent unionisation. However, it is also argued that with the expansion and mass delivery of services, white-collar workers find themselves in a similar situation as manual workers and behave and act in a similar manner to protect their interests through collective representation (Lockwood 1989). Since the mass delivery of services is mainly associated with public sector employment, the effect of unionisation can be expected to be either positive or neutral in public sector organisations and negative or neutral in private sector firms. Lastly, the effect of industry is included to control for possible systematic differences in ILMs across industries.

It is difficult to envisage the development of an ILM without the requisite administrative support needed to set up and monitor these employment systems. Jacoby (1984) argues that the personnel function was a necessary development which enabled the "replacement of a market-oriented, arbitrary and impermanent employment system by one that was more bureaucratic, rule bound and secure". While personnel departments are an established feature of most firms in the Cranfield survey, the relative importance of the function varies across firms. Two measures are used to assess the importance of the personnel function. The existence of a written document outlining a firm's human resource management strategy can be taken as a measure of the attention given to personnel matters. Secondly, the strength of the personnel function is evaluated by the extent to which the personnel department is given primary responsibility for major policy decisions in the areas of: pay and benefits; recruitment and selection; training and development; employee relations; health and safety and workforce expansion/reduction. We would expect one or both of these measures to be positively associated with the use of internal advertising. However, given the emphasis in the HRM literature extolling the benefits of performance-related pay (PRP) schemes, the relationship between a developed central personnel function and standard wage structures is difficult to specify.

A statistical analysis of the survey data revealed the following findings in relation to these issues.

The use of internal advertising to fill manual positions is positively associated with firms which recognise a trade union and have a strong personnel function. Recognising a union is the most important variable associated with internal advertising for manual positions, being almost twice as important as having a written personnel strategy. Contrary to expectations sector and size are not significant in any of the equations. In particular, the absence of a relationship between size and the use of internal advertising is surprising. It could be argued that it is the proportion of manual workers in a firm, rather than the overall size of a firm's workforce, which is critical. That is, firms with a high proportion of manual workers will, *ceteris paribus*, have a wider range of manual grades with vacancies and hence a greater propensity and opportunity to advertise internally. As expected, there is no relationship between unionism and the use of internal advertising for white-collar workers, nor with the extent of control exercised by the personnel department. But the importance attributed to personnel matters, as measured by the existence of a written document on personnel strategy, is significant, confirming the relationship between the personnel function and ILMs.

The relationship of the structural variables with the use of standard wage structures as measured by the absence of PRP schemes for manual and clerical workers is difficult to specify. There is no theoretical or empirical reason to expect size to be related to the use of PRP schemes. However, we would expect standard wage structures to be more prevalent in the public sector for both manual and clerical workers. Similarly, standard wage structures are likely to be associated with union recognition and a high level of unionisation, particularly for manual workers.

Once again, sector and size have no effect on the use of standard wages/salaries. Although the coefficient for white-collar workers is large and positive, indicating a relationship between public sector employment and standard wages, it fails to reach the required significance level.

Union recognition is positively and significantly related to standard wages for manual workers, though not for clerical workers. In both cases the actual level of union membership is not related to the use of standard wages. The attention given to personnel strategy is significantly and negatively related to the use of standard wages. Consequently, where a firm has a written strategy on personnel matters, it is more likely to use PRP schemes for all employees.

This contrasts with the positive association of strategy with the use of internal advertising to fill vacancies. Thus, a high priority accorded to personnel strategy encourages the use of some processes characteristic of ILMs but is also associated with exposing wages and salaries more closely with external performance criteria. It could be argued, albeit tentatively, that close attention to personnel strategy is linked with a restructuring of the employment system in firms within the core sector of the economy. This argument fits broadly with the limited case study results of firms who place a high priority on human resource management (Storey 1992).

Overall, the results confirm the importance of a recognised trade union for manual workers for both the allocation and pricing of labour and also, as we have seen, the importance of the personnel function in the determination of ILMs. However, the variables used to measure both the pricing and allocation of labour are limited in their coverage of both of these processes. An adequate measure would include: job tenure, internal mobility, job grades, the rules governing promotion, deployment, transfers, layoffs and, in the case of non-standard wages, the mechanisms by which wages are fixed. In their absence, the results reported here must be seen as tentative and inconclusive and requiring further research. In particular, it would be useful to assess the relationship between different ILM arrangements and employee relations practices.

CONCLUSIONS

The survey data indicates that in a majority of cases, recruitment and selection will be completed through a combination of HR function and line management involvement. Line management's responsibility in this area has increased in the past three years. In relation to recruitment methods, external advertising is favoured for management and/or professional/technical vacancies, whereas internal advertising is most common for clerical and/or manual grades. On the whole, larger organisations make more use of the internal labour market. Ownership is also an important factor here, with Irish-owned organisations appearing to make less use of the internal labour market in the recruitment process, across all employee categories. The application form, the interview panel, and the referee are the most commonly used selection methods, while others such as biodata, testing, assessment centres, and group selection methods are used only in minority of cases. With respect to gender in recruitment, while a large percentage of organisations do not target women, of those which do, a high percentage are unionised.

In relation to training and development, there has been a general increase in spending over the past three years, for all employee grades, and rather than such increases being determined by organisational size, they may largely be determined by environmental factors influencing the organisation. Staff communication training emerges as the area in which most managers have been developed over the past three years, confirming the increased importance attached to this area in recent years.

The way in which the employment relationship is organised and managed is an important factor in defining the climate of employee relations in a firm. The factors related to the presence or absence of an ILM are divided into structural factors and strategic human resource management issues. The use of internal advertising to fill manual positions is positively associated with firms which recognise a trade union and have a strong personnel function. There is no relationship between unionism and the use of advertising for white-collar workers. The relationship of the structural variables with the use of standard wage structures was measured by the absence of PRP schemes for manual or clerical workers. Size and sector have no effect on the use of standard wages/salaries. Union recognition is positively and significantly related to standard wages for manual workers. The attention given to personnel strategy is significant and negatively related to the use of standard wages. Consequently, where a firm has a written strategy on personnel matters, it is more likely to use PRP schemes for all employees. The results confirm the importance of a recognised trade union for manual workers, for both the allocation and pricing of labour.

Chapter 7

TRENDS IN FLEXIBLE WORKING PATTERNS IN IRELAND

Michael Morley and Patrick Gunnigle

INTRODUCTION

In recent years, we have witnessed the emergence of a debate among academics, personnel practitioners and the trade union movement on different ways of engaging and utilising labour. Subsumed under the overarching concept of "flexibility", the 1980s saw a huge increase in interest in the contribution various employment strategies might make both to organisational effectiveness and performance and increased opportunities for employees. And the debate continues. Pollert (1991) notes that prophesies of a "new" or "radical break" in the climate of production relations, the nature and the "future" of work have driven this debate into a "post-industrial futurology", one in which new types of work and new employment relations are being heralded as the novel and indeed path-breaking developments of the new era. Further grist to this particular mill is the suggestion that within the European context, the completion of the internal market will lead to more radical and atypical employment patterns across sectors.

THE CONTEXT FOR CHANGE IN IRELAND

Labour Market Changes and Unemployment

The most notable changes in the Irish labour market over the past 20 years have been the dramatic fall in the numbers employed in agriculture and the consistent growth in employment in the services sector which now accounts for almost 60 per cent of all employees (Table 7.1).

Much of this service sector growth in recent years has been concentrated in private services. In the period 1975–89, there was a significant increase in employment in financial and business services (42 per cent), professional services (21 per cent) and personal services (16 per cent) (Dineen 1992). Conversely, the fiscal rectitude policies of successive governments since the early 1980s have seen a concentration in employment in the public sector.

TABLE 7.1: EMPLOYMENT CHANGES BY SECTOR 1961–89 (000)

	1961	1975	1979	1985	1989
Agriculture	380 (36%)	238 (22%)	221 (19%)	171 (16%)	163 (15%)
Industry	257 (25%)	337 (31%)	365 (32%)	306 (28%)	306 (28%)
Services	415 (39%)	498 (47%)	559 (49%)	602 (56%)	621 (57%)

Source: Labour Force Surveys/CSO-1989.

While employment has remained relatively constant in industry as a whole, there has been a significant change in the sectoral distribution of industrial employment. In particular, the period since the 1970s has seen a substantial fall in the numbers employed in older indigenous manufacturing, with a large reduction in the numbers employed in the textiles, clothing and footwear sectors. During the same period, there were substantial increases in employment in foreign-owned firms, particularly in chemicals and engineering. Generally, job losses in the manufacturing sector tended to be concentrated in the lower-paid, labour-intensive industries catering for the home market, while companies (largely foreign-owned) in more capital-intensive export-oriented sectors fared much better.

Accompanying these changes in the sectoral distribution of employment, have been significant changes in work patterns. Principally as a result of the recession, the composition of the workforce has changed. The most significant influencing trend has been the sustained recession which has resulted in the creation of a pool of unemployed people prepared to do marginal work. This high unemployment has been a key concern among unions and employees, and has had the largely undesired effect of forcing individuals to consider different ways of working in order to retain jobs.

Unemployment figures increased dramatically during the 1980s and in early 1993 stood at approximately 20 per cent of the workforce. The onset of the second major economic recession in the early 1980s, combined with the rapid growth in the numbers joining the labour force, caused major problems for employment creation. The total numbers at work fell by 6.6 per cent in the 1979–85 period and unemployment increased by almost 230 per cent. Dineen (1992) suggests that the reasons for this dramatic growth in unemployment are part supply-driven (population growth and increased labour force participation rates) and part demand-driven (weak international demand abroad and fiscal rectitude at home).

Other important developments in employment structure over the past decade have been the growth in long-term unemployment, a lowering of the retirement age and a return of widespread emigration up to the late 1980s. Within this overall pattern, it is interesting that the participation rate of females in employment has increased. Clearly, the sectoral shifts in employment are favourably biased towards greater female employment, with females proportionately over-represented in those sectors which are seen to be expanding. Much of the growth in female participation rates has been in the areas of retail distribution, insurance and financial/business, professional and personal services.

Overall, at a macro level, the single greatest challenge facing the Irish economy is the need to tackle effectively the persistently high level of unemployment. Despite a pervasive feeling that the fundamentals of the economy are sound (low inflation, balance of payment surpluses, good employee relations, solid GNP growth), the country has increasingly struggled to provide jobs for its young, well-educated workforce. The openness of the Irish economy also means that any downturn in the world economy significantly impacts upon domestic economic performance, particularly in relation to export growth and emigration opportunities.

Non-standard Working Arrangements

It would appear that shifts in employment structure and the depressed economic environment have led to greater variation in the forms of employment, with a trend away from what are regarded as traditional employment arrangements towards more non-standard or atypical employment forms. Such employment is defined as any form of employment which deviates from the traditional full-time, permanent format, and indeed this trend is one of the most visible in employment practices in Ireland, as illustrated by tables 7.2 and 7.3.

TABLE 7.2: PART-TIME EMPLOYMENT 1979–89 (000)

	1979	1987	1989
Regular Part-time	35.5	65.6	70.3
Occasional Part-time	22.1	12.8	12.1
All Part-time	57.6	78.4	82.4
Part-time as % of Total	5.4%	7.1%	7.6%

Source: Labour Force Surveys/CSO/Dineen 1992.

TABLE 7.3: TEMPORARY EMPLOYMENT 1983–89 (000)

	Males	Females	TOTAL	Temp. as % of Total
1983	25.5	26.4	51.93	6.0%
1985	28.5	33.0	61.5	7.4%
1987	32.8	38.9	71.8	8.5%
1989	32.9	38.8	71.7	8.5%

Source: Labour Force Surveys/CSO/Dineen 1992.

Clearly, the increased incidence of non-standard employment forms must be viewed in the context of the broader changes in employment patterns: particularly the expansion in unemployment and the shifting employment patterns characterised by a fall in agriculture and manufacturing industry and the growth in the service sector, as highlighted. We noted that the growth in the services sector has been primarily confined to private (professional and personal) services, areas traditionally associated with non-standard employment. Furthermore, the public sector, which has traditionally been associated with typical employment forms, has undergone severe contraction in employment terms with the result that changes in the sectoral distribution of employment have favoured an increase in non-standard employment. While it has also facilitated a rise in female employment, the nature of the jobs lost and those created differs substantially. Areas of job loss, particularly manufacturing industry and the public sector, are associated with providing relatively secure employment, while conversely, areas of employment growth — most notably personal services such as contract cleaning and catering services — are associated with more insecure, less well-paid work.

One other key issue is that despite the growth in atypical employment, the majority of workers in the non-agriculture sector (almost 80%) remain in standard employment. Thus, while there would appear to be a definite trend towards atypical employment, the gradual incremental change must be viewed in the context of broader economic and labour market changes. It is also plausible to suggest that the apparent substitution of non-standard for standard employment is largely expedient and reactionary in the face of the difficult economic environment in which many organisations now find themselves. However, these changes do have the potential to remain in the longer term and become more widely accepted, partly because of the financial attractions to employers of reduced employment-related overheads and partly because of the continuing high levels of unemployment.

FIGURE 7.1: ATYPICAL/TOTAL EMPLOYMENT

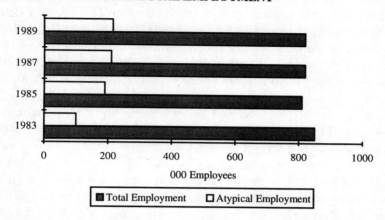

000 Employees

■ Total Employment   □ Atypical Employment

*   These figures are adjusted to allow for overlaps in atypical employment forms
(see Dineen 1992)
Source: Labour Force Surveys/CSO.

The Flexibility Debate

An associated issue is the contention that the flexible firm model as
advanced by Atkinson (1984) and characterised by a planned development of a core/periphery employment model is emerging in Irish organisations (Flood 1990). The core/periphery model of future employment
involves the breaking up of the existing hierarchical structure of the firm
so that radically different employment policies can be pursued for
different groups of workers. Within this scenario, the "core" is composed
of full-time staff, enjoying relatively secure challenging jobs with good
pay and employment conditions, while the "periphery" is composed of an
amalgam of temporary, part-time and contract groups with less favourable pay and employment conditions and less job security or training and
promotion opportunities. Based on a planned development of the core/
periphery employment model, the flexible firm scenario is an attempt to
increase flexibility in three key areas. Numerical flexibility which incorporates the use of non-standard employment forms allows the organisation to hire and/or shed labour flexibly in line with business demands.
Functional flexibility, incorporating multi-skilling and cross training is
dedicated to the establishment of a broader flexible skill set in the
organisation. Financial flexibility is based on the principle of linking pay
rates to labour and product market conditions and making pay increases
for individual employees variable and contingent upon performance.
Thus, as an organisational flexibility strategy, McInnes(1988) suggests
that such an approach is clearly labour-market led and is facilitated by

the reduced bargaining power of labour in times of high unemployment.

Recent Irish commentators note a definite trend towards greater flexibility (Suttle 1988, Flood 1990), particularly in relation to numerical flexibility in the services sector. This trend may in part be explained by the looseness of the Irish labour market and the consequent availability of people willing to work in temporary or part-time jobs (Gunnigle 1992).

Functional flexibility is defined as the expansion of skills within a workforce, or the ability of firms to reorganise the competencies associated with jobs so that the job holder is willing and able to deploy such competencies across a broader range of tasks. This process may result in employees moving into higher or lower skill areas, or a combination of both. It is often referred to as multi-skilling. Elger (1991) notes that the most striking feature of the findings on functional flexibility in the influential IMS study of large firms is actually the modesty, rather than the radicalism of the changes involved, and the centrality of reduced manning levels rather than up-skilling. For craft maintenance activities, 75 per cent of their manufacturing panel reported a "small enlargement of a maintenance craftsman's job", and 57 per cent had gained limited craft overlap, sometimes requiring training, but without violation of any group's "core trade". This is hardly revolutionary change. As Elger highlights:

> Despite the interpretative gloss, such findings accord quite closely with other evidence, in suggesting only minimal moves towards the super-craftsman and multi-skilling but rather more mundane change. Furthermore, the authors recognise that, while craft union leverage and the training costs involved in genuine multi-skilling were important influences on this pattern, many managements were primarily concerned to reduce waiting time rather than looking for any more radical change.

The evidence to date from Ireland on functional flexibility suggests that this form of flexibility is relatively rare and is largely confined to manufacturing industry (Suttle 1988). Some larger organisations have taken a number of initiatives in the area of multi-skilling, such as the ESB and TEAM Aer Lingus in the semi-state sector and Krups Engineering and Aughinish Alumina in the private sector. It has been argued, (Gunnigle & Daly 1992), that "add-skilling" or "extra-skilling" may be more appropriate descriptions of these developments than multi-skilling. This argument is based on the evidence that functional flexibility among skilled workers largely involves those categories receiving training in and agreeing to undertake other prescribed tasks in addition to their traditional trade — for example, fitters undertaking electrical/instrumentation work. There is, of course, evidence of organisations claiming to have total functional flexibility in their operations. However, as Gunnigle (1992) notes, such functional flexibility would appear to pertain only in unskilled assembly-type work where there is a minimal training requirement and it is thus relatively easy to deploy workers across a large range of tasks as required.

Financial flexibility consists of two elements. Firstly, it incorporates the ability of organisations to adjust pay rates to reflect market conditions, particularly the labour market. Secondly, it encourages the introduction of merit/performance-related reward systems whereby employees are paid at a rate dependant on their performance, using an assessment-based system or one relating payment to the individual's level of skills acquisition. In this respect, Keenan & Thom (1984) suggest that financial flexibility is often used to encourage functional flexibility. While it is difficult to identify a clear picture in the area of financial flexibility, in Chapter 5 on Reward Practices, we highlighted a trend towards greater financial flexibility with respect to the increased incidence of variable pay systems. However, it was also noted that this trend is much less evident if one examines the application of performance- related payment systems to different employee categories, with such systems being largely confined to managerial and professional employees. In relation to the second aspect of financial flexibility (adjusting pay rates to reflect prevailing market conditions), there have been two prominent examples of "two-tier" pay systems in Bank of Ireland and Aer Lingus (Flood 1989). Both of these involved the introduction of a new entry grade at pay levels considerably below those pertaining for those who traditionally carried out such work. On the whole, there would appear to be little evidence of the widespread incidence of this form of flexibility, despite the fact that the state of the labour market facilitates such developments.

Despite the appeal of the flexible firm scenario in some quarters, the research evidence to date suggests that change in this area would appear to be much more closely aligned with gradual incrementalism rather than with a radical post-industrial futurology, possibly because of the inherent weaknesses in the model. It has been criticised both for its conceptually weak base and for the practical difficulties associated with its introduction.

LIMITATIONS OF THE CORE/PERIPHERY EMPLOYMENT MODEL

Pollert (1988) advances four key conceptual limitations. Firstly, the model asserts that segmentation between a core and a periphery is a new departure. However, labour market analysis was always based on a dual market, segmented between the internal/external labour market. It simply argues that there are two labour markets when it may be better to argue that the labour force is divided into many parts using different segmentation criteria. Secondly, it suggests that skills such as crafts, engineering and systems analysis are brought in on a subcontracting basis and that craftsmen, engineers and systems analysts are thus not part of the core workforce. However there is little empirical evidence for this. The model also ignores sexual segmentation. The construction of a core workforce, argues Pollert, is as much due to male domination of certain activities to the exclusion of women as it is to management strategy. Thirdly, the rationale for having a core and a periphery may be a result more of managements' efforts to control labour than of an attempt to encourage flexibility. This issue needs more explicit recognition in the model. Fourthly, along with analytical and descriptive problems, the model has problems on a prescriptive level. In linking manpower policy to business strategy, the model diverts attention away from long-term training needs by providing an excuse to move them to the periphery. It may be concentrating on labour as the chief strategic problem, at the expense of structural, organisational, control and growth strategy issues.

Keenan & Thom (1988) also highlight a number of practical problems associated with the model. Firstly, they suggest that efforts to develop and implement the model can create more problems than the model actually solves, particularly where subcontracted labour is being used as redundancies are occurring. Secondly, by having such a distinction in the workforce, the insecurity of employment and the lack of career prospects may stimulate resentment and frustration in the periphery. Furthermore, in terms of a societal cost, a two-tier workforce creates unhealthy distinctions. Moreover, such a distinction may lead to a further widening of the skills gap and future skill shortages, thus inhibiting national ability to compete with other industrialised nations.

Overall, considering the initial high level of general enthusiasm for the flexible firm model, it is somewhat surprising that it is left to the original authors to dispel some of the enthusiasm for their claims. In their article entitled "Is Flexibility Just a Flash in the Pan?" Atkinson & Meager (1986) highlight that:

> Although the observed changes were widespread, they did not cut very deeply in most firms, and therefore the outcome was more likely to be marginal, ad-hoc and tentative, rather than a purposeful thrust to achieve flexibility.

The extant literature therefore reveals several strands within the flexibility debate. It is argued that competitive pressures are increasingly forcing organisations to increase their capacity to employ or shed labour more rapidly in order to achieve a better fit between workforce size and fluctuations in the demand for goods and services. Consequently, non-standard employment in the form of temporary/casual workers, fixed-term contracts, home-workers and subcontracting is seen to follow. Other types of flexibility are also seen to be emerging in the form of shift work and finally, functional flexibility concerned with the relaxation of demarcation lines and the adoption of broader job descriptions. However, the research evidence to date would appear to be suggesting that while flexibility is on the increase, this is occurring in a relatively piecemeal fashion in reaction to depressed labour and product market conditions, rather than as a systematically planned emergence of the totally flexible firm. However, such apparently expedient responses to environmental conditions may well be sustained when the environment changes, as organisations become more anxious to retain the advantages of certain flexibility forms (Hakim 1991). The purpose of the remainder of this chapter is to inform the flexibility debate further by providing a deal of timely systematic information on trends in flexible working patterns in Ireland.

SURVEY FINDINGS ON FLEXIBLE WORKING PATTERNS IN IRELAND

The survey collected information on three key areas. Firstly, questions relating to the changes that have occurred in the use of non-standard working arrangements over the past three years were asked. Secondly, we sought to examine, at organisational level, the proportion of the work-force on short/fixed-term contracts. Thirdly, and finally, the study attempted to examine the extent to which there had been a major change in the specification of jobs for various categories of employees over the past three years. These are three areas of inquiry that are central to the flexibility debate.

Change in the Use of Non-standard Working Arrangements
While some increases in flexibility throughout the 1980s, particularly in relation to part-time working, were confirmed by the Workplace Industrial Relations Surveys in the UK, there was little overall change in employers' use of various forms of non-standard employment over the second half of the 1980s. In the Irish context the PWCP reveals a some-what mixed pattern with evidence of both stability and some change in this area (Table 7.4).

TABLE 7.4: CHANGES IN WORKING ARRANGEMENTS

	Increase	Same	Decrease	Not Used	Missing
Weekend Work	20.4%	43.5%	13.0%	18.2%	4.8%
Shift Work	14.1%	42.4%	6.3%	29.7%	7.4%
Overtime	21.2%	38.7%	28.3%	5.2%	6.3%
Part-time Work	31.2%	23.8%	6.3%	27.5%	11.2%
Temporary/Casual Work	34.6%	33.5%	13.8%	8.9%	9.3%
Fixed-term Contract	30.9%	26.0%	3.3%	27.9%	11.9%
Home-based Work	3.0%	7.4%	—	68.8%	20.8%
Govt. Training Schemes	11.2%	25.3%	1.1%	43.9%	18.6%
Subcontract	29.7%	27.1%	4.5%	27.9%	10.7%

N = 269

Source: Price Waterhouse Cranfield Project (Ireland); University of Limerick 1992.

It would appear that Irish managements, much like their counterparts abroad, have attempted to go some way towards ensuring that labour inputs are more responsive to environmental conditions, but not to the extent, that one might, perhaps, expect. Thus, a large percentage of respondents suggest that working arrangements have remained unchanged, most notably in relation to weekend work (43.5 per cent), shift work (42.4 per cent) and overtime (38.7 per cent). However, these three are an exception with respect to their classification and they do not often occur in discussions on atypical employment because they tend to be undertaken by "core" rather than "peripheral" employees. Therefore, turning to what might be described as "flexible strategies for a more responsive organisation", significant increases are recorded for part-time work (31.2 per cent), temporary/casual work (34.6 per cent), fixed-term contracts (30.9 per cent) and subcontracting (29.7 per cent). Home-based work is by far the least used flexibility strategy in Ireland, with 68.8 per cent of respondents suggesting that this strategy is not employed. Overall therefore, looking at the data in aggregate, the result is one of relative stability. A number of differences do occur between the public and private sector which are worth highlighting (Table 7.5).

The increase in weekend work over the last three years was far greater in the private sector than in the public sector (24 per cent as opposed to 8.6 per cent). Similarly, in relation to shift work, there is a 19.7 per cent recorded increase for the private sector, but no increase for the public sector. Conversely, where an increase occurred in the use of part-time work, temporary/casual work, fixed-term contracts and government training schemes, such an increase was larger in public than in private sector companies. Finally, there are no substantial differences between the trends recorded for overtime and subcontracting, as flexibility strategies, in the public and private sectors.

TABLE 7.5 (a): TRENDS IN WORKFORCE FLEXIBILITY: PUBLIC

	Increased	Same	Decreased	Not Used
Weekend Work	8.6%	51.7%	6.9%	24.1%
Shift Work	—	55.2%	3.4%	32.8%
Overtime	19.0%	43.1%	24.1%	6.9%
Part-time Work	39.7%	31.0%	5.2%	13.8%
Temporary/ Casual	39.7%	39.7%	5.2%	6.9%
Fixed-term Contract	46.6%	32.8%	3.4%	13.8%
Home-based Work	—	5.2%	—	72.4%
Govt. Training Schemes	17.2%	29.3%	—	36.2%
Subcontract	31.0%	19.0%	3.4%	34.6%

N = 58

TABLE 7.5 (b): TRENDS IN WORKFORCE FLEXIBILITY: PRIVATE

	Increased	Same	Decreased	Not Used
Weekend Work	24.0%	42.6%	14.2%	15.8%
Shift Work	19.7%	39.3%	7.1%	27.9%
Overtime	22.4%	39.3%	29.0%	3.8%
Part-time Work	26.8%	23.0%	7.7%	32.8%
Temporary/ Casual	32.2%	32.2%	16.9%	9.8%
Fixed-term Contract	26.2%	24.6%	2.75	32.8%
Home-based Work	3.3%	8.2%	—	70.5%
Govt. Training Schemes	9.3%	24.6%	1.6%	47.0%
Subcontract	29.0%	30.6%	4.4%	18.0%

N = 183

Source: Price Waterhouse Cranfield Project (Ireland); University of Limerick 1992.

The data was also disaggregated to test for differences between unionised and non-unionised organisations (Table 7.6).

A number of key points emerge from this table. Firstly, non-unionised organisations appear less likely to use shift work as a flexibility strategy than their unionised counterparts, with 61 per cent of non-unionised respondents suggesting that they do not use shift work, compared with 25 per cent of unionised respondents. Secondly, the use of overtime as a flexibility strategy has increased more in unionised environments (25 per cent), than in non-unionised (12 per cent). However, the decrease is also greater in unionised organisations (33 per cent), suggesting perhaps that while unionised organisations continue to rely heavily on overtime, they may be turning to other methods in ever-increasing numbers, in an attempt to achieve a more flexible responsive organisation. Thirdly, and perhaps somewhat surprisingly, part-time work also appears more common in unionised organisations. While 26 per cent of unionised organisations suggest they do not use part-time work, approximately 50 per cent of non-unionised organisations suggest it is not used. Furthermore, the increase that has occurred in the use of part-time work has been far greater in unionised companies (38 per cent), than in their non-union counterparts (22 per cent). Fourthly, and conversely, in relation to temporary/casual work, the increase that occurred in non-unionised companies over the last three years outweighs that which occurred in unionised environments (45 per cent and 35 per cent respectively). Fifthly, the evidence suggests that fixed-term contracts appear to be more common in unionised organisations. The results reveal that while 28 per cent of unionised companies do not use such contracts, the corresponding figure for non-unionised organisations is 47 per cent. Furthermore, the increase in the use of these contracts over the last three years in unionised organisations outweighs that which occurred in non-unionised (37 per cent and 25 per cent respectively). Sixthly, while 52 per cent of unionised and 55 per cent of non-unionised organisations suggest that they do not use government training schemes, the increase that has occurred in their use has been greater in the unionised sector (15 per cent *v.* 9 per cent). Finally, while home-based work remains relatively uncommon for both unionised and non-unionised companies, there has been a relatively large and equal increase in the use of subcontracting.

TABLE 7.6 (a): WORKFORCE FLEXIBILITY: UNIONISED

	Increased	Same	Decreased	Not Used
Weekend Work	21% (42)*	48% (95)	13% (26)	18% (36)
Shift Work	16% (32)	51% (100)	7% (14)	25% (49)
Overtime	25% (49)	38% (74)	33% (65)	3% (7)
Part-time Work	38% (71)	28% (51)	8% (14)	26% (48)
Temporary/Casual	36% (67)	39% (74)	16% (30)	9% (16)
Fixed-term Contract	37% (68)	31% (57)	4% (7)	28% (51)
Home-based Work	3% (4)	8% (13)	—	89% (142)
Govt. Training Schemes	15% (25)	30% (51)	2% (3)	52% (87)
Subcontract	34% (63)	29% (54)	5% (9)	30% (56)

* Actual numbers in parenthesis.

TABLE 7.6 (b): WORKFORCE FLEXIBILITY: NON-UNIONISED

	Increased	Same	Decreased	Not Used
Weekend Work	21% (11)*	40% (21)	17% (9)	21% (11)
Shift Work	12% (6)	24% (12)	4% (2)	61% (31)
Overtime	12% (6)	55% (28)	20% (10)	14% (7)
Part-time Work	22% (11)	26% (13)	4% (2)	61% (31)
Temporary/Casual	45% (24)	28% (15)	9% (5)	15% (8)
Fixed-term Contract	26% (13)	25% (13)	—	47% (24)
Home-based Work	8% (4)	14% (7)	—	78% (39)
Govt. Training Schemes	8% (4)	33% (17)	—	55% (28)
Subcontract	26% (14)	34% (18)	4% (2)	36% (19)

* Actual numbers in parenthesis.
Source: Price Waterhouse Cranfield Project (Ireland); University of Limerick 1992.

Table 7.7 highlights the influence of organisational ownership on non-standard employment patterns. Weekend work appears to have increased more in Irish-owned and US-owned organisations (21 per cent and 22 per cent respectively), than in UK-owned organisations (8 per cent). Shift work is much more common in US-owned companies with only 12 per cent suggesting they do not use it, compared with 40 per cent of Irish-owned and 42 per cent of UK-owned companies.

TABLE 7.7 (a): WORKFORCE FLEXIBILITY: THE INFLUENCE OF OWNERSHIP (IRISH)

	Increased	Same	Decreased	Not Used
Weekend Work	21% (31)*	52% (76)	10% (15)	17% (25)
Shift Work	10% (14)	46% (66)	5% (7)	40% (57)
Overtime	20% (28)	44% (63)	29% (42)	6% (9)
Part-time Work	40% (56)	30% (42)	7% (9)	22% (31)
Temporary/Casual	36% (50)	37% (51)	14% (19)	12% (16)
Fixed-term Contract	34% (47)	30% (41)	2% (3)	33% (46)
Home-based Work	5% (6)	11% (13)	—	83% (99)
Govt. Training Schemes	19% (25)	31% (40)	19% (25)	47% (61)
Subcontract	33% (46)	29% (40)	4% (6)	33% (45)

* Actual numbers in parenthesis

TABLE 7.7 (b): WORKFORCE FLEXIBILITY: THE INFLUENCE OF OWNERSHIP (UK)

	Increased	Same	Decreased	Not Used
Weekend Work	8% (1)*	46% (6)	23% (3)	23% (3)
Shift Work	8% (1)	50% (6)	—	42% (5)
Overtime	8% (1)	54% (7)	39% (5)	—
Part-time Work	39% (5)	23% (3)	8% (1)	31% (4)
Temporary/Casual	50% (7)	21% (3)	14% (2)	14% (2)
Fixed-term Contract	33% (4)	17% (2)	—	50% (6)
Home-based Work	—	8% (1)	—	92% (11)
Govt. Training Schemes	—	31% (4)	—	69% (9)
Subcontract	4% (6)	21% (3)	7% (1)	29% (4)

* Actual numbers in parenthesis

TABLE 7.7 (c): WORKFORCE FLEXIBILITY: THE INFLUENCE OF OWNERSHIP (US)

	Increased	Same	Decreased	Not Used
Weekend Work	22% (11)*	18% (9)	18% (9)	24% (12)
Shift Work	27% (13)	49% (24)	12% (6)	12% (6)
Overtime	28% (14)	34% (17)	38% (19)	—
Part-time Work	18% (14)	21% (9)	9% (4)	52% (23)
Temporary/Casual	45% (22)	39% (19)	10% (5)	6% (3)
Fixed-term Contract	40% (18)	33% (15)	2% (1)	22% (10)
Home-based Work	2% (1)	—	—	98% (42)
Govt. Training Schemes	5% (2)	24% (10)	2% (1)	67% (28)
Subcontract	36% (17)	30% (14)	6% (3)	26% (12)

* Actual numbers in parenthesis
Source: Price Waterhouse Cranfield Project (Ireland); University of Limerick 1992.

Following the same trend, there has been a much larger increase in the use of shift work in US-owned companies (27 per cent), than in their Irish and UK counterparts (10 per cent and 8 per cent respectively). Overtime continues to remain relatively popular in Irish-owned organisations, with 19.6 per cent of respondents saying it has increased in the last three years. Similarly, 28 per cent of US-owned companies maintain that an increase has occurred, the corresponding figure for UK-owned companies being a mere 8 per cent. Part-time work appears more common in Irish and UK-owned companies. A total of 52 per cent of US-owned companies suggest that part-time work is not used, the corresponding figure for Irish and UK-owned companies being 22 per cent and 31 per cent respectively. Furthermore, the increase in the use of part-time work has been far greater in Irish- and UK-owned companies than in their US-owned counterparts. The results reveal a large increase in temporary/ casual work across organisations, regardless of ownership, with the largest increase occurring in UK-owned companies (50 per cent). Similarly, the use of fixed-term contracts has increased across ownership categories, with an increase of 34 per cent in Irish-owned organisations, 33 per cent in UK-owned companies and 40 per cent in US-owned organisations. Furthermore, it appears that US-owned companies are more likely to have this type of working arrangement than are UK organisations. Only 22 per cent of US-owned companies do not use this type of contract, whereas half of all responding UK-owned companies do not employ fixed-term contracts. The corresponding figure for Irish-owned companies is 33 per cent. Home-based work, as might be expected, is used by only a small minority of companies across ownership categories, with the data revealing that 83 per cent of Irish, 92 per cent of UK-owned and 98 per cent of US-owned responding companies do not use this type of non-standard employment. Government training schemes appear to have been embraced much more strongly by Irish-owned companies than by their UK- or US-owned counterparts. While 19.4 per cent of Irish organisations record an increase in the use of such schemes, no UK-owned and only 5 per cent of US-owned companies record a similar increase. Finally, in relation to subcontracting, the results reveal a sizeable increase across ownership categories, the increase being largest (43 per cent) in UK-owned companies.

In summary, while the pattern of responses is mixed, clearly suspicion of atypical/non-standard employment (for whatever reasons) has not prevented many organisations in Ireland from introducing some changes in working arrangements over the last three years. While presumably the "takers" have gone this route of non-standard employment in an attempt to ensure a better fit between labour inputs/costs and demand fluctuations, the surprising result must surely be the large number of organisations which remain "non-takers", those which have chosen not to adopt these types of strategies. Thus, while there is a trend towards non-standard employment in Ireland, the evidence reveals that this change must be viewed as a gradual incremental one, rather than as a radical departure from past practice, and, as mentioned, this finding bears out the results of the Workplace Industrial Relations Surveys in the UK.

Proportion of the Workforce on Non-standard Contracts
One could argue that the relative stability emerging from the analysis thus far is in some way surprising, as the state of the Irish labour market clearly facilitates the use of such non-standard employment strategies. However, our results are further strengthened and substantiated by reference to the proportion of an organisation's workforce which is covered by such contracts. The aggregate results are presented in Table 7.8.

TABLE 7.8: PROPORTION OF WORKFORCE ON NON-STANDARD CONTRACTS

	< 1%	1–10%	11–20%	> 20%
Part-time Work	39%	29%	5%	6%
Temporary/Casual	26%	43%	9%	5%
Fixed-term Contract	37%	20%	5%	13%
Home-based Work	44%	1%	—	—
Govt. Training Schemes	46%	11%	—	—

N=269
Source: Price Waterhouse Cranfield Project (Ireland); University of Limerick 1992.

The results reveal that while part-time work is common, it is so for a relatively small proportion of responding organisations workforces. Thus, 39 per cent of respondents suggest that less than 1 per cent of their respective workforces are on part-time contracts, with the percentage falling to 6 per cent for more than 20 per cent of the workforce. The pattern is somewhat similar for temporary/casual contracts, but with a larger proportion of the workforce (1–10 per cent) likely to be employed on a temporary/casual basis. Fixed-term contracts are more common at the higher end of the scale and thus have greater coverage, with 13 per cent (35 companies) having more than 20 per cent of their respective workforces employed on this basis. Home-based work and government training schemes are again much less common, and while approximately 45 per cent of respondents use such methods, they cover less than 1 per cent of the workforce in a majority of cases.

There are some sectoral differences here (see Appendix 1, Table 7A). Part-time work appears to cover a larger proportion of individuals in the public sector. Thus, while 27 per cent of private sector organisations have between 1 and 10 per cent of the workforce employed on a part-time basis, the corresponding figure for public sector respondents is 41 per cent. Similarly, 10 per cent of public sector respondents have between 11 and 20 per cent of their workforce employed part time, the figure for the private sector being only one quarter of that. In relation to temporary/ casual work, some differences also occur. The results reveal that in the private sector 74 per cent of respondents employ up to 10 per cent of the workforce on a temporary/casual basis. The equivalent percentage in the public sector is 66 per cent. Furthermore, while 7 per cent of private sector respondents employ between 11 and 20 per cent on a temporary/ casual basis, over 12 per cent of public sector respondents employ between 11 and 20 per cent of their workforce on that basis.

Fixed-term contracts are common across both sectors, though the public sector does have a slightly higher proportion of its workforce covered by such contracts. Similarly, while both home-based work and government training schemes are used in both sectors, a proportionately higher percentage of public sector employees are covered by the latter.

We also sought to examine the extent to which union presence/ absence might impact upon the use of such contracts (see Appendix 1, Table 7B). No substantial differences are recorded for part-time work, with 85 per cent of unionised companies and 87 per cent of non-unionised companies having up to 10 per cent of the workforce employed on a part-time basis. The trend in relation to the use of temporary/casual contracts, home-based work and government training schemes is similar, with few highly significant differences occurring between unionised and non-unionised organisations. Finally, there does appear to be a difference in relation to the use of fixed-term contracts. While 17 per cent of respondents from non-unionised organisations suggest that more than 11 per cent of their workforce is employed on this basis, a larger 25 per cent of unionised organisations have more than 11 per cent of their workforce covered by such contracts.

In relation to the impact of organisational ownership on the proportion of the workforce covered by non-standard contracts, (see Appendix 1, Table 7C) a number of key findings emerge from the data. Firstly, part-time work is common across ownership categories, but UK-owned organisations are likely to have a proportionately higher percentage of their workforce employed on this basis. Secondly, with respect to temporary/casual contracts, Irish- and US-owned organisations appear to have a larger proportion of their employees employed on this basis (17 per cent for both for more than 11 per cent of the workforce). The equivalent percentage for UK-owned companies is only 8 per cent. Thirdly, while fixed-term contracts also appear common across ownership categories, they are more common in Irish- and UK-owned companies for larger proportions of the workforce, than in US-owned companies. Thus, 18 per cent of Irish-owned companies and 20 per cent of

UK-owned have more than 20 per cent of their workforce employed on a fixed-term basis, while only 4.5 per cent of US respondents have more than 20 per cent of their workforce covered by fixed-term contracts. Finally, ownership does not appear to impact significantly on the use of home-based work or on the use of government training schemes with respect to the proportion of the workforce covered.

Change in Job Specification

In the context of an increased interest in functional flexibility during the 1980s, the Price Waterhouse Cranfield Project sought to examine the extent to which organisations were changing job structures for different categories of employees. Respondents were asked whether there had been a major change in the specification of jobs in their organisation for management, professional/technical employees, clerical and manual employees, and were given a four-item scale (i.e. jobs were made more specific; there was no major change; jobs were made wider/more flexible; or don't know). The aggregate results are presented in Figure 7.2.

FIGURE 7.2: CHANGE IN SPECIFICATION OF JOBS OVER LAST THREE YEARS

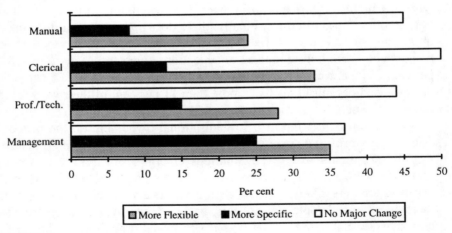

N=269
Source: Price Waterhouse Cranfield Project (Ireland); University of Limerick 1992.

Again, the pattern here is one of relative stability, with some change occurring. While 38 per cent of respondents maintain that no major change has occurred in the specification of management jobs, between 40 and 50 per cent maintain that no change has occurred in professional/ technical, clerical and/or manual jobs. However, where change has occurred, it was more likely to be in the direction of flexibility, for all categories, than that of making jobs more specific. This again is consistent with our argument on gradual incremental change in the direction of flexibility, rather than radical path-breaking developments.

TABLE 7.9 (a): CHANGE IN THE SPECIFICATION OF JOBS: PUBLIC

	Management	Prof./Tech.	Clerical	Manual
More Specific	19% (11)*	12% (7)	9.0% (5)	7% (4)
No Change	59% (34)	60% (35)	55.0% (32)	55% (32)
More Flexible	22% (13)	12% (7)	29.0% (17)	16% (9)
Don't Know	—	—	1.7% (1)	—

*   Actual numbers in parenthesis

TABLE 7.9 (b): CHANGE IN THE SPECIFICATION OF JOBS: PRIVATE

	Management	Prof./Tech.	Clerical	Manual
More Specific	27.0% (49)*	16.0% (29)	13.0% (24)	10.0% (19)
No Change	31.0% (56)	39.0% (72)	46.0% (85)	44.0% (80)
More Flexible	41.0% (75)	36.0% (66)	34.0% (63)	27.0% (49)
Don't Know	0.5% (1)	0.5% (1)	1.1% (20)	1.6% (3)

*   Actual numbers in parenthesis
Source: Price Waterhouse Cranfield Project (Ireland); University of Limerick 1992.

When the data is disaggregated to test for sectoral differences, three key findings emerge. Firstly, a slightly higher percentage of jobs, for all categories of employees, have been made more specific in the private sector. Secondly, a higher percentage of jobs, again for all categories of employees, have undergone no major change in the last three years in the public sector, particularly in relation to management and professional/ technical employees, with 59 per cent and 60 per cent respectively witnessing no change in the public sector. The equivalent percentages for their counterparts in the private sector are 31 per cent for management and 39 per cent for professional/technical employees. Thirdly, a significantly higher percentage of jobs across employee categories have been made more flexible in the private sector, the largest differences again occurring in managerial and professional/technical grades.

TABLE 7.10 (a): CHANGE IN THE SPECIFICATION OF JOBS: UNION

	Management	Prof./Tech.	Clerical	Manual
More Specific	24.0% (50)*	15.0% (31)	10.0% (21)	10% (20)
No Change	40.0% (82)	45.0% (94)	52.0% (107)	49% (102)
More Flexible	36.0% (75)	28.0% (58)	32.0% (67)	27% (55)
Don't Know	0.5% (1)	0.5% (1)	1.5% (3)	1% (2)

*   Actual numbers in parenthesis

TABLE 7.10 (b): CHANGE IN THE SPECIFICATION OF JOBS: NON-UNION

	Management	Prof./Tech.	Clerical	Manual
More Specific	26% (15)*	14% (8)	16% (9)	7% (4)
No Change	35% (20)	40% (23)	44% (25)	30% (17)
More Flexible	26% (15)	30% (17)	30% (17)	14% (8)
Don't Know	—	—	—	2% (1)

*   Actual numbers in parenthesis
Source: Price Waterhouse Cranfield Project (Ireland); University of Limerick 1992.

The results relating to differences in unionised and non-unionised organisations are interesting, particularly because the popular literature portrays trade unions as a constraining force on the introduction of arrangements that allow for increased levels of functional flexibility. Indeed, the Workplace Industrial Relations Survey in the UK reported that managers in unionised workplaces where changes had been made were more than twice as likely to report constraints as their non-union counterparts (see Millward et al. 1992). While our data does not measure the actual extent to which trade unions have constrained the introduction of functional flexibility, it does give the reader an indication of how similar the picture actually is in unionised and non-unionised environments.

Consequently, it is at least suggestive of two possible scenarios. Either trade unions have not in fact exerted influence in relation to curtailing flexibility in unionised establishments, or possibly, managements in non-union companies have not used, to the full extent, the supposed free hand that they possess. At any rate, there are few differences between unionised and non-unionised organisations in Ireland with respect to changes in the specification of jobs for managerial, professional/ technical, clerical or manual employees.

TABLE 7.11 (a): CHANGE IN THE JOB SPECIFICATION BY OWNERSHIP (IRISH)

	Management	Prof./Tech.	Clerical	Manual
More Specific	30.0% (47)*	16.0% (24)	14% (22)	11% (17)
No Change	45.0% (70)	51.0% (79)	55% (85)	46% (71)
More Flexible	26.0% (40)	22.0% (34)	28% (43)	17% (27)
Don't Know	0.6% (1)	0.6% (1)	1% (2)	1% (2)

*   Actual numbers in parenthesis

TABLE 7.11 (b): CHANGE IN THE JOB SPECIFICATION BY OWNERSHIP (UK)

	Management	Prof./Tech.	Clerical	Manual
More Specific	43% (6)*	21% (3)	—	—
No Change	21% (3)	36% (5)	57% (8)	64% (9)
More Flexible	36% (5)	29% (4)	43% (6)	21% (3)
Don't Know	—	—	—	—

*   Actual numbers in parenthesis

TABLE 7.11 (c): CHANGE IN THE JOB SPECIFICATION BY OWNERSHIP (US)

	Management	Prof./Tech.	Clerical	Manual
More Specific	6% (3)*	4% (2)	2% (1)	6% (3)
No Change	29% (15)	33% (17)	44% (23)	39% (20)
More Flexible	60% (31)	56% (29)	46% (24)	46% (24)
Don't Know	—	—	—	—

*   Actual numbers in parenthesis
Source: Price Waterhouse Cranfield Project (Ireland); University of Limerick 1992.

Our results indicate some key differences with respect to ownership. Firstly, US-owned companies have made jobs more specific for all categories of employees only in a minority of cases. UK- and Irish-owned companies report much higher percentages in this respect. Secondly, Irish owned organisations have undergone the least change in the specification of jobs for management and professional/technical categories, 45 per cent and 51 per cent remaining the same.

Conversely, UK-owned organisations have changed clerical and manual job specifications least, with 57 per cent of clerical and 64 per cent of manual undergoing no major change in the last three years. Thirdly, US-owned organisations have made jobs most flexible across employee grades. Thus, in US companies, 60 per cent of managerial, 56 per cent of professional/technical, 46 per cent of clerical and 46 per cent of manual employees have had their jobs made more flexible in the last three years. Irish-owned companies were approximately 50 per cent less likely to introduce such flexibility changes.

THE IMPLICATIONS FOR EMPLOYEE RELATIONS

On the whole, non-standard employment forms do not necessarily signify the emergence of a flexible firm scenario, but rather, as Flood (1988) suggests, a segmented labour market at industry sector level. The evidence presented here indicates a definite trend towards greater flexibility on a gradual incremental basis, but the emergence of the flexible firm is clearly not supported. However, the move towards greater flexibility, particularly in the context of a two-tier system has, according to Flood (1989), two key implications for the nature and conduct of employee relations: unionisation of those in non-standard employment and management/union relations.

Unionisation of Those in Non-standard Employment

Flood (1989) suggests that individuals employed on a non-standard/ atypical basis can be expected to seek trade union membership, whereas trade union influence may in fact decline for core/standard employees. The extent to which this will occur is difficult to predict because traditionally there has been a low unionisation rate among those employed on a non-standard basis, particularly among those in personal services. Two key reasons can be cited for this low rate of unionisation: Firstly, unions have never relied heavily on such segments for membership; and secondly, individuals employed on a non-standard basis are likely to be passive about unionisation, fear of unemployment being one of the key reasons for such passivity.

Bain (1983) advanced a hypothesis that where the features of an industry enable substantial degrees of unionisation among full-time core employees, the unionisation of peripheral employees is likely to follow. Conversely, if such a propensity to unionise is missing among core employees, then peripheral employees unionisation rates will also be low. Applying this to the Irish situation, it follows that attempts at unionisation may bring little by way of results. Our ever expanding service sector is noted for its low rate of unionisation among full-time employees, a fact that does not auger well for the emergence of a strongly unionised peripheral workforce, at least in this sector.

Overall, in the Irish situation, one way of reversing the downward trend in union membership would be to instigate a recruitment drive among peripheral employees. However, this poses some difficulty, as peripheral employment is most likely to occur in our growth sector (services), a sector that has traditionally proved difficult to unionise, even amongst full-time core employees.

Management/Union Relations

In line with the dualism which may occur in people management strategies in the core/peripheral scenario, it is similarly suggested that such a dualism might occur in management/union relations. Flood (1989) suggests that those companies who move towards the utilisation of peripheral employees may increasingly experience dual patterns of individual conflict (i.e. low levels amongst core and higher levels amongst peripheral employees).

CONCLUSIONS

The most notable changes in the Irish labour market over the past 20 years have been the dramatic fall in the numbers employed in agriculture and the consistent growth in employment in the services sector, which now accounts for almost 60 per cent of all employees. While Irish managers have attempted to go some way towards ensuring that labour inputs are more responsive to environmental conditions, a large percentage of respondents suggest that working arrangements have not changed that much. From the research, it appears that non-unionised organisations appear less likely than their unionised counterparts to use shift work as a flexibility strategy. However, overtime as a flexibility strategy has increased more in unionised than in non-unionised environments. While 17 per cent of non-unionised establishments suggest that more than 11 per cent of their workforce is employed on the basis of fixed-term contracts, 25 per cent of unionised establishments have more than 11 per cent of their workforce covered by such contracts. Overall, while there is a trend towards non-standard employment in Ireland, the evidence reveals that this change must be viewed as a gradual incremental one, rather than as a radical departure from past practice. This is relatively surprising, as the state of the Irish labour market would appear to facilitate the use of such non-standard employment strategies.

Chapter 8

EMPLOYEE RELATIONS IN SMALL FIRMS

Juliet McMahon

INTRODUCTION

Up until the mid-1970s Irish industrial policy concentrated mainly on attracting large multinational companies to set up in Ireland. In recent years there has been a growing realisation of the importance of the small enterprise to the economy, in terms of wealth and job creation. Recent developments have increased the importance of the small firm even more: foreign multinationals experiencing increasing uncertainty in world markets can no longer be relied on to provide an answer to Ireland's unemployment problems, and the shedding of labour by existing large companies has resulted in an ever expanding small firm sector.

This chapter examines the current state of knowledge of employee relations in the smaller firm and attempts to give some insight into the particular characteristics of employee relations in these firms. For the purposes of this chapter a "small firm" will be defined as one employing 100 people or less.

Relevant data from the Price Waterhouse Cranfield study will be incorporated into each section and analysed to provide an overview of general trends in employee relations in Irish small firms, and to examine whether the current Irish situation reflects the views of existing research, most of which emanates from the UK.

THE SAMPLE

Within the total sample, there were 84 companies which employed 100 people or less. As would be expected, the large majority of respondent companies were Irish owned, but it was interesting to note that of the 77 companies that replied to the question on ownership, 26 per cent (20 firms) were foreign owned.

TABLE 8.1: SMALL FIRMS: OWNERSHIP

Ownership	No. of Companies	% of Companies
Ireland	57	74.0%
Germany	6	7.8%
UK	4	5.2%
US	7	9.1%
Netherlands	1	1.2%
Switzerland	1	1.3%
Other	1	1.3%

N=77

Source: Price Waterhouse Cranfield Project (Ireland); University of Limerick 1992.

Surprisingly, quite a high percentage of the sample identified their product markets as European or worldwide — almost 40 per cent (Table 8.2). This does not support the conventional view that small firms cater mainly for local markets, and could indicate a growing awareness on the part of small-firm owner/managers of the need to penetrate markets other than the domestic one, in order to survive a single market. However, further research would obviously be necessary in order to determine this.

TABLE 8.2: PRODUCT MARKET OF SAMPLE SMALL FIRMS

Market	Number of Firms	% of firms
Local	7	8.3%
Regional	6	7.1%
National	37	44.0%
European	18	21.4%
Worldwide	15	17.9%
Missing	1	1.2%

N=84

Source: Price Waterhouse Cranfield Project (Ireland); University of Limerick 1992.

The sample contained companies from most sectors as is illustrated in Table 8.3 below.

TABLE 8.3: INDUSTRY SECTORS OF SAMPLE SMALL FIRMS

Sector	Number of Firms	Percentage of Firms
Agriculture	7	8.3%
Non-energy Mineral	6	7.1%
Metal Manufacturing	12	14.3%
Other Manufacturing	10	11.9%
Building/Civil Engineering	2	2.4%
Dist. Trades/Hotels	10	11.9%
Transport/Communications	1	2.4%
Banking and Finance	6	7.1%
Personal Services	1	1.2%
Health	5	6.0%
Other Services	5	6.0%
Education	4	4.8%
Fire, Police and Quangos	13	15.5%
Missing	2	1.2%

N=84

Source: Price Waterhouse Cranfield Project (Ireland); University of Limerick
    1992.

EMPLOYEE RELATIONS IN SMALL FIRMS: AN OVERVIEW

The issue of employee relations has not received a great deal of attention in literature relating to small firms. Curran (1981), complained that the growing increase in interest in this area as a source of jobs "has not been matched by an increase in concern with the quality and character of employment in small firms." Given that small firms are responsible for a large proportion of employment in the private sector, this neglect of employee/employer relations in such firms becomes increasingly unacceptable in policy and research terms. The nature of the work process in smaller enterprises and the precise ways in which employer and employee construct their mutual relations and sustain them in order to produce output must be understood if training policies, financial support, employment and industrial relations law etc. are to be effective in meeting the needs of firms, employees, and the economy.

Most existing research into small business concentrates on the problems and personalities of owners rather than employees. However, as Goss (1991) points out, this does not mean that there are not firmly held beliefs about how such workers think, feel, and behave. The most widespread view is that employee relations in small firms are more harmonious than in their larger counterparts, and job satisfaction is greater. This "small is beautiful" philosophy is continuously reinforced by politicians, the media, and popular economists. Unfortunately this "conventional wisdom" finds its basis in a number of studies whose methodology and empirical foundations are questionable to say the least.

The two most influential studies carried out on the topic of small firms were those of Ingham (1970), and the Bolton Report (1971). Ingham suggested that the low level of bureaucracy associated with small firms created the potential for close personal relationships between the employer and those employed, and between fellow workers, and hence resulted in high levels of attachment. He then sought to relate the realisation of this potential to the attitudes and aspirations held by workers in small firms. He suggested that over time employees tend to generate distinct orientations to work, attaching more or less importance to economic/non-economic rewards. Those holding a non-economic orientation would place a higher value on rewards such as job satisfaction and pleasant interpersonal relationships. Such employees would, he suggested, self select to work in small firms. Although Ingham stressed that his thesis was contingent on a situation of full employment, it has still been criticised by more contemporary researchers (Curran and Stanworth 1981, Storey 1982, Goss 1991) on a number of counts. It exaggerates the amount of choice open to job seekers. It does not take into account the selection preferences and practices of employers. The sample he used was too narrow and not representative of small-firm employees as a whole.

The Bolton Report was very influential as it formed the basis for much subsequent UK government policy.

> In many respects the small firm provides a better environment for the employee than is possible in most large firms. Although physical working conditions may sometimes be inferior in small firms, most people prefer to work in a small group where communications present fewer problems: the employees in the small firm can easily see the relationship between what they are doing and the objectives and performance of the firm as a whole. Where management is more direct and flexible working rules can be varied to suit the individual ... no doubt mainly as a result of this, the turnover of staff in small firms is very low and strikes and other kinds of industrial dispute are relatively infrequent.[1]

Major criticisms of this "industrial harmony" thesis are that it is

---

[1] Bolton, 1971, p. 21.

founded largely on the uncorroborated opinions of employers, supplemented by a rather narrow reading of Ingham's earlier study (Curran and Stanworth 1981), and that it uses the technique of proof by assertion to a large extent (Brady 1982).

Curran and Stanworth (1981) also highlight the monolithic character of much of the research into small firms:

> They implicitly suggest a pattern of industrial relations in the small enterprise, regardless of the many other factors which can influence these relations. The small enterprise is represented in almost every sphere of economic activity ... and it is most unlikely that patterns of worker management relations will not reflect this diversity.

This inability of researchers to encompass the sheer variety of employment contexts in which small firms are found leads, they claim, to over-generalisation. More recent research has attempted to cope with the above weaknesses and has continued to develop a more subtle and credible picture of employer–employee relations in the small enterprise. Above all, researchers call into question the notion that employee relations will usually be harmonious in small firms. Henderson and Johnson (1974) argued that the fact that small firms are highly vulnerable economically could well have implications for achieving and maintaining stable employer–employee relations. Curran and Stanworth (1981) support this assertion when they argue that in order to remain competitive, small-firm employers will have to respond quickly to changes in the market, making adjustments in work systems or even labour-force size. From the workers' point of view, this means greater insecurity in employment. Such economic insecurity operates to make employee and employer each aware that their mutual interests cannot always coincide. Small-firm owner-managers are antipathetic to a methodical and systematic approach to management: they "pride themselves on their informal approach" argued Henderson and Johnson (1974, p. 29), but this again may result in an unplanned, hazard-prone approach to employing others. Curran and Stanworth (1979) and Scott et al. (1989) found that the proportion of employees who felt relations with their employers were close was much lower than would have been expected from the Bolton Report's characterisation. Scott et al. (1989) found that industrial subcultural differences were pronounced, with employers' and workers' attitudes as well as their relations varying considerably. The research of Goss (1985, 1991) shows that small- enterprise employees do not differ fundamentally from large-firm workers in terms of their attitudes, and labour turnover levels in small firms do not indicate any great attachment to the firm or employer. In an Irish context, the work of Gunnigle and

Brady (1984) found evidence that industrial relations is not as harmonic as might be expected. Quite a number of the small firms in their study had considerable problems in the industrial relations area.

From the research, a number of key areas of employee relations emerge which need to be examined briefly. Firstly, from a managerial perspective, the attitudes and approaches small-firm employers bring with them to the workplace. These are discussed under frames of reference and management styles. Secondly, the more practical and visible aspects of employee relations are discussed — such as conflict resolution, recruitment and training, and rewards.

UNITARY FRAME OF REFERENCE

A common perception of employee relations in small firms is that they are practised very much from a unitary frame of reference. This perception possibly comes from the extensive literature on the entrepreneurial personality (Kets de Vries 1977, Goffee and Scase 1982), which attributes to owner-managers such traits as: a high locus of control, and reluctance to delegate. That this frame of reference actually exists in small firms is backed up by research. Scott et al. (1989), in an extensive survey of over 400 owner-managers, found that conflict was conventionally explained away in personal terms — as the result of an employee with "wrong" attitudes, someone who "did not fit in" or was "a trouble-maker". In other words, what might be seen as an employee relations issue in other contexts — resulting, for example, from employees having different views from employers, or inconsistencies of managerial practice, or organisational and work arrangements — are not perceived as such by small-firm employers.

Marchington (1982) suggests that unitary and pluralistic frames of reference differ in three basic respects.

Firstly, they see a different role for trade unionism as a "legitimate rival source of leadership". From a unitary perspective no role is seen for trade unions. Research by Gunnigle and Brady (1984) indicated that a majority of small-firm owner-managers saw no role for trade unions in their firms. Consequently, claims for trade union recognition arose as a particularly problematic area for employers. In their survey, most owner-managers said that, in the event of their employees joining a trade union, they would adopt a different management style, and a number said they would close.

Secondly, management prerogative is viewed differently. A manager with a unitary frame of reference will be less likely to accept curbs on managerial prerogative. Again, Gunnigle and Brady found that the vast majority of owner-managers in their sample were strongly opposed to any curbs placed on management prerogative, stressing the need for flexibility and change.

Thirdly, attitudes towards conflict will be different — in relation both to possible sources of conflict and to management's approach to conflict resolution. From the unitary perspective, (given the assumption of common purpose and harmony) conflict, if it arises, will be attributed to anything but a divergence of interests. A substantial number of owner-managers in the Gunnigle and Brady survey tended to blame industrial relations problems on individual "trouble-makers" or "activists". From the above it would seem that there is considerable evidence that small owner-managers veer towards a unitary frame of reference with regard to employee relations. How this impacts on conflict resolution, procedures and communication and other employee-relations related issues will be discussed below.

MANAGERIAL STYLES IN THE SMALL FIRM

Given the evidence for a unitary frame of reference among small-firm employers, it could reasonably be expected that this would manifest itself in the style of management adopted in smaller workplaces and indeed much of the dominant views on employer–employee relations in such companies can be summed up in the notion of paternalism: "The entrepreneur operates a quasi familial unit with employment relations embedded within a wider set of personal concerns", Curran (1986). The popular perception is of a harmonious relationship between employer and employee. Henderson and Johnson (1974), suggest that because many small firms start off as family businesses, the head of the business may continue to treat the employees as part of a family. This can, of course, work to the benefit of both parties, but it can also cause problems in the employer–employee relationship. For example, employers with a paternalistic attitude towards their employees would not readily accept a desire on the part of their employees to join a trade union.

Looking at Table 8.4 it would seem that quite a sizeable proportion of the sample companies did recognise trade unions (61 per cent). Relative to trade union recognition in larger companies covered by the study, it emerges that there is a difference of about 23 per cent (84 per cent of firms with more than 200 employees recognised trade unions), but compared with the study as a whole, this deviation narrows to about 16 per cent (76 per cent of all firms recognised trade unions). Therefore, contrary to the situation in other countries such as the UK and US, trade union recognition in Irish small companies seems quite high. Indeed it was higher than expected, given the results of earlier research.

TABLE 8.4: TRADE UNION RECOGNITION

Trade Union Recognition	Number of Firms	% of Firms
Yes	51	60.7%
No	32	38.1%
Missing	1	1.2%

N=84

Source: Price Waterhouse Cranfield Project (Ireland); University of Limerick 1992.

Owner-managers may also have an unrealistic perception of employee goals in that they may expect a lot more convergence between their goals and employee goals than may actually be the case. It is also more likely that the small-firm owner-manager with a paternalistic attitude will not make any great attempt to formalise communication and consultation. 23 per cent of the sample companies stated that they have no formal methods by which employees can communicate their views to management. (This is discussed in more detail below.)

However, as Curran and Stanworth (1981) point out:

> The owner/manager exercises an entrepreneurial function combining the factors of production — including labour — to produce goods and services at a price for a market. *Only within these constraints is the exercise of managerial initiative more or less free* but equally these constraints strongly effect non-managerial participants' thinking and behaviour. The outcome of these influences shapes the social dynamics of the small enterprise.[2]

In other words, even though small-firm owner-managers tend towards a unitary frame of reference and paternalistic styles of management, there are other factors in the internal and external environment which constrain managerial choice and can affect approaches if not attitudes to management. For instance, nature of the product market, or as Goss (1991) suggests, the dependence of the employer upon certain employees and vice versa, and the power of the workers individually or collectively to resist the exercise of proprietorial prerogative. Gunnigle and Brady (1984) also support the contingency view of managerial style in small

---

[2] Curran and Stanworth, 1981, p. 153.

firms. They identified two main typologies: family paternalism, and prag-matic paternalism (where some minimum level of procedural formalisa-tion is accepted). Goffee and Scase's (1982) study of small firms mainly in the construction industry, (where employees were often as skilled as their employer) found evidence of a managerial style which they labelled "fraternalism" where the employer is in effect a "first among equals".

Perhaps the best attempt to date at identifying managerial typologies without falling into the trap of generalisation is that of Goss (1991). Employers, he argues, adopt modes of control felt to be congruent with the expectations of their employees. Using the two dimensions of employer–employee dependence, and power of employees to resist pro-prietorial prerogative, he develops the following model.

FIGURE 8.1: TYPES OF MANAGEMENT STYLE IN SMALL FIRMS

Ability of employees to resist the exercise of proprietorial prerogative
High ·· **Low**
Extent of employers'   1.Fraternalism
economic dependence   2. Paternalism
upon employees   3. Benevolent Autocracy
4. Sweating
Low

Briefly, the styles are as follows; **Fraternalism** reflects a high level of employer dependence upon workers who provide labour that is both vital to the success of the business and in short supply in the labour market. **Paternalism** arises when the employer's dependence upon labour is less pressing and where the position of the workers is such as to limit their power to resist proprietorial prerogative. Unlike fraternalism which seeks to organise workers without clearly defined hierarchical control, the differentiation of employer and employed is at the centre of paternalism. At the same time, however, this strategy also seeks to foster the identifi-cation of subordinates with their superiors. **Benevolent Autocracy** emphasises the "closeness of the links between employer and employee but does not seek to cultivate the employment relationship in directions which extend beyond the workplace or which lead to expectations of employer obligations towards employees that override the exigencies of the market" (Goss 1991, p. 79). **Sweating** exists where concessions to employees are deemed largely unnecessary by employers, as workers can be recruited and replaced readily without disrupting business activities.

Here the principal factor in the employment relationship is cost rather than stability or trustworthiness.

Stanworth (1991) welcomes Goss's typologies as they highlight the complexities of small firm employer–employee relations in a systematic fashion, attempt to introduce a multidimensional approach to analysis, and get away from the "all is good" or "all is evil" view of employee relations in the small firm. The major weakness, he asserts, is that Goss fails to emphasise that more than one of the typologies may exist in the same company at one time. Also, the benevolent autocracy typology is too broad — Stanworth suggests that even further categorisation is required if more adequate analysis is to be produced. Nevertheless, this move by contemporary researchers away from the over-simplistic, over-general analysis of managerial attitudes and approaches is indeed welcome and will provide a useful framework for future research.

TRADE UNIONS

It has already been discussed above how the unitary frame of reference and paternalistic attitude of many owner-managers can mitigate against the presence of trade unions in the smaller firm. Statistics show that trade union presence is indeed lower in small companies than in their larger counterparts (Millward et al. 1992, Gunnigle and Brady 1984).

The Price Waterhouse Cranfield study would seem to bear this out: a third of the sample had no trade union presence, and in a further 31 per cent, less than half of the employees were members of a trade union (Table 8.5) . In firms with over 200 employees only 12 per cent had no trade union presence and a further 10 per cent had between 1 per cent and 50 per cent of employees in a trade union.

TABLE 8.5: TRADE UNION DENSITY

Proportion of Staff in Trade Union	% of Companies	Number of Companies
0	33.3	28
1–25%	15.5	13
26–50%	15.5	13
51–75%	13.1	11
76–100%	21.4	18
Don't Know	1.2	1

N=84

Source: Price Waterhouse Cranfield Project (Ireland); University of Limerick 1992.

Gunnigle (1989) also found that the nature of trade union activity in small firms is often quite different from that in large firms: the level of trade union activity in unionised small firms tends to be lower; shop-steward structures are less well developed; and there tends to be little interaction with trade unions at official level. Consequently, he argues, despite a trade union presence, the actual role of trade unions in representing members in small firms is often a diluted one. It must be pointed out, however, that the weakness of unionisation is not due only to the influence of small-firm employers. Stanworth (1991) argues that trade unions themselves often shy away from attempts to organise small-firm employees. Apart from increasingly tough opposition by owners to such attempts (McGovern 1989), each small enterprise yields relatively few members, and because labour turnover is often high, having organised employees, the union may well find a few months later that the whole exercise needs to be repeated. In other words, it is not always cost effective for unions to organise small firms.

Structural factors also influence levels of unionisation. Small firms are said to employ large numbers of women and younger employees — groups which were never traditionally targeted by trade unions. Small companies are very often found in the private services sector which also has a poor record of trade union organisation. Data from the Price Water-house study showed that the majority of small firms have less than 50 per cent union density. As has been seen above, although trade union recognition was higher than expected, trade union density, in keeping with previous research, was quite weak, and this could reflect a reluctance on the part of trade unions to organise the sample firms, or a reluctance on the part of employees to join.

It remains to be seen whether the current trend of larger unionised companies shedding employees and becoming part of a growing small firm sector (Millward et al. 1992) will have any effect on levels and role of trade unions in such companies. The much quoted literature on the declining power of trade unions would lead to an expectation that trade union influence within companies would also be declining, especially if owner-managers of such companies are as unitarist and anti-union as they are depicted to be. Of the companies within the sample which recog-nised trade unions, 20 per cent maintained that trade union power had decreased over the previous three years, as opposed to 74.5 per cent who maintained it had increased or remained the same — hardly evidence of a dramatic decline in trade union power (Table 8.6)

TABLE 8.6: CHANGING INFLUENCE OF TRADE UNIONS

Trade Union Influence	Number of Firms	% of Firms
Increased	8	15.7
Decreased	10	19.6
Same	30	58.8
Don't Know/Missing	3	5.9

N=51

Source: Price Waterhouse Cranfield Project (Ireland); University of Limerick 1992

CONFLICT AND CONFLICT RESOLUTION

One of the major assertions of early research was that because levels of overt conflict (strikes, work to rule, etc.) are low in small firms relative to large firms, it follows that employee relations are trouble-free and harmonious, and small-firm employees have a greater attachment to the firm. While acknowledging the lower incidence of overt conflict, most contemporary researchers would question the subsequent assumption of industrial harmony. Newby (1977) argues that the persistence of low conflict levels may not so much reflect the commitment of employees, or the "all one happy family" view of the enterprise, but rather may reflect a pragmatic acceptance of the status quo where there is a perceived lack of alternatives. In other words, employees tailor their responses to the situation. Therefore, the situation elicits from workers behaviour (as opposed to attitudes) which gives the appearance of industrial harmony. This assertion is backed up by research (Curran and Stanworth 1979, and Goss 1988) which found that small-firm workers did not display higher levels of attachment to their employers than their counterparts in larger firms. Goss (1991) argues that research evidence, far from supporting the industrial harmony thesis, suggests that conflict is common to small firms, but that it tends to manifest itself at an individual level, (workers will tend to leave or be dismissed rather than be involved in conventional industrial action) or be neutralised before it develops to the point of expression. Gunnigle and Brady (1984) also found that in Irish small companies overt conflict tended to be low. However, several companies in their survey stated that management–employee relations had often been very bad but that this rarely resulted in industrial action. Gunnigle (1989) suggests several reasons for this. Poor trade union organisation means that employees are not well organised to take collective action. Also, the frequency and personal nature of management–employee contacts may inhibit employees and make them reluctant to engage in industrial action because of the negative consequences it may entail.

With regard to conflict resolution, Gunnigle and Brady (1984) found that owner-managers were very reluctant to refer issues to a third party. Only three respondents in their sample had ever used the conciliation service of the Labour Court, and only two firms had had a case dealt with by the full Labour Court. However, quite a number of small firms had issues dealt with by a rights commissioner or the Employment Appeals Tribunal. This reflects the recent findings of Millward et al. (1992), who found that difficulties and referrals over dismissal tend to arise more commonly in smaller than large establishments. These findings lend credence to the assertion that conflict does exist in small companies, but at a more individual level.

USE OF PROCEDURES

Millward et al. (1992) found that small firms were less likely than large companies to have formalised procedures, except in the area of discipline. Gunnigle and Brady (1984) also found similar results in their survey of Irish companies. In their sample 16 firms out of a total of 23 stated that they had no formal communication mechanisms in operation in their company. The reason expressed for this was usually that the close relationship between employer and employee made formal communications mechanisms unnecessary, or that the owner-manager was too busy to get involved in setting up formal procedures. Only seven firms had grievance procedures in operation, and it was also noted that the procedures that existed were not very sophisticated. The main view expressed in relation to grievance procedures was that there was no need for formal procedures, as all differences were settled informally. It should be noted that this was the view as expressed by management.

In relation to discipline, the respondents seemed to be aware of the general legal context and custom and practice in the area of discipline administration. However, 14 firms out of 23 had no disciplinary procedure in operation, and of the seven who had, five were written and two unwritten.

The existence of trade unions did not seem to influence the use of formalised disciplinary procedures. The authors concluded that while there was a greater awareness of underlying principles of dealing with discipline in the workplace, this did not always manifest itself in the use of formalised procedures.

Results from the Price Waterhouse Cranfield Study show that 23 per cent of small firms had no formal communications mechanisms in place for employee–management interaction. A more detailed breakdown of the main methods of employee management communication is shown in Table 8.7.

TABLE 8.7: MAIN METHODS OF EMPLOYEE MANAGEMENT COMMUNICATION

Mode	Yes	No	Missing
Immediate Superior	84.0% (71)*	0	13
Trade Union(s)	45.2% (38)	20.2% (17)	29
Workforce Meetings	40.5% (34)	21.4% (18)	32
Quality Circles	8.3% (7)	32.1% (27)	50
Suggestion Boxes	9.5% (8)	29.8% (25)	51
Attitude Survey	2.4% (2)	38.1% (32)	50
No Formal Methods	23.8% (20)	10.7% (9)	55
Other Methods	10.7% (9)	—	0

* Actual numbers in parenthesis.

N = 84

Source: Price Waterhouse Cranfield Project (Ireland); University of Limerick 1992.

RECRUITMENT AND TRAINING

As already stated, Ingham's thesis of worker self selection into small or large firms has been extensively criticised by more recent research. Curran and Stanworth's criticism, that the element of choice open to workers is overemphasised, is supported by the suggestion of Blackburn and Mann (1979) that getting a job is not so much the result of a careful rational choice process as a host of influences over which the employee has no control. Many of these influences have become more severe in the 1980s as unemployment rises. Goss (1991) argues that less well trained, less experienced, younger workers tend to work in small firms not as a result of self selection, but because their lack of training and previous experience ruled out the possibility of working in large firms.

The importance of employer preferences is highlighted by Blackburn and Hankinson (1989), who found that the attitude of recruits was an important criterion for their selection. This was particularly marked for lower skilled grades reflecting their plentiful supply. Curran and Stanworth (1979), reported that small firm employers had a preference for younger workers because not only were they cheaper, but they were thought to be more flexible in their work attitude. However, employer preference is not without its own constraints: The dual or segmented labour market theories developed by researchers such as Kreckel (1980), and Rainnie & Scott (1982), suggest that large firms have preferences for certain types of workers — the well qualified and experienced with a stable work history — and are prepared to pay well, offer a wide range of fringe benefits, and internal career opportunities to secure their preferred employees. Small enterprises, on the other hand, cannot match the reward packages offered by large firms, most cannot afford the fringe benefits or offer the same career opportunities. (For instance, in the Cranfield study it emerged that only 4.8 per cent of the sample small firms offered any formal career planning). As a result, small companies become restricted to recruiting from the "secondary" labour market — that is, those with low skills, little experience, and unstable work history. This idea of the dual labour market is supported to some degree by various studies (Hitchens & O'Farrell 1988, Blackburn & Hankinson 1989) which found that the greatest problem facing many small firms was the availability to them of skilled staff, especially at middle management level. More recently, however, it has been argued that dual labour-market theories have exaggerated the divisions within the overall labour market. Also the recession of the 1980s has had the effect of unfreezing existing labour-market conditions (Curran 1986). Large firms may be much less able or willing to offer high rewards, job security, and career prospects, as they face more uncertain environments.

Data from the Price Waterhouse Cranfield study indicate a somewhat haphazard approach to recruitment, and maintenance of employee records: less than half of the respondents carried out manpower planning, 38 per cent compared with 83 per cent of their larger counterparts.

Over 50 per cent of respondents did not maintain any records on turnover, and a large proportion did not have any database of age profiles, qualifications and training, or absenteeism (Table 8.8).

TABLE 8.8: MAINTENANCE OF EMPLOYEE RECORDS

Data/Records Maintained	Yes	No	Missing
Staff Turnover	28.6% (24)*	51.2% (43)	20.2% (17)
Age Profiles	31.0% (26)	48.8% (41)	20.2% (17)
Qualifications/Training	47.6% (40)	38.1% (32)	14.3% (12)
Absence Levels	44.0% (37)	36.9% (31)	19.0% (16)

* Actual numbers in parenthesis.
N = 84
Source: Price Waterhouse Cranfield Project (Ireland); University of Limerick 1992.

This compares very poorly with results obtained from larger companies within the study. As can be seen from Table 8.9, the majority of companies with over 200 employees maintained such records, enabling them to adopt a strategic approach to recruitment and training. Of particular significance is the difference in maintenance of training records in small and large companies, especially in light of research by O'Farrell (1990) (see below), which highlights the need for much more positive attitudes and approaches to training in small firms in Ireland, which he maintains are of an inferior standard, giving rise to inferior quality products.

**TABLE 8.9: EMPLOYEE RECORDS
(COMPANIES WITH 200+ EMPLOYEES)**

Data/Records Maintained	Yes	No
Staff Turnover	68.8%	15.9%
Age Profile	58.8%	20.3%
Qualification/Training	71.7%	15.9%
Absence Levels	65.2%	21.0%

Source: Price Waterhouse Cranfield Project (Ireland); University of Limerick 1992.

With regard to training, the work of Hitchens and O'Farrell (1988, 1990) is of particular interest in an Irish context. In various studies comparing small Irish companies with their counterparts in Scotland, Northern Ireland, and England, they invariably found that Irish companies were less competitive in terms of price and labour and quality. Quality of skills at all levels and inadequate training were identified as the major proximate causes of manufacturing problems.

> Contrary to the assertions and prescriptions of many policy makers and commentators, the human capital weaknesses of small companies are not confined to management. Variations in quality of output and the substandard design and quality of many firms is a problem of inadequate expertise and skills at several levels; managerial, intermediate/supervisor, and production employees. Small firm workforce from top to bottom are: undereducated, under trained, and under skilled. This skills gap especially at the intermediate supervisor level means that the owner/manager becomes involved in sorting out simple problems because the intermediate skill level is missing or inadequate. Low skills also transmit themselves into low productivity by ruling out sophisticated technologies. Most small

firms managers do not perceive that their companies are lacking in quality of skills in part because they are part of the low skill syndrome.[3]

Results of studies such as that by Blackburn and Hankinson (1989) demonstrated that training is often perceived as an unaffordable luxury. They found that the low participation in formal training was attributable to its expense and considered inappropriateness. Expense included not only the fees of the course, but also its cost in terms of absence from the firm, since it involved the cost of unproductive labour. These authors also found that training resulting in highly specialised staff was considered inappropriate because of the need for staff with multiple skills to cope with the highly flexible nature of the work. However, results from the Price Waterhouse Cranfield study seem to indicate an increased commitment to training on the part of respondent firms, in that almost one third indicated that they had increased the money spent on training for most grades of staff over the previous three years.

TABLE 8.10: CHANGES IN MONEY SPENT ON TRAINING (ALLOWING FOR INFLATION) OVER THE LAST THREE YEARS

Type of Staff	Increased	Same	Decreased	Don't Know	Missing
Managerial	29.8% (25)*	35.7% (30)	7.1% (6)	13.1% (11)	14.3% (12)
Professional	31.0% (26)	28.6% (24)	9.5% (8)	9.5% (8)	21.4% (18)
Clerical	27.4% (23)	36.9% (31)	9.5% (8)	10.7% (9)	15.5% (13)
Manual	17.9% (15)	20.2% (17)	10.7% (9)	11.9% (10)	39.3% (33)

*   Actual numbers in parenthesis.
N = 84
Source: Price Waterhouse Cranfield Project (Ireland); University of Limerick 1992.

Interestingly, the Price Waterhouse Cranfield data highlighted that a majority of the sample firms (52.4 per cent) *did* carry out some form of analysis of training needs. However, this was carried out most often as a result of employee requests and/or line management requests, and to a lesser extent through performance appraisal. The use of training audits emerged as the least utilised method.

The effectiveness of training was monitored by 60 per cent of respondents, but again the most popular methods of assessment tended to be informal, such as informal feedback from line management (46.4 per

---

[3] O'Farrell, 1988, p. 413–14.

cent) and/or trainees (44 per cent). More formalised methods of evaluating training effectiveness appeared less popular — such as tests (7 per cent).

Hitchens and O'Farrell (1988) also noted that Irish managers, on average, were less critical of sample products shown to them, had less technical knowledge of their products, were less aware of the needs of the market and were not as well informed concerning the key competitive criteria in their specific industry segments. Interestingly, the exceptions to this were managers who had worked abroad or had gained most of their experience in an M.N.E., or foreign nationals who had been trained abroad. To increase the competitiveness of Irish small industry, they recommend a shift in state aid away from fixed to soft assets — for example, training at all levels, R&D, and quality control.

REWARDS

Gunnigle (1989) maintains that small firms are much more likely to be wage followers than leaders. He found that a majority of Irish small firms always implemented the terms of national wage agreements. Wallace (1982) found that the trend of paying less than the going rate of wage settlements seems more evident among small than among large firms. Scott et al. (1989) argue that the heterogeneity of the small-firm sector makes it difficult to make generalisations about wage determination and in their study found evidence of a considerable variation by sector. In particular, the hi-tech sector did not fit the image of the small firm as paying lower wages than larger firms. Indeed, within this sector they found evidence in many instances of more attractive packages being offered to professional employees in small companies than in larger ones. They do point out, however, that the greater career potential offered by large firms can negate the attractiveness of initial superior benefits on offer to professional/technical staff in small companies.

The Price Waterhouse Cranfield Study provides some interesting data on variations in pay determination for different grades of employee (Table 8.11). For managerial and professional/technical employees — notoriously difficult for small firms to recruit — the emphasis seems to be on individual rates. This is most noticeable in the case of managerial staff, and could be a reflection of the market power of such employees. In other words, to attract competent managers, small firms must be willing to negotiate reward packages acceptable to particular individuals.

In relation to manual and clerical employees, the Price Waterhouse Cranfield data would seem to support the earlier findings of Gunnigle (1989), that small firms tend to be wage followers and implement the terms of national wage agreements, although there was some evidence of individually determined rates for clerical staff. Individual rates of pay did not seem to be an issue to any great extent for manual employees and reflects the traditional approach to pay determination for such employees in Ireland even in larger companies.

TABLE 8.11: LEVELS OF PAY DETERMINATION

Level of Pay Determination	Managerial	Professional/ Technical	Clerical	Manual
National/Industry Level	28.6%	32.1%	50.0%	51.0%
Regional	0.0%	0.0%	2.4%	2.4%
Company Level	34.5%	26.2%	27.4%	14.3%
Establishment	9.5%	10.7%	13.1%	11.9%
Individual	52.4%	34.5%	26.2%	9.5%

N = 84.

Source: Price Waterhouse Cranfield Project (Ireland); University of Limerick 1992.

THE PERSONNEL FUNCTION IN THE SMALL FIRM

If current literature holds true — that is, if small-firm owner-managers retain a unitary perspective and are unwilling to delegate authority, then it would be expected that the owner-manager would tend to assume responsibility for most decision making within the firm.

Of the respondent firms, only 22.6 per cent had a personnel department, as compared with 86.3 per cent of larger firms. This could be a reflection of a reluctance on the part of owner-managers to relinquish authority, but is more likely to be related to the size factor in that the volume of personnel-related work is not great enough to warrant the setting up of a specialist department.

TABLE 8.12: EXISTENCE OF PERSONNEL DEPARTMENT

Does Firm Have Personnel/HR Department?	Number of Firms	% of Firms
Yes	19	22.6%
No	64	76.2%
Missing	1	1.2%

N = 84.

Source: Price Waterhouse Cranfield Project (Ireland); University of Limerick 1992.

CONCLUSIONS

The understanding of employer–employee relations in the small enter-prise has developed greatly over recent years as research gives a more complex analysis of the attitudes and approaches of managers and the effect of external factors on the small firm. Such an understanding is essential and needs to be developed even further in light of the increasing importance of the small firm to the Irish economy. If small firms are to operate to their maximum potential, then it is important that policy makers are aware of the needs of this sector and of the best methods of encouraging and developing growth. For instance, appropriate training and development facilities and programmes have already been targeted as a crucial area.

Unfortunately most of our knowledge on employee relations in small firms comes mainly from Britain, which, although useful to a certain extent, addresses an environment substantially different from that facing Irish small companies: a labour market with a large number of ethnic minority groups; different government policies; and a larger domestic market, to name but a few. The most relevant research in the Irish context to date would seem to be the work of Gunnigle and Brady (1984). This study, however, concentrated only on managers, and therefore cannot give us a fully balanced insight into the state of employee relations in Irish small firms. Also, it is necessary to update this work in order to be aware of more recent trends. For instance, the Price Waterhouse Cran-field study raises questions over the conventional view of trade union recognition in Irish small firms. A better understanding of small-firm employers/employees could help to tackle such problems as high turn-over, skill problems, conflict, labour costs, and ultimately competi-tiveness.

The industrial harmony theory that prevailed in earlier studies of employee relations in small firms has been challenged by more recent studies, which have attempted to develop a more subtle and credible picture of employer–employee relationships in such companies. There is considerable evidence from contemporary research, of a largely unitarist perspective among managers of small firms. Results from the Cranfield survey would tend to support this in relation to private-sector small companies in Ireland.

Even though small-firm owner-managers tend towards paternalistic styles of management, this is impacted upon by internal and external fac-tors, particularly the power of workers to resist the exercise of mana-gerial prerogative. Trade union presence tends to be lower in small com-panies. This reflects not only managerial ideology, but also a reluctance on the part of trade unions to organise employees of small firms. The low levels of conflict evident in small firms does not necessarily support the "industrial harmony" thesis, but often reflects an inability on the part of employees to challenge the existing power structure. Small companies are less likely to have formalised procedures, for example, in the areas of grievance, and discipline. A number of studies identify inadequate training as a major proximate cause of manufacturing problems in small Irish companies, and therefore a source of uncompetitiveness. Small companies tend to be wage followers rather than leaders. However, this is not always the case, especially in hi-tech small companies which must offer superior remuneration packages in order to attract scarce, highly skilled employees.

Chapter 9

EMPLOYEE RELATIONS IN GREENFIELD SITES[1]

Patrick Gunnigle

INTRODUCTION

This chapter considers some preliminary research findings on employee relations practices in companies establishing at new (Greenfield) sites. In particular, it focuses on management approaches or styles in employee relations and draws on previous work by the author. A major characteristic of the Human Resource Management (HRM) literature is the suggestion that organisations are giving greater strategic consideration to personnel and employee relations considerations (Fombrun et al. 1984, Beer et al. 1985, Guest 1987, 1989). This is particularly felt to be the case at Greenfield sites where managements are less constrained by established practice and are felt to have greater scope to develop desired employee relations approaches (Guest 1987, 1989). For the purposes of this chapter management style in employee relations incorporates the philosophy and principles guiding management action and behaviour on labour matters. It incorporates managerial values and beliefs about how employees should be managed, and forms the basis for the subsequent development of policies in areas such as reward systems, communications and collective bargaining.

Organisations clearly differ in their approaches to workforce management and specifically the area of employee relations. Commentators have attempted to explain such variances by reference to a range of external

---

[1] This paper is based on the findings of a study on industrial relations practices in Greenfield sites conducted by the author in the period 1991–93. For further information see:

(i) Gunnigle, P., "Management Approaches to Employee Relations in Greenfield Sites", *Journal of Irish Business and Administration Research,* Vol. 13, 1992.

(ii) "Collectivism and the Management of Industrial Relations in Greenfield Sites", paper presented to the International Industrial Relations Association, Fourth European Congress, Helsinki, Finland, August 1994.

and internal factors, such as product market conditions, competitive strategy and top management ideology, which influence employee relations. A particular organisation's employee relations style will reflect the interplay of factors in the organisation's internal and external environment. An important aspect of such explanations is the idea of strategic choice. In considering management styles in employee relations, strategic choice addresses the degree to which senior management possesses and exercises strategic choice in developing personnel and employee relations policies and practices. The notion of strategic choice infers that senior management possesses some room for manoeuvre and, while environmental factors may constrain the range of choice, senior management retains considerable power in making decisions on "appropriate" styles, policies and practices.

As we have seen, Ireland has traditionally been associated with a strong collectivist, "employee" relations emphasis — generally referred to as the "pluralist" model (Roche 1990). Many commentators have argued that the past decade has seen a shift away from this pluralist model towards some variant of Human Resource Management (HRM). However, a persistent problem with such analyses is the tendency to view HRM styles as essentially homogenous, adopting similar philosophies and policies.

Nevertheless, as we highlighted in Chapter 3, research evidence in Ireland and abroad points to the existence of numerous variants of HRM (Soft HRM, Neo-pluralism and Hard HRM) incorporating different approaches to workforce management (Guest 1989, Kennoy 1990, Storey 1992, Gunnigle 1992b). While there are differences in these HRM variants, it is significant that they are all characterised by greater integration of employee relations considerations in strategic decision making and the development of complementary policies to improve human resource utilisation. HRM, therefore, constitutes a particular perspective on workforce management which can take numerous forms, all of which contrast with the traditional pluralist employee relations model. In the *traditional employee relations* model human resource considerations rarely concern strategic decision makers, and relations between management and employees are grounded in the pluralist tradition, with a primary reliance on adversarial collective bargaining.

EMPLOYEE RELATIONS AT GREENFIELD SITES

Turning to the issue of Greenfield sites, it would, therefore, seem that management's range of personnel/employee relations policy choice straddles a continuum from the traditional pluralist employee relations perspective to some variant of HRM (as highlighted in Chapter 3). In Ireland, there have been tentative suggestions that the traditional pluralist model is being replaced by approaches incorporating either a variant of traditional pluralism (neo-pluralism) or a unitarist perspective involving a range of HRM policies designed to eliminate employee needs for collective representation (neo-unitarism) However, the position remains unclear with some commentators arguing that there has been substantial change in management approaches to employee relations in the 1980s involving greater sophistication in management approaches, while others are less convinced, pointing to the lack of empirical evidence and to the deep rooted pluralist traditions of Irish employee relations.

THE RESEARCH

This chapter is based on findings from a research project on employee relations in Greenfield sites in the Republic of Ireland. For the purposes of this study Greenfield sites are defined as "locations where an organisation establishes a new facility in a start-up mode incorporating design of plant". Only organisations which started operations in the period 1987–91 and have more than 100 employees were included in the study. In total some 53 Greenfield companies were identified which met the study definition. A notable point here is that the incidence of large Greenfield site start-ups in Ireland is relatively small. Also, US companies account for over half the total number of "large" Greenfield start-ups in Ireland. It is important to add a note of caution. It is possible that there are other large Greenfield sites which have not been identified. However, given the scope of the search in this study, it is unlikely that these would amount to more than a handful of firms. This chapter is based on preliminary analysis of interviews, questionnaire responses, financial and other company data relating to these companies.

COMPANY PROFILE

A summary profile of the firms studied is outlined in Table 9.1. The most notable issues emerging from this is the dominance of US-owned firms in the sample population and the concentration of new firms in what have been termed "high technology sectors". Of the firms studied, approximately 51 per cent (27 companies) were US owned. The remaining 26 firms consisted of eleven (mainly) Irish, six Japanese, five German, and three "other" European companies, as well as one "other non-European/ US"-owned company. These 53 companies employed some 11,000 employees giving an average company size of 207 employees. While the study investigated a range of personnel/employee relations areas, this chapter focuses on a number of key issues which are felt to be indicative of management approaches to employee relations, namely:

(i)   Trade union recognition and membership;

(ii) Membership of employer associations;

(iii) Payment practices;

(iv) Management-communications

(v)   The nature of the personnel function.

TABLE 9.1: PRINCIPAL ACTIVITY BY COUNTRY OF ORIGIN

	Irish	US	European	Japanese	Other	TOTAL
Metal Manufacturing & Engineering						
* Mechanical Engineering	0	2	4	1	0	7
* Office/Data Processing Machinery	0	6	0	3	0	9
* Electrical & Instrument Engineering	1	6	2	1	0	10
Chemicals & Pharmaceuticals	0	1	1	0	0	2
Other Manufacturing						
* Textiles and Clothing	3	0	0	0	0	3
* Printing and Publishing	1	0	0	0	0	1
* Rubber and Plastics	0	1	1	1	1	4
Information/Data Processing	0	5	0	0	0	5
Software	1	6	0	0	0	7
Food & Drink	2	0	0	0	0	2
Transport/Communications Services	2	0	0	0	0	2
Other Services	1	0	0	0	0	1
	11	27	8	6	1	53

Source: Gunnigle, 1994.

OBJECTIVES

A central theme of this study is that Greenfield sites offer management an ideal opportunity to consider what type of employee relations style it wishes to pursue and to develop personnel and employee relations polices which help establish, reinforce and sustain that particular style. It is further contended that an examination of management practice in Greenfield sites should provide valuable insights on the degree to which employee relations considerations are taken into account in strategic decision making and thus should serve either to confirm or reject the hypothesised trends identified in much of the HRM literature which point to the emergence of a greater strategic perspective in employee relations management.

FINDINGS ON EMPLOYEE RELATIONS IN GREENFIELD SITES

The Role of Trade Unions

The role of trade unions is seen as a key indicator of management approaches to employee relations in Greenfield companies. This aspect incorporates both the extent of union recognition and, where unions are recognised, the nature of management–trade union relations. Given the dominance of both US and "high technology" firms in the sample, one would anticipate a high incidence of non-union firms. As can be seen from Table 9.2 this was indeed the case. The incidence of non-unionism was mainly related to ownership and industrial sector. Indeed non-unionism was predominantly confined to US-owned firms, with only four (15 per cent) of the 27 US-owned firms recognising trade unions. In contrast most Irish (82 per cent), European (100 per cent) and Japanese (67 per cent) companies recognised trade unions. An interesting theme to emerge from the interviews conducted in a majority of Japanese and European companies was their preference for single union recognition or "one grieving voice" as stated by the general manager of a large Japanese company.

It was interesting that only one of the 23 US-owned firms in the computer/electronics, software and information/data processing sectors recognised a trade union. Indeed of the four unionised US firms there seemed to be particular and unique reasons in each instance which facilitated union recognition. In three cases the new Greenfield companies were wholly-owned subsidiaries of US corporations which had established operations in Ireland over a decade ago and had recognised trade unions in those companies. This experience was instrumental in the decision to recognise trade unions in the new Greenfield facility. The other remaining US firm which recognised unions operated in a craft-based sector employing skilled employees who were traditionally highly unionised, thus making union recognition probable.

Interviews among non-union firms revealed that, for the great majority, the decision to pursue the non-union route was determined at corporate headquarters (HQ). This indicated something of a paradox with later findings that personnel/HR practices at the Irish establishment were generally different from those adopted at corporate HQ (discussed below). When this issue was explored with respondents, the common response was that corporate HQ tended to establish broad parameters of personnel/employee relations policy (such as the preference to avoid union recognition), and that local management had flexibility in the day-to-day implementation of personnel policies. In general it seemed that the impact of corporate headquarters in influencing establishment level employee relations was greater in non-union firms than in unionised ones.

TABLE 9.2: UNION RECOGNITION BY COUNTRY OF OWNERSHIP

Union Recognition	Irish	US	European	Japanese	Other	TOTAL
Yes	9	4	8	4	0	25
No	2	23	0	2	1	28

Source: Gunnigle, 1994.

As can be seen from Table 9.3, most firms which recognised trade unions had closed shop agreements with one or more trade unions. Also, union recognition was generally confined to manual grades.

Only two firms (both Irish) recognised trade unions for white-collar or managerial grades. Membership levels for manual grades were quite high with 22 (88 per cent) of the 25 companies which recognised trade unions reporting between 80 and 100 per cent union membership among manual grades. Indeed 16 firms (64 per cent) reported that all their manual employees were trade union members. Again, the pattern emerging is that foreign-owned companies tended to have a more proactive and structured approach to trade unions, while Irish companies were more reactive in their approach. As discussed below, this was strongly linked to the life-cycle stage of the company.

Turning to the impact of trade unions upon workplace-level employee relations, the aggregate evidence suggest that a majority of companies (56 per cent) which recognise trade unions feel that unions have either a "major" or "considerable" impact on workplace employee relations (see Table 9.4) On the other hand, it appears significant to note that respondents in 44 per cent of unionised firms felt that unions had either a "minor" or "little/no impact" on workplace employee relations.

TABLE 9.3: CLOSED SHOP AND UNION MEMBERSHIP LEVELS (UNIONISED COMPANIES)

	Irish	US	European	Japanese	TOTAL
Union Recognition but No Closed Shop	2	1	1	1	5
Closed Shop Agreement with One Union	6	1	7	3	17
Closed Shop Agreement with More Than One Union	1	2	0	0	3
Average Union Membership among Manual Grades	80.5%	87.5%	99%	96.5%	N/A
Average Union Membership among White-collar Grades	12.0%	0%	0%	0%	N/A
Average Union Membership among Managerial Grades	17.0%	0%	0%	0%	N/A

N = 25
Source: Gunnigle, 1994.

TABLE 9.4: IMPACT OF TRADE UNIONS IN WORKPLACE EMPLOYEE RELATIONS

	Irish	US	European	Japanese	TOTAL
Major Impact	1	0	1	0	2 (8%)
Considerable Impact	4	2	3	3	12 (48%)
Minor Impact	3	2	4	0	9 (36%)
Little/No Impact	1	0	0	1	2 (8%)

N = 25
Source: Gunnigle, 1994.

Membership and Utilisation of Employer Associations

Membership of employer associations is also seen as a useful indicator of preferred managerial approaches to employee relations. Membership of employer associations has traditionally been associated with the pluralist employee relations model. The majority of Greenfield firms surveyed (62 per cent) were employer association members (in all but one instance, members of the Federation of Irish Employers [FIE]).[2] The decision to join an employer association was largely associated with country of ownership and trade union membership (see Tables 9.5 and 9.6). While just over half of the US- and Irish-owned firms were employer association members, over 86 per cent of "other" foreign owned companies were members of employer associations.

TABLE 9.5: EMPLOYER ASSOCIATION MEMBERSHIP AND UTILISATION BY COUNTRY OF OWNERSHIP

	Employer Association Membership		Utilisation of Employer Association Services		
	Yes	No	Direct Involvement in Establishment Level Employee Relations	Employee Relations Advice	General Personnel/ HR Advice
Irish	6	5	2	5	5
US	14	13	2	14	14
Japanese	4	2	1	4	4
European	8	0	7	8	8
Other	1	0	0	1	1
TOTAL	33	20	12	32	32

N = 53
Source: Gunnigle, 1994.

Employer association membership was positively related to trade union recognition. As expected, companies which recognised trade unions were significantly more likely to join trade unions. Of the 25 unionised firms, 22 (88 per cent) were employer association members while only 11 (39 per cent) of the 28 non-union firms were members.

Only some 36 per cent of the companies which were members of employer associations used association executives directly in workplace employee relations interactions. The more general pattern was for organisations to use the employer association primarily as a source of information and advice across a range of personnel issues including industrial relations.

---

[2] The Federation of Irish Employers (FIE) has since merged with the Confederation of Irish Industry to form the Irish Business and Employers Confederation (IBEC).

**TABLE 9.6: EMPLOYER ASSOCIATION MEMBERSHIP AND UTILISATION
BY TRADE UNION RECOGNITION**

	Employer Association Membership		Utilisation of Employer Association Services		
	Yes	No	Direct Involvement in Establishment Level Employee Relations	Industrial Relations Advice	General Personnel/ HR Advice
Non-union Firms	11 (39%)	17 (61%)	0	11 (100%)	11 (100%)
Unionised Firms	22 (88%)	3 (12%)	14 (56%)	21 (84%)	21 (84%)

N = 33
Source: Gunnigle, 1994.

Payment Practices

An interesting issue arising from the data on pay policies (see Table 9.7) is that the great majority of firms surveyed had a conscious strategy of maintaining wage levels at, above or below the normal going rate for their industrial sector. It is particularly interesting that non-union companies were generally not pay leaders (that is, wage rates were not above industrial and regional norms). Of the 13 companies which had a conscious policy of paying above the norm for their industrial sector, eight recognised trade unions. Indeed, the majority of non-union firms had a conscious policy of ensuring pay levels remained at the norm for their sector and/or region. Equally, the presence or absence of trade union recognition did not produce any significant trend among the companies whose pay rates were below the norm for their sector. Four of the "low pay" firms were non-union and six recognised trade unions.

An important issue in the context of analysing change in employee relations is the incidence and nature of performance-related pay systems. In particular, the incidence of performance-related pay (PRP) based on formal performance appraisals for all employees' grades is seen as a significant indicator of a preference for a more individualist (as opposed to collectivist) approach to employee relations. Table 9.7 indicates that 25 (47 per cent) of the 53 firms studied used PRP for all employee grades. The incidence of PRP for all employees was strongly linked to union recognition and company ownership. Of the 25 firms which used PRP for all employees, 21 (84 per cent) were non-union and 18 (72 per cent) were US owned. Interestingly, only a minority of the Irish and other foreign-owned firms used PRP for all employees.

This pattern is reinforced in the use of performance appraisal to aid PRP decisions. Of the 22 firms which used performance appraisal to aid PRP decisions 21 (95 per cent) were non-union and 20 (91 per cent) were foreign owned (18 US owned).

TABLE 9.7: PAY LEVELS AND INCIDENCE OF
PERFORMANCE RELATED PAY

	Pay Levels			Conscious Pay Strategy		Performance Related Pay (for all employees)		Performance Appraisal Helps Decide Pay Increases (for all employees)	
	Below Norm	At Norm	Above Norm	Yes	No	Yes	No	Yes	No
Irish	1	7	3	6	5	3	8	2	9
US	4	15	8	26	1	18	9	18	9
Japanese	1	4	1	6	0	1	5	1	5
European	3	4	1	5	3	3	6	0	8
Other	1	0	0	1	0	1	0	1	0
TOTAL	10	30	13	44	9	26	28	22	31
	(19%)	(24%)	(83%)	(83%)	(17%)	(47%)	(53%)	(41%)	(59%)

N = 53
Source: Gunnigle, 1994.

Management–Employee Communications

Another key aspect of organisation-level employee relations is the nature of management–employee communications. This study focused on the communications fora used by management in communicating with employees, and the type of information communicated using such fora. A majority of firms surveyed (58.5 per cent) communicated formally with all employee categories on business strategy (see Table 8.8). However, only a minority of firms (40 per cent) communicated formally with all employee grades on financial performance. The majority of US firms communicated formally with all employees on business strategy and financial performance. The issue is less clear cut among Irish-owned and other foreign-owned firms. Approximately 40 per cent of "other foreign-owned firms" communicated formally with all employees on business strategy and 20 per cent communicated formally on financial perfor-mance. Only some 18 per cent of Irish firms (two out of eleven firms) communicated formally with all employees grades on business strategy and 27 per cent communicated formally on financial performance.

Interviews with respondent firms confirmed this trend and suggested that the nature and scope of communications fora were more sophisticated in the great majority of US-owned firms — particularly in the computer/high technology sectors. Differences in communications tended to focus on the range of formal communications mechanisms used, the level of senior management involvement in, and the commitment to, these mechanisms. The more sophisticated firms tended to use a range of communications mechanisms with particular emphasis on direct communications with individual employees. The most common approaches focused on "cascade" mechanisms with briefings for different employee levels augmented by communications through line management, general workforce meetings and other written and oral communications. Apart from a few exceptions, firms with less sophisticated approaches were either Irish or "other" foreign owned, and tended to rely primarily on collective communications fora, particularly collective bargaining, basic written communications and normal line-management–employee interactions.

TABLE 9.8: FORMAL COMMUNICATIONS WITH ALL EMPLOYEES

	Formal Communications on Business Strategy		Formal Communications on Financial Performance	
	Yes	No	Yes	No
Irish	2	9	3	8
US	23	4	15	12
Japanese	4	2	2	4
European	2	6	1	7
Other	0	1	0	1
TOTAL	31	22	215	32

N = 53
Source: Gunnigle, 1994.

Personnel Management and the Specialist Personnel Function

A final aspect of management approaches to employee relations considered in this chapter is the role of the specialist personnel function. Of the 53 companies, 38 (72 per cent) had a specialist personnel function. This seemed largely dependent on ownership and size. Only four of the eleven Irish companies (36 per cent) had a specialist personnel function, while the majority of US (79 per cent), Japanese (83 per cent), and other foreign companies (66 per cent) had specialist personnel functions. In terms of job title of the senior personnel practitioners, 16 (42 per cent) incorporated the term "human resources" and 13 (34 per cent) used the term "personnel". Of the senior personnel practitioners, 33 (87 per cent) reported to the chief executive or equivalent. However, none of the senior personnel practitioners in the firms studied had a seat on the board of directors. The major reason given for this somewhat surprising finding was that most firms with a specialist personnel function were subsidiaries of larger, foreign-owned companies. Consequently, there was no potential for board-level involvement in the Irish operation although at corporate level the personnel function may indeed have been represented at (corporate) board level. Nevertheless, it does seem significant that even in the (few) Irish companies with a personnel function and among the small number of foreign-owned companies with an Irish board of directors, the senior personnel practitioner did not have a seat on the board. However, senior personnel practitioners were part of the top management team in 29 (76 per cent) of the 38 firms which had a specialist personnel function.

At the more generic level, the picture emerging in relation to the impact of personnel considerations on major business policy decisions is somewhat mixed. Over 60 per cent of respondents indicated that personnel considerations had at least a "considerable" impact on major business policy decisions. However, some 18 respondent firms (38 per cent) reported that personnel considerations had little influence on major business policy decisions.

TABLE 9.9: SPECIALIST PERSONNEL FUNCTION

Respondent Firms with a Specialist Personnel Function*	71.7%
Job Title of Senior Personnel Practitioner Incorporates Term "Human Resources"†	42.0%
Job Title of Senior Personnel Practitioner Incorporates Term "Personnel"†	34.0%
Senior Personnel Practitioner Member of Board of Directors†	0%
Senior Personnel Practitioner Member of Top Management Team†	76.3%

*   N = 53
†   N = 38
Source: Gunnigle, 1994.

As indicated in Table 9.10 some 34 per cent of firms had a written personnel/human resource (P/HR) strategy and a further 28 per cent of firms had an unwritten P/HR strategy. Written P/HR strategies were particularly common in US firms. Interview data confirmed a strong preference among US-owned American firms, particularly in the electronics/ information technology sectors, to have explicit policies across a range of personnel areas. While almost 60 per cent of US companies had a written P/HR strategy, only 9 per cent of Irish companies had such a strategy. Although the evidence is quite tentative, it seems that Irish firms are less likely to have such explicit policies. Japanese firms seem likely to have broad mission statements but less likely to develop these into explicit P/HR strategies. An interesting trend which arose in interviews with senior management was a growing preference for less explicit P/HR policy statements. Senior managers felt that companies should avoid committing themselves in writing to particular personnel policies, since these might inflate expectations and restrict management flexibility to initiate policy changes. This development may be due, at least partially, to the trading difficulties currently being encountered by some firms seen as the major exponents of "soft HRM" practices, such as Digital and Wang. A number of management respondents felt that broad strategy statements allowed greater flexibility to tailor personnel policies and practices to business needs.

An interesting issue explored with the 42 foreign-owned companies was the degree to which P/HR policies at the Irish establishment varied from those adopted at corporate headquarters. Interestingly, a majority of the 42 foreign-owned companies reported that their polices were either slightly or substantially different from those adopted at corporate headquarters.

TABLE 9.10: PERSONNEL/HUMAN RESOURCE STRATEGY

P/HR Strategy	Irish	US	European	Japanese	Other	TOTAL
Yes — written	1	16	0	1	0	34% (18)
Yes — unwritten	2	7	3	3	0	28% (15)
No	8	4	5	2	1	38% (20)

N = 53
Source: Gunnigle, 1994.

The general trend in relation to the nature of the personnel function and its impact on employee relations was that foreign-owned, and specifically US companies, were most likely to have a particular desired approach to employee relations, as generally manifested in an explicit P/HR strategy. In all but the smaller US-owned firms, a specialist personnel function was vested with responsibility for the implementation of specific policies and practices to effect the desired employee relations style. Irish firms were less likely to have either a particular desired employee relations style or P/HR strategy, and tended to view employee relations issues as somewhat peripheral to the business and to deal with them in a largely ad hoc manner.

The most influential factor affecting management approaches to employee relations seemed to hinge on the life-cycle stage of the firm. US and other foreign-owned companies were generally larger and more mature than their Irish counterparts, had a developed corporate culture and an explicit desired employee relations style. The role of management at the Irish operation, and specifically the responsibility of the personnel function, was to develop effectively the desired corporate culture and complementary employee relations style. Apart from two particular exceptions, the Irish companies studied were more embryonic in nature. They also tended to act as suppliers to a few major customers and were largely price takers in their product market. The management teams were generally quite small in number, and, because of the market vulnerability of the firms, tended to focus primarily on cost control and aggressive marketing. There was little perceived need for employee relations policies, and a specialist personnel function was seen as an un-affordable overhead. However, it seemed significant that the one older, more mature Irish company did actually have an explicit P/HR strategy and a specific desired employee relations style. Indeed, this firm's decision to establish a Greenfield operation was strongly influenced by management's desire to adopt more "novel" workforce management practices, particularly in the area of multi-skilling and performance-related pay, and this was felt to be more feasible in a Greenfield situation.

Discussion

The aggregate evidence presented in this chapter points to emergent patterns of employee relations management which diverge from the pluralist model and incorporate many HRM characteristics. However, in only a minority of cases could these emergent employee relations patterns be classified as "soft" Human Resource Management (Keenoy 1990, Storey 1992). Indeed a number of the organisations studied adopted employee relations styles which more closely approximated to "hard" HRM. Characteristics of this approach were most obvious in the adoption of atypical employment forms (particularly temporary working and subcontracting) and intense performance management techniques to improve cost effectiveness while meeting required performance standards and "bottom line" financial criteria.

Greenfield sites offer management an ideal opportunity to consider what type of employee relations style it wishes to pursue and to develop personnel polices which help establish and reinforce that particular style. A key strategic issue for Greenfield companies is the decision on where to locate the new operation. Interviews with respondent firms revealed that the main factors which influenced location decisions were:

(i) Financial incentive package;

(ii) Labour availability and skills;

(iii) Access to single European market (foreign companies only);

(iv) Labour costs; and

(v) Layout/configuration of site facility.

It was significant that the majority of companies, and almost all US-owned companies, saw the availability of skilled labour as a central positive factor influencing location of new start-up facilities. Employee relations per se did not feature as a significant management concern in establishing Greenfield site facilities. It was, however, interesting that firms which had an explicit policy of paying below the going rate for their sector, tended to locate in more peripheral regional locations where average pay rates were lower than those pertaining in more industrialised urban centres.

The majority of companies surveyed (particularly in the foreign-owned sector) had a conscious P/HR strategy and adopted particular policies to nurture this approach. Most companies with a conscious P/HR strategy linked its rationale to broader business concerns. The most commonly stated reason was the need to ensure flexibility of business operations. Higher quality levels and increased employee commitment and productivity were also commonly mentioned. A prominent feature among the Greenfield companies which did not recognise trade unions or had closed shop agreements with one union was a desire to ensure labour flexibility in the operations of the business. This objective was particularly prominent in the computer/electronics sector.

The evidence presented in this chapter points to higher levels of proactivity in employee relations, particularly in US companies. Many of these pursued some of the features of HRM such as sophisticated recruitment and socialisation of new employees, internal labour market emphasis incorporating employee development, and a wide range of communications devices. A particular feature was an emphasis on direct dealings with the individual employee (Guest 1989). The most common feature of higher individualism was performance-based reward systems tied to individual employee appraisals, direct employee communications and a focus on individual employee development. Union avoidance strategies were another common feature in the "HRM companies". Interviews and survey data from the Greenfield companies in this study seem to confirm the trend identified by McGovern (1989), who pointed to increasing opposition to union recognition. McGovern suggests that the rapid levels of change, characteristic of the electronics industry, demanded high levels of flexibility in work practices and thus made non-union approaches more appropriate in avoiding labour rigidities and de-marcation. This chapter on employee relations in Greenfield companies identifies a strong desire among most US-owned companies to avoid union recognition. This goal, according to management respondents, was generally effected through rigorous selection and prompt handling of workplace grievances. Interestingly, high pay does not seem to feature commonly as a union avoidance strategy.

On the impact of country of ownership on employee relations styles, the evidence here suggests that the most visible examples of HRM-type polices are in foreign-owned companies, particularly of US origin. This is in line with the suggestion of Guest (1989) that *American* companies, reflecting their home culture of anti-unionism, individualism and famili-arity with HRM, will generally pursue the non-union path in establishing Greenfield sites. While the evidence here is quite tentative, it seems that *Japanese* companies are more likely to seek single-union closed-shop agreements, while *European* companies seem less preoccupied with personnel/employee relations considerations and are likely to adopt more traditional approaches.

Alongside the emphasis on individualism, discussed above, is evi-dence of changing management approaches to collectivism as a means of managing workplace employee relations. The concept of collectivism in-corporates the degree to which management acknowledges the right of employees to collective representation, and their consequent influence on management decision making (Purcell, 1987). High collectivism is mani-fested in mechanisms for employee representation such as trade unions or works councils. It incorporates both the existence of such mechanisms and the spirit in which management approaches their operation, particu-larly the degree to which management actively supports employee involvement or alternatively seeks to minimise its impact on the orga-nisation. The trend emerging in Greenfield sites indicates a move from collectivism to individualism via sophisticated recruitment, rewards and employee development policies. This move from collectivism to individualism does not mean that collectivist structures are abandoned. Rather, it seems that in-house fora such as works committees are preferred to trade unions but that such fora are largely communications vehicles with little or no scope for negotiations. It also seems that where US- or Japanese-owned companies recognise trade unions, the union's role in workplace employee relations is often quite limited. The evidence in relation to employer associations is also indicative of change in the role of collectivism in employee relations management. Employer associations have traditionally been integral to the pluralist employee relations model. However, growth of the non-union sector, particularly in Greenfield sites, and a related expansion of individualistic HRM-type policies means that, for such companies, membership of an employers' association (in essence a trade union of employers) is often perceived as incompatible with a management approach based on individual dealings with employees. The Irish Business and Employers Confederation partially responded to this development by establishing an advisory and consultancy service designed to cater for non-union firms while not conferring the traditional status of association member. The evidence from this study seems to indicate that this strategy has met with some success, as a substantial proportion of recently established non-union firms are now joining employer associations.

CONCLUSIONS

The most striking feature of management approaches to employee relations in the companies studied is the prominence of a planned and co-ordinated approach to employee relations management in the majority of foreign-owned companies. Most Irish companies, on the other hand, seem to adopt a more "incidentalist" approach to employee relations. In general, however, the study findings indicate a move away from the traditional pluralist model based on adversarial collective bargaining with trade unions. The emerging trend in preferred management approaches to employee relations among most foreign-owned firms is one of higher individualism and constrained collectivism. Such a trend is evidenced by policies designed to mitigate attempts to achieve trade union recognition, or where unions are recognised, to prescribe tightly their role in workplace employee relations.

It is felt that company life cycle and industrial sector, as well as ownership per se, are key factors impacting on management approaches to employee relations. Proactivity in employee relations was most evident in companies with tight corporate cultures and was often reflected in a higher level and better resourced personnel function. Most such foreign companies were US owned and operated in "high technology" sectors. Foreign-owned companies tended to be more secure in their product market and the Greenfield operation in Ireland was generally established as part of a conscious business plan. Within this context it is hardly surprising that such organisations tended to have explicit corporate cultures and desired employee relations styles. On the other hand, most Irish Greenfield companies were characterised by more organic growth and were relatively "small players" in their product market. Again, the fact that such companies did not have conscious employee relations styles reflects a context of more ad hoc development of the firm as a whole and a more insecure position in their product market(s).

It was interesting that two of the companies studied had established new operations at a Greenfield site as a preferred alternative to expanding their existing Irish facility. This indicates some support for the contention of Emery (1980) that Greenfield sites offer opportunities to establish "a new paradigm of work relationships". This was particularly the case in the instance of the single mature Irish company which established at a Greenfield site because it offered the company greater opportunity to adopt management practices which differed considerably from the more traditional approaches adopted in the parent company.

This study suggests that the incidence of large non-union firms in Ireland is no longer confined to a few prominent household names such as IBM and Digital. Indeed, the evidence presented here points to the emergence of a vibrant non-union sector among Greenfield manufacturing and service companies. This trend is likely to be accentuated by the increasing numbers and visibility of companies successfully pursuing the non-union route. These provide useful models for new organisations considering establishing on a non-union basis. The current industrial policy focus on high technology industries and internationally traded services also seems likely to accentuate this trend.

This chapter has attempted to sketch the employee relations choices facing managements establishing at Greenfield sites. Of particular significance in the Irish context is the degree to which more individualist approaches are being adopted and replacing traditional pluralism. In evaluating current Irish developments, there has been a trend incorrectly to equate notable examples of HRM with widespread pervasiveness of such approaches. However, this study points to a trend towards patterns of employee relations management in Greenfield companies which diverges from the traditional pluralist model. If this trend were to continue, as seems likely given the current thrust of industrial policy, the traditionally significant role of trade unions in manufacturing industry may be severely eroded. It is, of course, plausible to argue that the depressed economic climate and record unemployment levels and relative immaturity of firms in the study population militate against union membership drives. Equally, it could be suggested that the traditional legitimacy and acceptance of trade unions, as manifested in the emergent corporatist structures characteristic of contemporary Irish industrial relations creates a socio-economic climate conducive to ensuring the maintenance of high levels of trade union recognition and density. However, the increased visibility of non-union models, combined with competitive pressures and continuing high levels of unemployment are likely to ensure that the adoption of patterns of employee relations management which diverge from the pluralist model will both endure and expand into the 1990s.

Chapter 10

HUMAN RESOURCE STRATEGY AND THE NON-UNION PHENOMENON

Patrick Flood, Bill Toner and Thomas Turner

INTRODUCTION

As late as a decade ago, the non-union company scarcely rated a mention in employee relations literature in Ireland or Britain. The IDA (Murray et al. 1984) found that 13 per cent of all manufacturing companies in Ireland with more than 250 employees (and 7 per cent of firms in the 50–100 category) were non-union, while Brown (1981) found in the UK that 24 per cent of manufacturing firms employing more than 50 did not recognise trade unions. However, in the 1970s, non-union companies were not considered a significant part of the employee relations scene. In Ireland, union density rose steadily during the period 1945–80 from 25.3 per cent to 55.4 per cent (Roche and Larragy, 1989). Thus, it appeared to commentators only a matter of time before all significant concentrations of employees became unionised. Beaumont (1987) considers that the limited presence of behavioural scientists in the employee relations research community was also a factor in the neglect of non-union firms with their strong human relations culture. Bassett's (1988) study suggests in a similar vein that it was easier for researchers to scrutinise union procedures and structures: "By contrast non-unionism is amorphous, decentralised, inaccessible". Another reason for the lack of interest in non-union firms was the high degree of legitimation given to unions in the UK (mainly by Labour governments) between 1964 and 1979. In particular, in the UK, the Employment Protection Act of 1975 (now amended), as well as incorporating statutory recognition procedures, conferred a number of legal rights on recognised trade unions, such as the right to be consulted on various issues and the right to certain information. This legislation appeared to place non-union employees in the role of outsiders in the employee relations arena. Similarly, in Ireland, there has been strong support for union recognition from the Labour Court and from the high degree of legitimation given to trade unions under the various social partnership arrangements which commenced in the 1970s.

By the mid-1980s the climate had changed considerably in the UK and Ireland. Bassett (1988) quotes 17 examples of companies in the UK de-unionising. Within a relatively short period, therefore, non-union companies had become a significant reality. It would be a mistake, however, to think that this signified a dramatic change in employee relations practice in Britain or Ireland. Larger manufacturing and service organisations, including units in the public sector, are still much more likely to be unionised than not. An important exception to this, as pointed out in Chapter 9, is the influx of US manufacturing subsidiaries, many of which are non-union. However, as Beaumont (1987) suggests, any significant non-union US presence may in fact precede the current recession. A recent CBI analysis of pay negotiations in the 1980s (Ingram and Cahill 1989) throws doubt on the widespread belief that the unions are weak in the UK and in retreat, at least in regard to the ordinary bread-and-butter issues. Similarly, Irish unions are also still strong in this area. What has changed in the 1990s is that non-unionism has come out of the closet. It is not now uncommon for the managers of non-union firms to go public about their non-union policies, in seminars and even in published articles, (see, for instance, Peach, 1983). There are several possible reasons for this new openness. Firstly, there is the increasing confidence of non-union companies such as IBM and Digital, which is partly a result of the alleged success of their HRM policies in removing the triggers to unionisation — such as insecurity, perceived inequity, poor supervision, etc. Research by Toner (1985) in the Irish context indicated that, in the large non-union companies studied, there was little demand for union representation amongst employees.

Secondly, a distinction is emerging between the backstreet non-union "sweat shops" and the large non-union companies. These large non-union companies, because of their size and profile, would be a ready target for unionisation if they did not employ union substitution policies. As a consequence, Barbash (1984) argues "management finds itself doing many of the things the union does, but without having to suffer the union presence", and in the process has become more open about its employee relations policies. Thirdly, a dominant anti-union ideology in the US has been gaining increasing currency on this side of the Atlantic. This opposition to unions is being expressed particularly through the management of US subsidiaries in Europe, including Ireland. Thus, non-unionism has acquired increased legitimacy and visibility, with the prospect that this will sooner or later be translated into a growth in the non-union sector not explainable by structural changes or changes in the business cycle (Bain and Elsheikh 1976, Bain and Price 1983). Is it true, as Bassett (1986) claims that "non-unionism and its sharpest form — union derecognition — looks set to continue and to grow and to be a feature of the industrial relations pattern"?

UNION AVOIDANCE AND COMPETITIVENESS

There have always been commercial organisations which have attempted to gain competitive advantage by preventing or discouraging union membership among employees. The main perceived advantage for management has been the ability to pay lower wages than unionised competitors, and the ability to make potentially unpopular decisions without facing an organised challenge from the workforce. Whether unionisation does, in fact, affect competitiveness is a debated point. In fact, in the 1970s an interesting school of thought developed in the United States which suggested that unionisation went hand in hand with higher productivity. A number of researchers working at Harvard University, notably Freeman and Medoff (1979), and Brown and Medoff (1978), found that industries in states with high rates of unionisation seemed to have achieved higher productivity than the same industries in the states with low unionisation. A number of criticisms have been made of their analysis (some of the criticisms coming from the same researchers). One criticism has been that their comparisons of productivity were based on value added, and therefore it is possible that the apparently superior performances from the unionised sectors were due to monopoly effects. This would arise where one or more unionised companies had a virtual monopoly in a particular market, and thus higher wages negotiated by unions could be passed on to consumers in the form of higher prices. Although in recent years the Harvard researchers have revised their views to some extent, their research does suggest that in many situations unions do not inhibit productivity as much as popularly supposed (see Freeman and Medoff 1984, for details of this research). However, Metcalf (1990) concluded from a review of the research on the economic effect of unions in Britain that unionisation is associated with lower productivity or, at least, has no effect.

Another criticism, which is particularly pertinent in the present context, is that even if unions do not reduce productivity, they do reduce profits, and thus, at least in the longer term, competitive advantage. Research into union effects on profitability have been surprisingly limited, and related mainly to the US. Here, in one important study, Clarke (1984) found that unionism decreased the pre-tax rate of return on capital by 4.1 per cent, or by 19 per cent relative to the sample mean. In the case of firms with low market share (less than 10 per cent), Clarke found that unions reduced profits by 4.7 per cent or by 40 per cent relative to the sample mean of 11.1 per cent. But no change was discerned by Clarke in the case of firms with more than 35 per cent of market share. In other studies, Ruback and Zimmerman (1984) found that there were substantial falls in equity value associated with union representation, and Connolly, Hirsch and Hirschey (1985) found that unions were able to capture rents associated with intangible capital investments in R&D, rather than with short-lived advertising expenditures. This latter finding would suggest that unions may impact negatively on long-term growth. Obviously a great deal depends on the character of the union movement in a particular country, and on union density. It seems unlikely that the larger Japanese manufacturing companies have lost out significantly through union representation: firstly, because all large manufacturing companies in Japan are unionised (albeit by Japanese-style company unions); and secondly, because these same companies have demonstrated their ability to compete internationally, make large profits, and invest heavily in R&D. To return to the US research of the 1970s, Freeman and Medoff (1979) postulated a number of reasons why unions might enhance productivity, and many of these arguments still have force. Their main argument is that unions lock workers into jobs by gaining better pay and conditions for them. Thus, turnover of experienced workers is reduced, speeding up learning effects; quality can be more easily maintained; and waste is kept to a minimum. Because investment in training is not lost through high turnover, more training is likely to be given in the future.

Other points put forward by Freeman and Medoff (1984) include such arguments as — unions, through shock effects, smarten up management; better communication channels enable workers to suggest improved ways of doing things; and the better morale of unionised workers improves their performance. Table 10.1 summarises some further US studies on the impact of unions on shareholder value, profitability and productivity.

The research findings listed in Table 10.1 suggest that union recognition is more likely to be associated, in the US context, with a decline in shareholder wealth.

TABLE 10.1: IMPACT OF UNION ACTIVITIES ON ORGANISATIONAL PERFORMANCE IN US (AS REPORTED IN RESEARCH STUDIES)

Union Event	Productivity	Profit/Share Price Effect	Time Period
Election (Ruback & Zimmerman)	N/A	Union Loss reduces shareholder equity by 1.86%; union win reduces shareholder equity by 3.84%	1962–84
"Unexpected" Wage Settlement (Abowd)	None	Each $1.00 gained by either side cost other side $1.00	1975–82
Concession Bargain (Becker)	N/A	Increases shareholder equity by 8%	1982–83
Two-Tier Agreement (Thomas & Kleiner)	N/A	Increases shareholder equity by 1% to 4.1%	1983–86
Strikes (Neumann, Becker & Olson)	N/A	Reduces shareholder equity by 1% to 4.1%	1962–82
Grievance Activity (Ichiowski; Katz, Kochan & Weber; Kleiner, Nickelsburg & Pilarski)	1 standard deviation increase in filings productivity by 1.5% to 6.7% related grievances	Increase from zero to average level of grievances by 14.6%	1970–80

Source: Kleiner 1990.

These negative results, Kleiner (1990) argues may also help explain why low-wage firms, which have potentially the most to lose from an organised drive, are the most likely to engage in union avoidance techniques.

Even in the Irish context, there is still a widespread perception among managers that unions are at best a necessary evil. The following is a list of supposed disadvantages of unions quoted by managers and researchers (see Toner 1987):

- Unions raise employment costs.
- Unions make change more difficult.
- Unions encourage trivial grievances.
- Unions impede communication.
- Unions promote an adversarial industrial relations climate.
- Unions inhibit individual rewards.
- Unions provide a platform for trouble-makers.
- Unions impose restrictions on production.
- Unions inhibit flexibility.
- Unions impose unnecessary high-manning level.

A THEORETICAL EXPLANATION OF THE NON-UNION PHENOMENON

Kochan, Katz and McKersie (1986) have developed a comprehensive and integrated theoretical framework which attempts to explain the emergence of the contemporary non-union phenomenon. Few attempts have been made to test the validity of their framework, particularly in a European environment. Although their model is influential and cited in many academic texts, it has received little empirical scrutiny. Figure 10.1 outlines an adapted version of the Kochan et al. model of the emergence of non-union employment relationships. It can be seen from this model that the emergence of non-union companies and the diffusion of the non-union system is integrally linked with a broad range of explanatory factors. These include the external environment, managerial values and business strategies, coupled with the impact of the firm's employee relations/HRM policies and practices. These are seen as contributing forces to union recognition or non-recognition.

FIGURE 10.1: EMERGENCE OF NON-UNION EMPLOYMENT RELATIONSHIPS

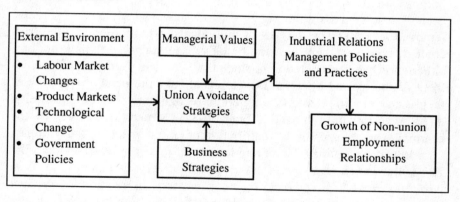

Source: Adapted from Kochan, T. & Katz, H.

The External Environment Variables

The external environment variables outlined by Kochan et al. (1986) include labour market and workforce demographics, product markets, technological change and government policies. The implication here is that where labour markets are slack, unions are weakened, implying a greater freedom on the part of managers to choose the non-union option. Workforce demographics are also significant — for example, increasing levels of female participation in the labour market (females having a lower propensity to unionise). Product markets are also seen as being highly significant. The product market impacts upon employee relations in a number of different ways. Irrespective of whether the firm is union or non-union, where labour costs-containment pressures are particularly high, these will have a highly significant impact on the type of employee-relations strategies pursued at the level of the firm. For example, if labour costs are a large proportion of total costs and if the organisation is pursuing a strategy of low-cost leadership, then it can be expected that very tight, codified labour relations policies and practices will be pursued at the level of the firm, with a view to containing labour costs at the minimum level. In the US, for example, where there is a non-union wage differential of some 15–20 per cent (Hirsch and Addison, 1986) it can be seen why firms wishing to contain labour costs opt for the non-union strategy. That is, by going non-union it is frequently cheaper. However, in the Irish case, no comparable data is available to show the union–non-union wage mark-up. Technological change is also seen as being important. It can erode jobs which are traditionally the domain of trade unions: blue-collar, low- and semi-skilled occupations. Government policies are also particularly important. For example, in the US there has been a resurgence in the right to work laws which again, perhaps, removed incentives on the part of individuals to join unions. In the Irish context, however, there has traditionally been support for trade unions, although it has been noted that, since the 1980s, the Industrial Development Authority and Shannon Development have not been as directive as they used to be in recommending union recognition to incoming foreign direct investors into Ireland (Toner, 1987). Structural changes in the economy and changes in the distribution of employment similarly impact upon the opportunities for non-unionism in a particular economy. *The Price Waterhouse data set allows us to test for a limited number of these variables in either a direct or proxy method.* In relation to product markets, we use two separate variables available in the Price Waterhouse data set. These include: firstly, the market into which the firm is selling; and secondly, the industry sector. Firms exporting internationally are more likely to experience greater competitive pressures than those selling a product or service in the home market, and are consequently more likely to view trade unions as an extra cost burden. Given the small number of companies (182) involved, they have been grouped into four industry categories: manufacturing, services, utilities and others. The large proportion of manufacturing firms in the sample has been further divided into those firms which produce electronic and computer-related products and which are defined as advanced manufacturing, and the remainder which are defined as traditional manufacturing (e.g. food, drink, textiles, paper, etc.) Unfortunately, within the Price Waterhouse data set we cannot calculate measures for government policies and technological change.

Business Strategies and Union Recognition

Every firm either implicitly or explicitly pursues a particular business strategy. A variety of different types of business strategy can be identified, all of which impact significantly upon the type of employee relations strategies which are pursued at the level of the firm. Schuler (1992) and Kochan et al. (1986) classified competitive strategies into two major approaches:

(i)   A strategy to be the lowest cost producer of goods or services in an industry;

(ii) A strategy to supply products or services that are extremely high in quality or technologically innovative in such a way as to differentiate the product or service from competing firms.

The latter strategy, it is argued, allows the firm to sell the product at a price premium. According to researchers such as the Boston Consulting Group (Buzell and Gale, 1990) this approach generates significant above-average returns to firms pursuing such a strategy. The important point to note here is that the business strategy and the type of product markets which the firm is facing have a significant impact on the type of employee relations and human resource management policies and practice which are pursued at the level of the firm. It can be expected that for firms who are aiming to be the lowest cost producer (low cost leadership) in a particular industry (and particularly where labour costs are a high percentage of the cost of manufacture), this will have a significant impact upon managerial strategies to control costs, including labour costs, at the level of the firm. By contrast, the firm which is pursuing a differentiation strategy may be generating a significant stream of revenue to the firm in a growth situation, which will lead to an entirely different set of competitive pressures at the level of the firm, which impacts upon the human resource management policies and practices being pursued there.

It is generally agreed that firms wish to match their business strategies and human resource management strategies. If the external environment is one of rapid change, turbulence and reactivity, then, ideally, the human resource management strategy at the level of the firm will recognise these external dimensions and develop a coherent approach aimed at matching human resource strategy to the external environment. Thus, for example, a premium may be placed upon highly flexible innovative and entrepreneurial employees in a highly reactive market. Such a strategy is likely to exclude trade unions from any role in the organisation and view them as a potential obstacle to the goals of flexibility and innovation. The Price Waterhouse data allows us to test for the effect of an explicit P/HR strategy on union recognition. The centrality and importance of a human resource strategy can be expected to vary inversely with union recognition.

The Role of Managerial Values in Shaping Union Recognition

In relation to managerial values, Kochan et al. (1986) would argue that these have a tremendous impact upon the decision of an organisation to recognise trade unions. As Kochan et al. (1986) point out, managerial values act as a lens through which environmental pressures or opportunities pass in the process of producing organisational responses. Options that are inconsistent with accepted values are rejected, discounted as being outside the range of all acceptable alternatives, or not even consciously considered. For example, deep-seated opposition to unions is seen as a key element in the ideology of American management. Thus, country of origin could potentially be a very powerful explanatory variable of union recognition or non-recognition. For example, one would expect (Guest, 1992) that foreign investors of US origin would be likely not to recognise trade unions. Japanese companies would be expected (because of the traditional arrangements in their home country) to go for a single union deal — it being the closest approximate to the establishment-based unions in Japan. Irish and European companies would be expected to recognise trade unions. In relation to the Price Waterhouse data set, the only variable which allows us to assess managerial values is the proxy variable of country of origin. This is used as a test for whether the country of origin has an impact upon union recognition. This could be expected to be particularly significant in Greenfield sites where one would expect that revealed managerial preferences in relation to unions would be most significantly exposed. For example, it would be expected and it has already been shown (Gunnigle, 1992) that US companies in Greenfield-site situations are very unlikely to recognise trade unions, at least at the early stage, until such time as contextual and environmental factors cause them to recognise trade unions (see Chapter 9).

Union Avoidance Strategies

Two very different strategies in relation to union avoidance may be adopted. The first of these may be described as the union suppression approach — for example, strenuously resisting union-organising drives, including the use of coercive tactics by managers to stay union free. The second is the union substitution approach which focuses on removing the triggers to unionisation within the organisation. According to Kochan et al. (1986), it was mainly the large companies which utilised union substitution strategies in the United States. Large firms with significant financial resources are in a situation where they can employ specialised personnel and employee relations staff who act as replacements for typical union-provided functions — such as grievance channels, due process, wage negotiations etc. — within the organisation. Firms which are unable to bear the costs of sophisticated approaches, including the development of a significant employee relations staffing ratio, are more likely to opt for the union-suppression approach. This is because of the fact that managers in such organisations hold doctrinaire neo-unitarist values which do not countenance trade unions as being relevant to their particular organisational context, and as a result unions are vehemently opposed. Some evidence of this can be found in the Irish context in the research done by McGovern (1989) which indicates that there is considerable opposition to union recognition amongst small hi-tech and service companies.

There is a range of environmental and organisational conditions which appear to increase the probability that an employer will choose the direct suppression approach to union avoidance (Kochan et al. 1986). Among these conditions are: the presence of a hostile social and political environment towards unions; employment of low-wage or unskilled workers with few labour-market alternatives; an abundant supply of alternative workers; lower recruitment and training costs; low profit in a highly competitive industry; smaller firms; the lack of professional personnel staff and the willingness to litigate union challenges through administrative and judicial procedures. It is extremely difficult to measure how many firms actively oppose unions through such direct suppression approaches. However, McGovern's (1989) research suggests that direct suppression tactics may have increased in Ireland over the past ten years.

Strategies to Reduce Incentives to Unionise

The alternative approach focuses on eliminating the triggers to unionisation — for example, poor supervision, perceived inequities, low levels of job security and comparatively low levels of pay. Strategies used to eliminate triggers to unionisation typically include some of the following (Kochan and Katz 1988):

(i)   Pay and conditions, including fringe benefits equal to or greater than those paid to workers employed in comparable industries and firms;

(ii) A high rate of investment by organisations in training and career development;

(iii) Considerable effort to create secure employment and avoid lay-offs as much as possible;

(iv) Sophisticated systems of organisational communications and information sharing;

(v) Informal mechanisms for or encouragement of participation in decision making about how the work is to be carried out;

(vi) Development of a psychological climate that fosters and rewards organisational loyalty and commitment;

(vii) Creation of a rational wage and salary administration, performance appraisal, and promotion systems which reward merit and also recognise seniority;

(viii) A non-union grievance procedure usually without binding arbitration;

(ix) Location of new production facilities in rural areas or in areas only sparsely unionised;

(x) Use of employee selection devices which weed out workers who might or might not be pro-union.

The purpose of these policies is to create a workforce of employees who are simultaneously satisfied with their economic rewards from work, the intrinsic aspects of their jobs and their ability to influence decisions having to do with their work. Some of the best examples among mature companies which apply the above soft human resource management approaches to retaining a non-union status include: International Business Machines (IBM), Eastman-Kodak, Digital Equipment, Motorola, Marks and Spencers, and Wang. Toner's (1985, 1987) studies of large non-union companies in Ireland show that these companies develop a strong corporate culture built upon their employment practices, which acts to reduce the perceived demand for unions amongst their employees. Given the nature of the Price Waterhouse data available, it is only possible to test for the union substitution strategy in the subsequent analysis.

Employee Relations, HRM Policies and Union Avoidance
Human resource policies and practices of the above type can be expected to have a significant impact upon whether firms recognise trade unions or not (Beaumont 1991; Fiorito et al. 1987; Guest 1987; Milner and

Richards 1991). There are several ways in which HRM policies and practices could act to reduce the incentives for unionisation. If we accept as a starting point that perceived inequities, dissatisfactions with the work environment and rewards can create a requirement amongst employees for unionisation, then one can begin to view HRM policies and practices as perhaps substituting for the functions and activities which trade union services supply. If good pay and conditions are provided, individual developmental and training needs are catered for, and if extensive communication, briefing and information services to employees exist, then one of the major functions of trade unions — namely the negotiation and improvement of such conditions and services — is eroded.

An explicit HR strategy often includes references to creating a culture and climate which creates a sense of "mutuality" amongst employees and managers at plant level. This can have the effect of reducing the demands for unionisation. Pay for performance systems which recognise individual contribution and merit have also been found (Toner 1987) to be a common feature in large non-union companies. The provision of career development and training opportunities in firms, plus an above-average expenditure on training is also a characteristic of large non-union companies. Selection methods designed to filter out people who are prone to unionise have also been found to be one of a battery of techniques used by non-union companies (Foulkes 1980). Briefing and communication techniques also might be expected to be more extensive in large non-union companies than in their unionised counterparts. The extent to which line managers are dominant within firms could also be expected to have a significant influence on the way in which HR policies and philosophies are developed and promulgated at the top level of the organisation. For example, Kochan et al. (1986) make the argument that during the 1970s human resource professionals lost ground to line managers and that the motivation actually to pursue non-union alternatives was felt first by line managers and high-level corporate executives, not by employee relations and HRM practitioners responsible for interaction and negotiations on union matters. Indeed, many employee relations professionals in the US, the UK and Ireland have risen to positions of influence within companies by virtue of the fact that there was a need to develop strong collective bargaining arrangements in order to produce quiescent trade union organisation at workplace level. As Kochan et al. (1986) argue, if line managers or top executives were to translate their preferences for the non-union option into an active organisational strategy they would need:

(i) To exert influence over those employee relations decisions that

would influence the future dependence on unionisation of the firm;
and

(ii) To enlist the aid of staff specialists who shared their union avoidance values and possessed the technical expertise to design effective
work systems which would make it difficult for trade unions to
organise.

The rise in behavioural-science-trained human resource management
specialists in the 1960s provided this staff support and expertise. Thus, it
could be expected that firms which have a strong line management
orientation would be less likely to recognise trade unions. In relation to
the Price Waterhouse data set, the human resource management variables
which we included in our analyses were:

(i) The extent to which line management dominance was in evidence
within companies;

(ii) The extent to which a variety of HRM practices were present within
companies.

The latter category included using extensive recruitment filters, the use
of performance-related pay for manual workers, budgetary expenditure
on training and development, the use of training needs analysis and the
presence of performance appraisal training for line managers, and the
extent to which briefing and communication methods were present
within organisations. In the former case, line dominance is measured by
the extent of influence of line managers on HRM areas and the presence
of performance-appraisal training for line managers. Finally, size of
organisation and the proportion of white collar workers in the workforce
are entered as standard control variables. Both variables have been
shown to have a significant impact on union recognition in a number of
studies (Beaumont and Harris 1989; Fiorito et al. 1987; Milner and
Richards 1991).

EVALUATING THE DEVELOPMENT OF THE NON–UNION PHENOMENON

A statistical analysis of the survey data revealed the following findings in
relation to these issues (see Appendix 1, Table 10A).

The location of a firm's market has no significant relationship upon
union recognition. However, industrial sector is an important factor in
non-unionism. Advanced manufacturing firms are negatively and significantly associated with union recognition, while firms in the second

traditional manufacturing category are positively associated with union-isation. A plausible interpretation of this result is that firms in the former manufacturing sector are operating in a more constantly changing market both nationally and internationally, and hence, trade unions are viewed as a potential obstacle to the development of flexible work patterns. The differential effects of manufacturing sector on union recognition tend to confirm the linkage between the external environment and unionisation.

Neither the existence of an explicit HRM strategy or the nature of managerial values appears to have any significant relationship to union recognition. Firms which do not recognise a trade union are no more likely to have a written policy on HRM strategy than other firms. The structural control variables of size and the proportion of clerical workers are, as predicted, both significantly related to unionisation. Any possi-bility that the impact of the HRM variables can be attributed to these structural factors is thus removed.

Turning to the HRM policies and practices, the relationship between both measures of line management dominance are significant and are in the direction predicted: negatively related to union recognition, i.e. line management involvement in HR policy areas is higher in non-union organisations. While the training budget expenditure fails to reach the required significance level, the coefficient is negative as predicted, that is, training expenditure tends to be higher in non-union establishments but is not significant in this particular analysis. Alternatively, the use of a training needs analysis is significant but is not in the direction predicted and is positively related to union recognition. The extent of communi-cation methods used also fails to reach significance, but the relationship is in the expected direction. Lastly, performance-related pay is negatively associated with union recognition and has the largest coefficient score. However, it is more likely that PRP schemes occur as a result of a non-union environment than as part of an active process of union substitution.

The results from the HRM practices measured provide limited support for the hypothesis that they are used to substitute for unions. But, it can be argued, a more critical factor is the centrality of line management in influencing HRM policy.

CONCLUSIONS

The maintenance of a non-union stance, particularly as practised by US manufacturing subsidiaries, is largely held (aside from the impact of structural and business-cycle effects) to be as a result of the union substi-tution policies adopted by such organisations. The location of an orga-nisations's market was found to have no significant impact on whether it recognises trade unions or not. The industry sector in which an organisation operates is seen as a significant indicator of a non-union stance. This is particularly evident in the manufacturing sector where advanced manufacturing firms, operating in uncertain competitive product markets, are predominately non-unionised, while traditional manufacturing organisations are positively associated with union recognition. Both the managerial values and the existence of explicit HR strategies were found to be insignificant in relation to the union/non-union debate. With respect to the relationship between non-unionism and HRM practices, line management dominance is significant and is seen to be negatively related to union recognition, i.e. line management involvement tends to be higher in non-unionised companies. As with earlier results, this analysis reveals that the range of communications methods used is largely attributable to non-unionised environments. Training expenditure tends to be positively associated with non-union organisations, with non-union establishments tending to spend more than their unionised counterparts. Finally, a significant positive relationship exists between the use of performance-related pay and a non-union stance. However, this is more likely to be the result of operating in a non-union environment than of an explicit union-substitution policy.

Empirically, the weakest link in our evaluation of the non-union phenomenon in this chapter is the absence of any relationship between union recognition and managerial values together with business strategy. As we have seen, in the manufacturing sector, the external environment is related to union recognition through the effects of the product market. Generally, firms producing electronic and computer-related products are less likely to recognise trade unions than firms in the more traditional product markets. Surprisingly, no relationship was found between union recognition and service sector. Given the small sample size, however, companies in diverse areas of the service sector were merged together, with the possibility that distinctive differences were submerged in the aggregate. In the case of HRM policies and practices where line management dominates, firms are less likely to recognise a union. Regarding the use of various HRM practices in order to substitute for a union, the results are less certain. Although the use of performance-related pay schemes for manual workers is the strongest distinguishing characteristic between union and non-union firms, it is unlikely to be part of a strategy or campaign to substitute or keep out unions. If the major weakness in the model tested is the mediating filter of managerial values, it must also be pointed out that the measures used from the data set are far from comprehensive and represent at best a crude substitution for more detailed and reliable measures. Even so, an empirical test of the

Kochan et al. theoretical framework does not fit the data as predicted. In particular, the crucial link consisting of managerial values does not appear to bridge the external environment and HRM practices regarding an integrated approach to trade unions. This is not necessarily a fatal blow to the model, partly for the reasons discussed above, but it is a serious challenge to its validity in a European context where trade unions have greater legitimacy and higher levels of union density than in the United States.

Chapter 11

CONCLUSIONS

INTRODUCTION

There is little doubt that there have been changes in employee relations over the course of the 1980s. This is clearly evidenced by key recurrent themes in the management literature over the decade. During the decade, several factors achieved prominence which altered the context within which employee relations take place. Among the most notable of these were: general economic recession; persistently high levels of unemployment; the growth of the services sector, often typified by low collective representation; and the growth of non-standard employment forms. Though many of these trends were present prior to the 1980s, they have become increasingly salient in recent years and have exerted a significant influence on the nature and conduct of employee relations.

However, there is some confusion about the precise direction and extent of change in employee relations, with arguments oscillating between gradual incrementalism, and a complete transformation leading to radical path-breaking developments. Some commentators argue that these developments are prefacing a fundamental shift in power relationships within employee relations, thereby allowing an increasing management withdrawal from reliance on "union-management relations" based on collective bargaining and the substitution of a more individualised approach to management-employee relations (Dastmalachian et al. 1991). Employee relations management in Ireland has traditionally been associated with strong collectivist principles. In the terminology of the Donovan analysis, employee relations in Ireland has been grounded in traditional pluralist principles, described by Bill Roche (1990) thus:

> Over a wide range of industries and services, employers and unions have conducted their relations on the basis of the premise that their interests were in significant respects different and in opposition.... These differences of interest were reconciled on an ongoing basis through collective bargaining pure and simple.

In this pluralist model, management responsibility for employee relations in most larger organisations is vested in the specialist personnel function whose role is essentially reactive and short term in perspective; employee relations is the primary personnel activity, with the personnel function acting as the guardian of procedures and negotiator of employee relations harmony, through its responsibility for managing relations with the unions.

Overall, many of the commentaries on the pervasiveness of change in employee relations are vague on what exactly has changed and on the extent of such change. This research is an attempt to clarify aspects of the debate in Ireland.

EMPLOYEE RELATIONS

What then is the evidence for change? With respect to workplace employee relations, the research evidence presented in this book suggests that developments in business strategy and product markets are indeed creating greater organisational awareness of the impact of employee relations issues on organisational performance. In particular, it would appear that employers are increasingly seeking to adapt selected Human Resource Management (HRM) techniques. However, there is little evidence to support the widespread adoption of comprehensive HRM approaches. Rather, it appears that where HRM initiatives are adopted, this is occurring alongside, rather than in place of, collective bargaining. Indeed, the evidence from this research suggests that levels of trade union recognition, density and influence in Irish organisations remain quite robust, and that the pluralist model is alive and well. It would appear therefore that established employee relations institutions and approaches have remained largely intact and will continue to have relevance in the 1990s. However, it is clear also that selected HRM initiatives (initiatives for the pursuit of higher quality standards, employee involvement initiatives, direct communication mechanisms, etc.) will alter the nature of employee relations practice at the workplace level.

SPECIALIST PERSONNEL FUNCTION

It has also been suggested that there has been a reappraisal of the functioning and legitimacy of the personnel/human resource function in recent years. We examined the personnel function under four headings, namely, presence, role, activities and characteristics. The evidence indicates that the function is a central operating tenet among a majority of responding organisations and maintains a central role in workplace employee relations. However, trade union recognition, organisational size and ownership were seen to have a significant impact on the existence or otherwise of a dedicated personnel function, with unionised organisations — those of US or Japanese origin and larger organisations — more likely to have a specialist function. The current evidence points to the personnel practitioner occupying a prominent position in the organisational hierarchy. Personnel specialists in US-owned organisations are the most likely to operate at a strategic level. Furthermore, the data reveal that personnel specialists in non-unionised environments are less likely to be involved in the early stages of strategy formulation than those in unionised organisations. Finally, one of the most dramatic changes in the recent past in this sphere has been the large increase in line-management involvement in personnel activities, particularly in the area of employee relations.

A shift in emphasis in recent years appears to have occurred, where traditionally, employee relations and related matters had been the most pressing areas of concern for the personnel function. However, our research suggests that employee relations considerations rank only fifth in terms of priority areas, behind training and development, communications, quality, and health and safety. However, it is important to note that many of activities, such as quality or communications, have a significant employee relations dimension.

REWARD PRACTICES

Turning to the area of reward practices, the data illustrate that pay determination for most non-managerial employees is still conducted at national level, mainly under the terms and conditions of the Programme for Economic and Social Progress. Rewards for managerial employees, as has traditionally been the case, are predominantly determined at the level of the organisation. Overall, despite the fact that pay was determined outside the firm in a majority of cases, this did not mean that organisations were of necessity taking a "hands-off" approach. The results indicate an increased tendency towards linking the fortunes of individuals more closely to those of the firm, through the utilisation of variable pay mechanisms. This trend was most evident in the private sector.

The results also demonstrate an increased interest in the use of financial incentives. Such incentives varied not only on the basis of the criteria for reward allocation, but also on the actual aims such schemes sought to achieve. Merit/performance-related pay emerges as the most commonly used incentive among organisations, particularly for manual and clerical employees. US-owned organisations were, on the whole, far more likely than their Irish- or UK-owned counterparts to use this incentive mechanism. The utilisation of other incentives remains relatively low in the Irish context.

INTERNAL LABOUR MARKETS

On the issue of internal labour markets (ILMs), the data reveal that the use of internal advertising to fill manual positions is positively associated with firms which recognise a trade union and which have a strong personnel function. Trade Union Recognition emerges as a key variable associated with internal advertising for manual positions, being almost twice as important as having a written personnel strategy. Contrary to expectations, sector and size do not appear to be important determinants of the use of internal advertising to fill manual positions.

With respect to recruitment and selection in general, the data confirm that organisations have little difficulty in attracting candidates, given the current state of the labour market. Application forms, the interview and reference checks emerge as the most popular selection tools, with relatively little use being made of mechanisms such as psychometric testing. With respect to gender in recruitment, the data suggest that relatively few organisations specifically target women in the recruitment process.

Expenditure on training and development for all employee categories has increased over the past three years, a factor which may be determined by environmental factors impacting on the organisation. The data also reveal that the number of days' training received decreases as one moves down the organisational hierarchy. In terms of priority areas, staff communication emerges as the area in which most managers have been trained over the past three years. Finally, line-management responsibility for training and development policy decisions has increased, reflecting the trend of decentralisation of core personnel activities noted above.

FLEXIBILITY

There appears to have been a general increase in flexibility in recent years, but it appears to be occurring in a relatively incremental piecemeal fashion, rather than as a systematically planned emergence of the totally flexible firm. This relative stability is in some ways surprising as the state of the labour market clearly facilitates the use of such non-standard employment strategies. However, it is suggested that this gradual move towards greater flexibility has two key implications for the nature and conduct of employee relations. Firstly, previous research suggests that individuals employed on a non-standard basis can be expected to seek trade union membership, whereas trade union influence may in fact decline for core employees. Secondly, research indicates that those organisations which employ on a non-standard basis may experience dual patterns of individual conflict, i.e. low levels amongst core employees and higher levels amongst those in non-standard employment. Further research is clearly necessary to explore such issues effectively.

SMALL FIRMS

Turning to the situation in small firms, it is suggested that despite the widespread view that employee relations in small firms are harmonious, the "small is beautiful" philosophy has been much criticised in recent years. Trade union recognition among small firms in Ireland appears high, relative to the situation in the UK and the US. Such recognition is highest in small firms in the public sector. However, density appears low, perhaps reflecting the reluctance on the part of the trade union movement to organise in the smaller firm. With respect to changing trade union influence in the small firm sector, a majority maintains that it has remained the same or indeed increased over the past three years.

Small firms appear to exhibit a somewhat haphazard approach to recruitment and to the maintenance of records, particularly in relation to employee turnover. This clearly mitigates against the adoption of a more strategic approach in employment matters. While some analysis of training effectiveness is carried out, there is a heavy reliance on informal methods among small firms.

The results on reward practices in small firms are as might be expected, with individual determination governing pay rates for managerial and professional/technical employees.

NEWLY ESTABLISHED (GREENFIELD) FIRMS

In relation to the evidence on Greenfield sites, the research suggests that management approaches to employee relations in foreign-owned Greenfield companies incorporate characteristics of HRM, most notably among US-owned companies. Such organisations demonstrate more proactive managerial styles and place a greater emphasis on individualist management–employee relations. The evidence on Greenfield sites also points to the emergence of a vibrant non-union sector among such companies. It is suggested that this trend is likely to be accentuated by the increasing numbers and visibility of companies successfully pursuing this non-union route.

THE NON-UNION PHENOMENON

On the non-union phenomenon specifically, it is suggested that such companies have become a significant reality because the climate has changed, allowing non-unionism to "come out of the closet". One of the key reasons for this new openness appears to be the increasing confidence of non-union companies themselves. Using the research evidence to test a theoretical framework which attempts to explain the emergence of the contemporary non-union phenomenon, it was found that the location of the firms market has no significant relationship to union recognition. However, advanced manufacturing firms were negatively associated with union recognition, while traditional manufacturing firms were positively associated with unionisation. It is suggested that advanced manufacturing firms may be operating in more turbulent and dynamic product market conditions, and that trade union presence might inhibit the emergence of the flexibility required.

With respect to the relationship between non-unionism and HRM practices, line-management dominance is significant and is seen to be negatively related to union recognition, while performance-related pay is negatively associated with union recognition, occurring as a result of the non-union environment itself, rather than as a union substitution mechanism.

CONCLUDING COMMENTS

Overall, therefore, it appears that while the context of employee relations in Ireland is indeed changing, there remains a strong sense of continuity. In relation to the adoption of HRM techniques, it does not seem plausible to suggest that organisations will jettison all past practice in favour of such techniques, and by implication, that HRM is about to replace the traditional pluralist model of employee relations. There is simply insufficient evidence to support this "post-modernist" hypothesis that we are moving to a new paradigm of work relationships and employer–employee interactions. It would appear more plausible to argue that what we are witnessing is a dualist approach, with HRM techniques co-existing with, rather than replacing, traditional employee relations practices. While it is evident that some aspects of employee relations have altered noticeably in recent years, others have demonstrated a surprising imperviousness to change.

APPENDIX 1

TABLE 2A: DETERMINANTS OF UNION DENSITY AT ESTABLISHMENT LEVEL

Variables**	Equations	
	1	2
SIZE	.37 (3.52)‡	.2 (2.75)†
SECTOR	.2 (1.88)	.56 (6.8)‡
WC	-.06 (-0.5)	-.24 (-3.0)‡
MARKET	.02 (0.22)	
STATUS	-.16 (-1.5)	
PARTIME	.06 (0.62)	
COSTS		
US	-.09 (-0.8)	
Irish	.07 (0.64)	
EC	-.12 (-1.2)	
INDUSTRY		
AGRIC	.15 (2.2)*	
TMANUF	.22 (2.1)‡	29 (3.9)‡
TRANS		
BANK		
0		
R2(adjusted)	.21	.35
F Ratio	11‡	12‡

* $< .05$
† $< .01$
‡ $< .001$
t statistic in parentheses

** The absence of a statistical result for a variable indicates that the variable is not included in the equation. Exceptions are Industry type where for convenience only statistically significant variables are printed.

189

**TABLE 2A: DETERMINANTS OF UNION DENSITY
AT ESTABLISHMENT LEVEL (VARIABLE LIST)**

	Variable List
UNION DENSITY	1='1–25%' 2='26–50%' 3='51–75%' 4='76–100%'
SECTOR	1 = public sector, 0 = private sector
SIZE	1 to 9 for employee numbers from 1–5,000+
WC	1 to 6 indicating increasing proportion of white-collar employees
PARTIME	1 to 8 indicating increasing proportion of part-time to full time employees
STATUS	1 = multi-establishment, 0 = single establishment
MARKET*	1 = home market, 0 = international market
ORIGIN	1 = 'US' 2 = 'Ireland' 3 = 'EC' 4 = 'rest'
COSTS	1 to 6 indicating increasing labour costs to total costs
INDUSTRY	
AGRIC	Agriculture; Hunting; Fishing; Forestry
TMANUF**	Traditional Manufacturing
TRANS	Transport and Communication
BANK	Banking; Finance and Insurance

*   Given the small size of the Irish economy establishments are divided into those who produce for the home market and those who export to other countries.

** The absence of a statistical result for a variable indicates that the variable is not included in the equation. Exceptions are Industry type where for convenience only statistically significant variables are printed.

Source: Price Waterhouse Cranfield Project (Ireland); University of Limerick, 1992.

TABLE 2B: FACTORS DISTINGUISHING RECOGNITION FROM NON-RECOGNITION (LOGIT REGRESSION METHOD)

Variables	Equations	
	1	2
SIZE	.28 (2.7)**	.29 (2.4)*
WHITE COLLAR	-.2 (-2.03)*	-.2 (-1.83)
MARKET	-.008 (0.02)	-.03 (-.09)
STATUS	.14 (0.4)	.23 (0.62)
US**	-.3 (-0.87)	.02 (0.04)
Rest	4.27 (0.28)	4.4 (0.3)
EC	-.13 (-0.3)	-.28 (-0.6)
Industry***		
Finance and Banking	-1.67 (-2.6)†	-1.9 (-2.7)†
Advanced Manufacturing	-.97 (-2.67)†	-1.1 (-2.7)†
HRM Variables		
Communications		-.03 (-0.1)
Training		-.51 (-1.8)
Pay Systems		-.64 (-2.1)*
Functional FLEXI		.09 (0.32)
Numerical FLEXI		-.23 (-0.6)
HRM Strategy		-.2 (-0.7)
CHISQ	143	169
DF	(134)	(127)
R2(pseudo)	.48	.52

*   P< .05

†   P< .01

‡   P< .001

**   All coefficients indicate the difference between Ireland which is equivalent to the constant and other countries impact on the dependent variable.

*** Traditional manufacturing is equal to the constant to which all other can be compared.

Source: Price Waterhouse Cranfield Project (Ireland); University of Limerick, 1992.

TABLE 3A: EFFECTS OF HRM PRACTICES ON UNION DENSITY IN ESTABLISHMENTS

Variables	Equations	
	3	4
SIZE	.18 (2.7)†	.22 (3.2)†
SECTOR	.44 (5.4)‡	.48 (6.0)†
WC	-.25 (-3.4)‡	-.23 (-3.0)‡
MANUF	31 (4.5)‡	.3 (4.2)‡
TRANS	.15 (2.4)*	.15 (2.4)*
AGRIC	.13 (2.0)*	.14 (2.1)*
R(2)	.42	.38
F ratio	15‡	14‡

*   < .05
†   < .01
‡   < .001
t statistic in parentheses
Source: Price Waterhouse Cranfield Project (Ireland); University of Limerick, 1992.

TABLE 3B: UNION PRESENCE AND HRM PRACTICES

PAY	-.3 (-4.5)‡
BUDGET	.044 (0.7)
FLEXI	-.01 (-0.2)
NUMERI	.00 (0.14)
STRAT	-.09 (-0.37)
HRM	-.22 (3.2)†
HRM Variables	
STRATEGY	1 = Written HRM strategy, 0 = none
BUDGET	1 = Training budget greater than 5%
PAY SCHEMES	1 = Existence of performance pay and profit sharing, 0 = none
COMMUN	1 = Briefing on financial strategy for employees, 0 = none
FLEXI	1 = jobs made wider/more flexible over last 3 years, 0 = no change
NUMERIC	1 = over 20% of workforce, 0 = less than 20%

Source: Price Waterhouse Cranfield Project (Ireland); University of Limerick, 1992.

TABLE 3C: WORKING DAYS LOST — STRIKES 1946–92

Year	Working Days Lost
1946	15,018
1956	48,089
1966	783,635
1970	1,007,714
1975	295,716
1980	412,118
1982	434,253
1984	386,412
1986	315,550
1988	130,000
1990	204,000
1991	82,960
1992	189,623

Source : Department of Labour/UCD.

TABLE 4A: TRADE UNION RECOGNITION AS A DETERMINANT OF THE ROLE OF LINE MANAGERS IN EMPLOYEE RELATIONS

	Trade Union Recognised	Trade Union Not Recognised	Missing
Increased	30.0	19.3	40.0
Same	60.4	66.7	60.0
Decreased	3.4	7.0	—
Missing	6.3	7.0	—

Source: Price Waterhouse Cranfield Project (Ireland); University of Limerick, 1992.

TABLE 4B: ORGANISATIONAL SIZE AS A DETERMINANT OF THE ROLE OF LINE MANAGERS IN EMPLOYEE RELATIONS

	1–100	100–200	201–300	301–400	401–500	500–1,000	1,001–2,000	2,000+
Increased	19.0	20.0	37.1	35.0	33.3	34.4	11.1	50.0
Same	63.1	74.0	54.3	55.0	61.1	56.3	88.9	44.4
Decreased	8.3	4.0	2.9	5.0	—	—	—	—
Missing	9.5	2.0	5.7	5.0	5.6	9.4	—	5.6

Source: Price Waterhouse Cranfield Project (Ireland); University of Limerick, 1992.

TABLE 4C: ORGANISATION SECTOR AS AN INDICATOR OF TOP PRACTITIONER EXPERIENCE

	Private	Public
> 1 Year	1.6%	5.2%
1–5 Years	13.1%	24.1%
5+ YEARS	41.0%	27.6%
Missing	44.3%	43.1%

Source: Price Waterhouse Cranfield Project (Ireland); University of Limerick, 1992.

TABLE 5A: CHANGE IN NON-MONEY BENEFITS BY SECTOR

	Private	Public
Increased	28.8% (49)	—
Decreased	1.8% (3)	—
No Change	65.3% (111)	96.0% (48)

Actual numbers in parenthesis.
Source: Price Waterhouse Cranfield Project (Ireland); University of Limerick, 1992.

TABLE 5B: CHANGE IN THE USE OF NON-MONEY BENEFITS IN UNIONISED AND NON-UNIONISED ORGANISATIONS

	Trade Union Recognised	Trade Union Not Recognised
Increased	18.0% (34)	37.7% (20)
Decreased	2.1% (4)	—
No Change	75.7% (143)	60.4% (32)
Don't Know	4.2% (8)	1.9% (1)

Actual numbers in parenthesis.
Source: Price Waterhouse Cranfield Project (Ireland); University of Limerick, 1992.

TABLE 5C: CHANGE IN THE USE OF NON-MONEY BENEFITS BY COMPANY ORIGIN

	Rep. of Ireland	UK	USA
Increased	15.6%	35.7%	31.3%
Decreased	0.7%	—	2.1%
No Change	79.4%	64.3%	62.5%
Don't Know	4.3%	—	4.2%

N= 141   N=14   N= 48

Source: Price Waterhouse Cranfield Project (Ireland); University of Limerick, 1992.

TABLE 5D: RELATIONSHIP BETWEEN ORGANISATION SIZE AND THE INCIDENCE OF INDIVIDUAL/BONUS COMMISSION

	1–100	101–200	201–300	301–400	401–500	501–1,000	1,001–2,000	2,000+
Managerial	32.1	30.0	20.0	25.0	27.8	37.5	33.3	27.8
Prof./Tech	23.8	22.0	20.0	20.0	27.8	18.8	44.4	16.7
Clerical	19.0	10.0	11.4	10.0	16.7	9.4	11.1	11.1
Manual	8.3	12.0	11.4	15.0	22.2	6.3	33.3	11.1

Source: Price Waterhouse Cranfield Project (Ireland); University of Limerick, 1992.

TABLE 5E: RELATIONSHIP BETWEEN ORGANISATION SIZE AND THE INCIDENCE OF PROFIT-SHARING SCHEMES

	1–100	101–200	201–300	301–400	401–500	501–1,000	1,001–2,000	2,000+
Managerial	15.5	18.0	14.3	15.0	16.7	18.8	—	11.1
Prof./Tech	10.7	14.0	11.4	15.0	11.1	15.6	—	5.6
Clerical	9.5	8.0	8.6	15.0	16.7	15.6	—	5.6
Manual	7.1	8.0	8.6	15.0	11.1	15.6	—	5.6

N=84   N=50   N=35   N=20   N=18   N=32   N=9   N=18

Source: Price Waterhouse Cranfield Project (Ireland); University of Limerick, 1992.

TABLE 5F: PROFIT-SHARING IN UNIONISED AND NON-UNIONISED ENVIRONMENTS

	Trade Union Recognised	Trade Union Not Recognised	Missing
Managerial	14.0	21.1	—
Prof./Technical	10.6	15.8	—
Clerical	9.2	14.0	—
Manual	8.7	10.5	—

Source: Price Waterhouse Cranfield Project (Ireland); University of Limerick, 1992.

TABLE 5G: UTILISATION OF EMPLOYEES SHARE SCHEMES IN IRELAND, UK AND FDR

Country	Specific Law and Year Introduced	Prevalent Types	No. of Schemes/ Firms	Employees Involved	Employee Benefits	General Attitude	Tax Benefits
Ireland	SPS(1982)	SPS	139 schemes	Executives	Probably high	Favour-able	Modest
	SO (1986)	SO	87	35,000	Probably high	Favour-able	Modest
UK	SPS '78, SO '80, DSO '84, CPS '87, ESOPs '88, ESO '78	DSO, CPS, SPS, SO, ESOPs	7,282 schemes 30% of firms	2 million employees	Various	Very favour-able	Sub-stantial for firms and em-ployees
FDR	Some; on DPS since 1961;	ESO, DPS	1,600 firms	1.3 million	5% of firms annual balance	Mainly Favour-able	Minor till '84
	on ESO since 1984	PS	5,000 mainly small firms	5.4% of employees	6.8% of wages	Mainly Favour-able	none

SPS = share-based profit sharing,
SO = share options
DSO = discretionary share option
CPS = cash-based profit sharing
ESOPs = employee share ownership plans
ESO = employee stock options.
Source: Adapted from Festinger; IRN 36, 1990.

TABLE 6A: RECRUITMENT METHODS AND COMPANY SIZE

Recruitment Method	Managerial		Professional/Technical	
	<200	>200	<200	>200
From among Current Employees	46%	60%	30%	41%
Advertise Internally	38%	46%	37%	41%
Advertise Externally	68%	64%	70%	68%
Recruitment Agencies	42%	40%	44%	42%
Search/Selection Consultants	31%	38%	19%	28%
Job Centres	0.8%	—	0.8%	1%
Apprentices	—	—	10%	9%
	N=125	N=138	N=125	N=138

Source: Price Waterhouse Cranfield Project (Ireland); University of Limerick, 1992.

TABLE 6B: SELECTION METHODS BY ORGANISATIONAL SIZE

	Selection Methods							
Size	Appl. Forms	Interview Panel	References	Biodata Test	Psych. Test	Aptitude Centre	Assess. Selec	Group
<200	87%	90%	93%	3%	9%	22%	2%	6%
>200	88%	83%	86%	7%	29%	41%	7%	8%

N (<200) = 125
N (>200) = 138
Source: Price Waterhouse Cranfield Project (Ireland); University of Limerick, 1992.

TABLE 6C: INCREASED SPENDING ON TRAINING BY SIZE

	1–100	101–200	201–300	301–400	401–500	501–1,000	1,001–2,000	2,001+
Mgt.	29.8%	52%	51.4%	65%	66.7%	62.5%	55.6%	55.6%
Prof.	31%	54%	48.6%	60%	55.6%	43.8%	55.6%	61.1%
Cler.	27.4%	52%	42.9%	55%	50%	40.6%	55.6%	38.9%
Man.	17.9%	38%	37.1%	35%	55.6%	50%	44.4%	50%
N	84	54	35	20	18	32	9	18

N=266
Source: Price Waterhouse Cranfield Project (Ireland); University of Limerick, 1992.

TABLE 6D: ANALYSIS OF TRAINING NEEDS BY ORGANISATION SIZE

	1–100	101–200	201–300	301–400	401–500	501–1,000	1,001–2,000	2,001+
Yes	52.4%	60%	54.3%	75%	77.8%	84.4%	100%	83.3%
	(44)	(30)	(19)	(15)	(14)	(27)	(9)	(15)
No	45.2%	40%	45.7%	10%	16.7%	15.6%	0	16.7%
	(38)	(20)	(16)	(2)	(3)	(5)		(3)
Don't Know	2.4%	0	0	15%	1.1%	0	0	0
	(2)			(3)	(1)			

Actual number of firms in parenthesis.
Source: Price Waterhouse Cranfield Project (Ireland); University of Limerick, 1992.

TABLE 6E: ANALYSIS OF TRAINING NEEDS: PUBLIC *V.* PRIVATE AND UNIONISED *V.* NON-UNIONISED

	Private	Public	Unionised	Non Union
Yes	69.4%	53.4%	68.1%	52.6%
No	28.4%	44.8%	29.5%	45.6%

Missing cases = 5
Source: Price Waterhouse Cranfield Project (Ireland); University of Limerick, 1992.

TABLE 6F: FACTORS AFFECTING THE PRESENCE OF INTERNAL RECRUITMENT AND STANDARD WAGE/SALARY SYSTEMS

Dependent Variable:

Vacancies Advertised Internally	(1 = Yes, 0 = No)
Standard Wage System	(1 = Yes, 0 = No)

	Internal Advert		Standard Wages	
Equation	1	2	3	4
	Manual	**Clerical**	**Manual**	**Clerical**
Variables				
Sector	.24 (1.0)	1.00 (0.4)	.48 (0.8)	.69 (1.6)
Size	.01 (0.1)	.06 (1.6)	.06 (0.8)	.01 (0.2)
Recognition	.56 (2.0)*	.07 (0.3)	.87 (2.4)*	.39 (1.4)
Union Level	.03 (-0.4)	.09 (1.3)	.1 (1.3)	.1 (1.3)
HR Strategy	.31 (2.1)*	.34 (2.3)*	.7 (-3.1)†	.6 (3.8)‡
HR Control	.07 (2.3)*	.05 (-1.1)	.04 (1.2)	.04 (-1.2)
Pseudo R2	.49	.50	.45	.47
Chisq.	256	265	222	238
DF	(245)	(246)	(246)	(146)

* $P<.05$
† $P<.01$
‡ $P<.001$

Source: Price Waterhouse Cranfield Project (Ireland); University of Limerick, 1992.

TABLE 7A: PROPORTION OF WORKFORCE ON NON-STANDARD CONTRACTS: (i) PRIVATE

	Private			
	<1%	1–10%	11–20%	>20%
Part-time	45% (83)	27% (50)	3% (5)	6% (10)
Temporary/Casual	32% (58)	43% (78)	7% (12)	4% (8)
Fixed Term	41% (75)	20% (37)	2% (4)	10% (19)
Home Work	46% (84)	1% (2)	—	—
Government Training Scheme	48% (87)	9% (17)	—	—

Actual numbers in parenthesis.

Source: Price Waterhouse Cranfield Project (Ireland); University of Limerick, 1992.

TABLE 7A: PROPORTION OF WORKFORCE ON NON-STANDARD CONTRACTS: (ii) PUBLIC

Public				
	<1%	1–10%	11–20%	>20%
Part-time	24% (14)	41% (24)	10% (6)	5% (3)
Temporary/Casual	16% (9)	50% (29)	12% (7)	7% (4)
Fixed Term	31% (18)	24% (14)	14% (8)	17% (10)
Home Work	55% (32)	43% (25)	—	—
Government Training Scheme	48% (28)	17% (10)	—	—

Actual numbers in parenthesis.
Source: Price Waterhouse Cranfield Project (Ireland); University of Limerick, 1992.

TABLE 7B: PROPORTION OF WORKFORCE ON NON STANDARD CONTRACTS: (i) UNION

Union				
	<1%	1–10%	11–20%	>20%
Part-time	48% (83)	37% (64)	6% (11)	8% (13)
Temporary/Casual	29% (51)	54% (95)	9% (16)	6% (3)
Fixed Term	48% (78)	26% (42)	6% (10)	19% (30)
Home Work	93% (92)	1% (1)	—	1% (1)
Government Training Scheme	79% (100)	17% (22)	—	—

Actual numbers in parenthesis.
Source: Price Waterhouse Cranfield Project (Ireland); University of Limerick, 1992.

TABLE 7B: PROPORTION OF WORKFORCE ON NON STANDARD CONTRACTS: (ii) NON-UNION

Non-union				
	<1%	1–10%	11–20%	>20%
Part-time	55% (22)	33% (13)	8% (3)	5% (2)
Temporary/Casual	39% (18)	44% (20)	13% (6)	4% (2)
Fixed Term	46% (19)	32% (13)	5% (2)	12% (5)
Home Work	89% (25)	4% (1)	—	—
Government Training Scheme	69% (24)	20% (7)	3% (1)	3% (1)

Actual numbers in parenthesis.
Source: Price Waterhouse Cranfield Project (Ireland); University of Limerick, 1992.

TABLE 7C: PROPORTION OF WORKFORCE ON NON-STANDARD CONTRACTS BY OWNERSHIP: (i) IRISH

	Irish			
	<1%	1–10%	11–20%	>20%
Part-time	41% (53)	42% (54)	9% (11)	8% (10)
Temporary/Casual	28% (35)	54% (67)	10% (12)	7% (9)
Fixed Term	47% (54)	25% (29)	8% (9)	18% (21)
Home Work	92% (67)	2% (1)	—	2% (1)
Government Training Scheme	76% (73)	19% (18)	—	1% (1)

Actual numbers in parenthesis.

Source: Price Waterhouse Cranfield Project (Ireland); University of Limerick, 1992.

TABLE 7C: PROPORTION OF WORKFORCE ON NON-STANDARD CONTRACTS BY OWNERSHIP: (ii) UK

	UK			
	<1%	1–10%	11–20%	>20%
Part-time	39% (5)	46% (6)	—	15% (2)
Temporary/Casual	33% (4)	58% (7)	8% (1)	—
Fixed Term	50% (5)	30% (3)	—	20% (2)
Home Work	100% (7)	—	—	—
Government Training Scheme	78% (7)	22% (2)	—	—

Actual numbers in parenthesis.

Source: Price Waterhouse Cranfield Project (Ireland); University of Limerick, 1992.

TABLE 7C: PROPORTION OF WORKFORCE ON NON-STANDARD CONTRACTS BY OWNERSHIP: (iii) US

	US			
	<1%	1–10%	11–20%	>20%
Part-time	68% (26)	21% (8)	5% (2)	3% (1)
Temporary/Casual	29% (14)	54% (26)	13% (6)	4% (2)
Fixed Term	55% (24)	34% (15)	5% (2)	5% (2)
Home Work	93% (27)	—	—	—
Government Training Scheme	80% (24)	13% (4)	—	—

Actual numbers in parenthesis.

Source: Price Waterhouse Cranfield Project (Ireland); University of Limerick, 1992.

TABLE 10A: FACTORS AFFECTING UNION/NON-UNIONISM

External Environment	Beta Coefficients			t-Ratio
Product Market		.18		0.6
Utilities		.06		0.2
Services		.30		-0.9
Advanced Manufacturing*		-.89		-2.5
Other		.76		1.6
Business Strategy				
Explicit HRM Strategy		0.49		1.5
Managerial Values				
Country of Origin	US		-0.44	-1.2
	Ireland		-0.40	-1.3
	Rest of World	4.0		0.3
Structural Control Variables		0.17		2.1
Company Size		0.17		2.1*
White-collar Employees (%)		-0.25		-3.0†
E.R./HRM Policies and Practices				
Line Management Dominance		-0.12		-2.4*
Performance Appraisal Training		-0.80		-2.5*
Recruitment Filters		0.1		1.9
Training Budget Expenditure		-0.18		-2.5*
Training Needs Analysis		0.55		2.1*
Communications Methods		-0.09		-0.7
Performance Related Pay		-1.11		-3.4‡
Intercept		5.3		7.23‡

Df: 164
* P<.05
† P<.01
‡ P<.001

Source: Price Waterhouse Cranfield Project (Ireland); University of Limerick, 1992.

BIBLIOGRAPHY

Abowd, J., (1989), "The Effect of Wage Bargains on the Stock Market Value of the Firm", *American Economic Review*, September.

Appelbaum, S. and Shapiro, B., (1991), "Pay For Performance: Implementation of Individual and Group Plans", *Journal of Management Development*, Vol. 10, No. 7.

Armstrong, M. and Murlis H., (1986), *Reward Management, A Handbook of Salary Administration*, Kogan Page in association with the IPM & Peat Marwick McLantock.

Ashton, P., (1984), *Management in the Organisation: Analysis and Action*, Macmillan.

Atkinson, A.J., (1984), *Flexible Manning: The Way Ahead*, Institute of Manpower Studies.

Atkinson, J., (1984), "Manpower Strategies for Flexible Organisations", *Personnel Management*, August.

Atkinson, J. and Meager, N., (1986), "Is Flexibility Just a Flash in the Pan?", *Personnel Management*, September.

Bain, G.S. and Elias, (1985), "Trade Union Membership in Great Britain: An Individual Level Analysis", British Journal of Industrial Relations, Vol. 23, No. 4.

Bain, G.S. and Elsheikh, F., (1979), *Union Growth and the Business Cycle*, Basil Blackwell.

Bain, G.S. and Elsheikh, F., (1980), "Unionisation in Britain: An Interestablishment Analysis Based on Survey Data", British Journal of Industrial Relations, Vol. 18, No. 2.

Bain, G.S. and Price, R., (1983), "Union Growth: Dimensions, Determinants and Density", in G.S. Bain (ed.), *Industrial Relations in Britain*, Basil Blackwell.

Balkin, D. and Gomez-Mejia, L., (1987), (eds.), *New Perspectives on Compensation*, Prentice Hall.

Barbash, J., (1984), *The Elements of Industrial Relations*, University of Wisconsin Press.

Barrow, M. and Loughlin, H., (1992), "Towards a Learning Organisation: 1. The Rationale", *Industrial and Commercial Training*, Vol. 24, No. 1.

Bassett, P., (1986), *Strike Free,* Macmillan.

Beaumont, P., (1987), *The Decline of Trade Union Organisation*, Croom Helm.

Beaumont, P., (1991), "Trade Unions and HRM", *Industrial Relations Journal*, Vol. 22, No. 4.

Beaumont, P. and Gregory, M., (1980), "The Role of Employers in Britain", Industrial Relations Journal, Vol. 11, No. 5.

Beaumont, P. and Harris, R., (1989), "The North–South Divide in Britain, The Case of Trade Union Recognition", *Oxford Bulletin of Economics and Statistics*, 51.

Becker, B., (1987), "Concession Bargaining, The Impact on Shareholders' Equity", *Industrial and Labour Relations Review*, 40.

Becker, B. and Olson, C.A., (1986), "The Impact of Strikes on Shareholders' Equity", *Industrial and Labour Relations Review*, 39.

Beer, M., Spector, B., Lawrence, P., Mills, D. and Walton, R., (1985), *Human Resource Management: A General Manager's Perspective*, The Free Press.

Beer, M., et al., (1984), *Managing Human Assets*, Collier Macmillan.

Berridge, J., (1992), "Human Resource Management in Britain", *Employee Relations*, Vol. 14, No. 5.

Bevan, S. and Thompson M., (1991), "How are Companies Interpreting Performance Management?", *Personnel Management*, November.

Blackburn, R. and Hankinson, A., (1989), "Training in the Smaller Business, Investment or Expense?", *Industrial and Commercial Training*, Vol. 21, March/April.

Blackburn, R., A. and Mann, D., (1979), *The Working Class in the Labour Market*, Macmillan.

Booth, A., (1986), "Estimating the Probability of Trade Union Membership, A Study of Men and Women in Britain", *Economica*, 53.

Bowey, A. and Thorpe, R., (1986), *Payment Systems and Productivity*, Macmillan.

Breen, R., et al., (1990), *Understanding Contemporary Ireland*, Gill and Macmillan.

Brewster, C. and Bournois, F., (1991), "Human Resource Management, A European Perspective", *Personnel Review*, Vol. 20, No. 6.

Brinkerhoff, R., (1988), "An Integrated Evaluation Model of HRD", *Training and Development Journal*, February.

Brown, W., (ed.), (1981), *The Changing Contours of British Industrial Relations*, Blackwell.

Brown, C. and Medoff, J., (1978), "Trade Unions in the Production Process", *Journal of Political Economy*, 86 (3).

Buckley, R. and Caple, J., (1990), *The Theory and Practice of Training*, Kogan Page.

Buzzell, R.B. and Gale, B.T., (1987), *The PIMS Principles, Linking Strategy to Performance*, The Free Press.

Callan, T. and Farrell, B., (1991), *Women's Participation in the Irish Labour Market*, NESC.

Cappelli, P. and McKersie, R., (1987), "Management Strategy in the Re-design of Workrules", *Journal of Management Studies*, 24, September.

Carruth, A. and Disney, R., (1988), "Where Have Two Million Trade Union Members Gone?", *Economica, 55*.

Clarke, E., (1984), "Unionisation and Firm Performance; The Impact on Profits, Grown and Productivity", *American Economic Review*, 24, (4).

Clarke, K. and Clarke, K., (1991), "Personnel Management, Defence, Retrenchment, Advance?", *Personnel Review*, Vol. 20, No. 1.

Clarke, P., (1989), "Payment by Result Schemes: A Review of Trends", *Industrial Relations News*, No. 8, 23.

Clegg, H., (1976), *Trade Unionism under Collective Bargaining, A Theory Based on Comparisons of Six Countries*, Blackwell.

Collins, D. and Sinclair, J., (1991), "The Skills Time Bomb": Parts 1–3, *Leadership and Organisation Development Journal*, Vol. 12, Nos. 1, 2 and 5.

Connolly, R., Hirsch, B. and Hirschey, M., (1985), *Union Rent Seeking, Intangible Capital and Market Value of the Firm*, Mimeo, University of North Carolina at Greensboro, January.

Cook, D. and Ferris, G., (1988), "Strategic Human Resource Management and Firm Effectiveness in Industries Experiencing Decline", *Human Resource Management*, Vol. 25, No. 3.

Cordova, E., (1988), "From Full-time Wage Employment to Atypical Employment: A Major Shift in the Evolution of Labour Relations", *International Labour Review*, Vol. 125, No. 6.

Croke, N., (1993), "Trade Union Membership Participation in Centralised Bargaining", *Industrial Relations News,* No. 2, 14.

Curran, J., (1986), *Bolton Fifteen Years On, A Review and Analysis of Small Business Research in Britain, 1971–1986*, Small Business Research Trust.

Curran, J. and Stanworth, J., (1981a), "The Social Dynamics of the Small Manufacturing Enterprise", *Journal of Management Studies*, Vol. 18, No. 2.

Curran, J. and Stanworth, J., (1981b), "Size of Workplace and Attitudes to Industrial Relations in the Printing and Electronics Industries", *British Journal of Industrial Relations*, Vol. 14.

Curran, J. and Stanworth, J., (1979), "Self Selection and the Small Firm Worker: A Critique and an Alternative View", *Sociology*, Vol. 13, September.

Curson, C., (1986), *Flexible Patterns of Work*, Institute of Personnel Management.

Daly, A., (1989), *Pay and Benefits in Irish Industry*, Federation of Irish Employers.

Dastmalachian, A., Blyton, P. and Adamson, R., (1991), *The Climate of Workplace Relations*, Routledge.

Davis, T., (1987), "How Personnel Can Lose its Cinderella Image", *Personnel Management*, March.

Deery, S. and De Cieri, H., (1991), "Determinants of Trade Union Membership in Australia", *British Journal of Industrial Relations*, Vol. 29, March.

Dineen, D. A., (1992), "Atypical Work Patterns in Ireland: Short-term Adjustments of Fundamental Changes", *Administration*, Vol. 40, No. 3, Autumn.

Dineen, D., (1988), *Changing Employment Patterns in Ireland: Recent Trends & Future Prospects*, University of Limerick.

Dineen, D., (1988), *Employment Developments in the Irish Economy Since 1979*, University of Limerick.

Disney, R., (1990), "Explanations of the Decline in Trade Union Density in Britain: An Appraisal", *British Journal of Industrial Relations*, Vol. 29, No. 2.

Doeringer, P. and Piore, M., (1971), *Internal Labour Markets and Manpower Analysis*, Lexington Books.

Donnelly, E., (1987), "The Training Model: A Time for Change?" *Industrial and Commercial Training*, May/June.

Drew, E., (1987), "New Structures of Work: An Irish Perspective", *International Journal of Manpower*, Vol. 6, No. 2.

Edwards, R., (1979), *Contested Terrain*, Basic Books.

Eichel, E. and Bender, H., (1984), *Performance Related Pay, A Study of Current Techniques*, American Management Association.

Elger, T., (1991), "Flexible Futures? New Technology and the Contemporary Transformation of Work", *Work, Employment and Society*, Vol. 1, No. 4.

Emery, F., (1980), "Designing Socio-technical Systems for Greenfield Sites", *Journal of Occupational Behaviour*, Vol. 1, No. 1.

Federated Union of Employers, (1984), "Profit Sharing", *FUE Bulletin*.

Fiorito, J., Lowman, C. and Nelson, F., (1987), "The Impact of Human Resource Policies on Union Organising", *Industrial Relations*, Vol. 26, No. 2, Spring.

Flood, P., (1989), *Human Resource Management: Promise, Possibility and Limitations,* University of Limerick.

Flood, P., (1990), "Atypical Employment: Core–Periphery Manpower Strategies — The Implications for Corporate Culture", *Industrial Relations News,* Nos. 9 and 10.

Flood, P., (1990), *Trends & Developments Affecting Personnel Management Practice in the 1980s,* University of Limerick.

Fombrun, C., Tichy, N. and Devanna, M., (1984), *Strategic Human Resource Management,* John Wiley & Sons.

Foulkes, F., (1980), *Personnel Policies in Large Non-union Companies,* Prentice Hall.

Fowler, A., (1990), "Performance Related Pay", *Personnel Management Plus,* June.

Fowler, A., (1988), "New Directions in Performance Pay", *Personnel Management,* November.

Fox, R., (1987), "Training of the Employed: Statistics for Ireland", *AnCo,* October.

Freeman, R. and Medoff, J., (1979), "The Two Faces of Unionism", *Public Interest,* No 57, Fall.

Freeman, R and Medoff, J., (1984), *What Do Unions Do?,* Basic Books.

Freeman, R. and Pelletier, J., (1990), "The Impact of Industrial Relations Legislation on British Union Density", *British Journal of Industrial Relations,* Vol. 28.

Garavan, T., (1990), "Strategic Human Resource Development: Characteristics, Conditions and Benefits", *Journal of European Industrial Training,* August.

Gill, D., (1973), *Performance Appraisal in Perspective, A Study Of Current Techniques,* Institute of Personnel Management.

Gill, D., (1977), *Appraising Performance: Present Trends and the Next Decade,* Institute of Personnel Management.

Goffee, R. and Scase, R., (1986), "Are the Rewards Worth the Effort? Changing Managerial Values in the 1980s", *Personnel Review,* Vol. 15, No. 4.

Goffee, R. and Scase, D., (1982), "Fraternalism and Paternalism as Employer Strategies in Small Firms", in Day, G., (ed.), *Diversity and Decomposition in the Labour Market,* Gower.

Golderberg, V., (1980), "Bridges over Contested Terrain, Exploring the Radical Account of the Employment Relationship", *Journal of Economic Behaviour and Organisation,* 1.

Gordon, D., Edwards, R. and Reich, M., (1982), *Segmented Work, Divided Workers,* Cambridge University Press.

Goss, D., (1988), "Social Harmony and the Small Firm: A Reappraisal", *Sociological Review*, Vol. 36, No. 1.

Goss, D., (1991), *Small Business and Society*, Routledge.

Goss, D. and Jones, R., (1991), "The Role of Training Strategy in Reducing Skills Shortages", *Personnel Review*, Vol. 20, No. 2.

Grafton, D., (1988), "Performance Related Pay: Securing Employee Trust", *Industrial Relations News*, 17 November.

Granovetter, M., (1984), "Small is Bountiful: Labor Markets and Establishment Size", *American Sociological Review*, 49.

Green, G., (1991), *Industrial Relations*, Pitman.

Guest, D., (1987), "Human Resource Management and Industrial Relations", *Journal of Management Studies*, Vol. 24, No. 5.

Guest, D., (1989), "Human Resource Management, Its Implications for Industrial Relations and Trade Unions" in Storey, J., (ed.), *New Perspectives on Human Resource Management*, Routledge and Kegan Paul.

Guest, D., (1989), "Personnel and HRM, Can You Tell the Difference?", *Personnel Management*, January.

Guest, D. and Rosenthal, P., (1992), "Industrial Relations in Greenfield Sites", Mimeo: Centre for Economic Performance, Industrial Relations Conference, London, March.

Gunnigle, P., (1989), "Management Approaches to Industrial Relations in the Small Firm", in *Industrial Relations in Ireland: Contemporary Issues and Developments*, University College Dublin.

Gunnigle, P., (1992a), "Management Approaches to Employee Relations in Greenfield Sites", *Journal of Irish Business and Administrative Research*, Vol. 13.

Gunnigle, P., (1992b), "Changing Management Approaches to Employee Relations in Ireland", *Employee Relations*, Vol. 14, No. 1.

Gunnigle, P., (1992c), "Human Resource Management in Ireland", *Employee Relations,* Vol. 14, No. 5.

Gunnigle, P., (1994), "Collectivism and the Management of Industrial Relations in Greenfield Sites", paper presented to the International Industrial Relations Association, Fourth European Congress, Helsinki, Finland, August.

Gunnigle, P. and Brady, T., (1984), "The Management of Industrial Relations in the Small Firm", *Employee Relations*, Vol. 6, No. 5.

Gunnigle, P. and Daly, A., (1992), "Craft Integration and Flexible Work Practices", *Industrial and Commercial Training*, Vol. 24, No. 10.

Gunnigle, P. and Flood, P., (1990), *Personnel Management in Ireland, Practice, Trends and Developments*, Dublin: Gill and Macmillan.

Hague, R., (1989), "Japanising Geordie-Land", *Employee Relations*, Vol. 11, No. 2.

Hakim, C., (1991), "Impact of Changing Employment Patterns on Manpower Policy", paper presented to Institute of Public Administration (Dublin), Conference on Industrial Relations Outlook and New Employment Patterns.

Hannaway, C., (1987), "New Style Collective Agreements — An Irish Approach", *Industrial Relations News*, Vol. 13.

Hannaway, C., (1992), "Why Irish Eyes are Smiling", *Personnel Management*, May.

Harrison, R., (1990), *Employee Development*, Institute of Personnel Management.

Hay Associates, (1975), *Survey of Human Resource Practices*, Hay Associates.

Henderson, J. and Johnson, B., (1974), "Labour Relations in the Smaller Firm", *Personnel Management*, December.

Hillery, B., (1989), "An Overview of the Irish Industrial Relations System", in *Industrial Relations in Ireland: Contemporary Issues and Developments*, University College Dublin.

Hirsch, B.T., (1980), "The Determinants of Unionisation, An Analysis of Inter-area Differences", *Industrial and Labour Relations Review*, Vol. 33.

Hirsch, B.T. and Addison, J.T., (1986), *The Economic Analysis of Unions: New Approaches and Evidence*, Unwin Hyman.

Hirsch, B.T. and Berger, M., (1984), "Union Membership Determination and Industry Characteristics", *Southern Economic Journal*, Vol. 1.

Hitchens, D. and O'Farrell, P., (1988), "The Comparative Performance of Small Manufacturing Companies Located in the Mid West and Northern Ireland", *The Economic and Social Review*, Vol. 19, No. 3.

Handy, C., (1984), "The Organisation Revolution and How to Harness it", *Personnel Management*, July.

Hoevemeyer, V., (1989), "Performance Based Compensation, Miracle or Waste", *Personnel Journal*, July.

Horwitz, F., (1990), "HRM, An Ideological Perspective", *Personnel Review*, Vol. 19, No. 2.

Ichiowski, C., (1986), "The Effects of Grievance Activity on Productivity", *Industrial and Labour Relations Review*, 40, (October).

Ingram, P. and Cahill, J., (1989), "Pay Determination in Private Manufacturing", *Department of Employment Gazette*, June.

IPC., (1986), *A Guide to Employee Shareholding through Profit Sharing*, Irish Productivity Centre.

Jacoby, S., (1984), "The Development of Internal Labor Markets in American Manufacturing Firms", in Osterman P., (ed.), *Internal Labor Markets*, MIT Press.

Kamoche, K., (1991), "Human Resource Management; A Multi Paradigmatic Analysis", *Personnel Review*, Vol. 20, No. 4.

Katz, H.C., Kochan, T.A. and Weber, M., (1985), "Assessing the Effects of Industrial Relations Systems and Efforts to Improve the Quality of Working on Organizational Effectiveness", *Academy of Management Journal*, 28, (September).

Keenan, J. and Thom, A., (1988), "The Future through the Keyhole, Some Thoughts on Employment Patterns", *Personnel Review*, Vol. 17, No. 1.

Keenoy, T., (1990), "HRM: A Case of the Wolf in Sheep's Clothing?" *Personnel Review*, Vol. 19, No. 2.

Kelly, A. and Brannick, T., (1985), "Industrial Relations Practices of Multinational Companies in Ireland", *Journal of Irish Business and Administrative Research*, Vol. 7, No. 1 .

Kelly, A. and Brannick, T., (1988a), "Explaining the Strike Proneness of British Companies in Ireland", *British Journal of Industrial Relations*, Vol. 26, No. 4.

Kelly, A. and Brannick, T., (1988b), "The Management of Human Resources: New Trends and the Challenge to Trade Unions", *Arena*, August.

Kelly, A. and Brannick, T., (1991), "The Impact of New Human Resource Management Policies on US MNC Strike Patterns", unpublished, University College Dublin.

Kenny, J. and Reid, M., (1986), *Training Interventions*, Institute of Personnel Management.

Kerr, C., (1954), "The Balkinisation of Labour Markets" in E.W. Bakke et al., *Labor Mobility and Economic Opportunity*, Cambridge, Mass.

Kets de Vries, M., (1977), "The Entrepreneurial Personality: A Person at the Crossroads", *Journal of Management Studies*, February.

Kleiner, M., (1990), "The Role of Industrial Relations in Industrial Performance", in Fossum, J.A., (ed.), *Employee and Labour Relations,* Bureau of National Affairs.

Kochan, T.A., Katz, H.C. and McKersie, R.B., (1986), *The Transformation of American Industrial Relations*, Basic Books.

Kochan, T. and Katz, H.C., (1988), *Collective Bargaining and Industrial Relations*, Irwin.

Kreckel, R., (1980), "Unequal Opportunity: Structures and Labour Market Segmentation", *Sociology*, Vol. 14, No. 4.

Lash, S. and Ury, J., (1988), *The End of Organised Capitalism*, Polity Press.

Lawler, E., (1988), "Human Resource Management, Meeting the New Challenge", *Personnel*, January.

Lawler, E., (1988), "Pay for Performance: Making it Work", *Personnel*, October.

Legge, K., (1988), "Human Resource Management — A Critical Analysis" in Storey, J., (ed.), *New Perspectives on Human Resource Management*, Routledge.

Lewis, C., (1984), "What's New in Selection?", *Personnel Management*, January.

Locker, A. and Teel, K., (1977), "Survey of Human Resource Practices", *Personnel Practices Journal*, March.

Lockwood, D., (1989), *The Black Coated Worker*, Clarendon.

Long, D., (1986), *Performance Appraisal Revisited*, Institute of Personnel Management.

Long, P., (1988), "A Review of Approved Profit Sharing (Trust), Schemes in Ireland and the UK", unpublished dissertation, College of Commerce, Dublin Institute of Technology.

Mace, J., (1979), "Internal Labour Markets for Engineers in British Industry", *British Journal of Industrial Relations*, 17.

Marchington, M., (1982), *Managing Industrial Relations*, McGraw Hill.

Marsden, D., (1990), "Institutions and Labour Mobility, Occupational and Internal Labour Markets in Britain, France, Italy and West Germany", in R. Brunetta and C. DellAringa (eds.), *Labour Relations and Economic Performance*, Macmillan.

McGovern, P., (1989), "Union Recognition and Union Avoidance in the 1980s", in *Industrial Relations in Ireland: Contemporary Issues and Developments*, University College Dublin.

McBeath G. and Rands, N., (1989), *Salary Administration* (4th Ed.), Gower.

McInnes, J., (1988), "The Question of Flexibility", *Personnel Review*, Vol. 17, No. 3.

McKay, L., (1987), "Personnel: Changes Disguising Decline", *Personnel Review*, Vol. 16, No. 5.

McMahon, G. et al., (1988), "Multinationals in Ireland Three Decades On", *Industrial Relations News*, 11 February.

McMahon, G., (1988), "Rush the Recruitment — Rue the Results", *Management*, February.

Metcalf, D., (1990), "Union Presence and Labour Productivity in British Manufacturing, A Reply to Nolan and Marginson", *British Journal of Industrial Relations*, Vol. 28, No. 2.

Millward, et al., (1992), *Workplace Industrial Relations in Transition*, Aldershot, Gore.

Milner, S. and Richards, E., (1991), "Determinants of Union Recognition and Employee Involvement: Evidence from the London Docklands", *British Journal of Industrial Relations*, Vol. 29, No. 3.

Monks, K., (1992), "Models of Personnel Management: A Means of Understanding the Diversity of Personnel Practices", *Human Resource Management Journal*.

Mooney, P., (1980), *An Inquiry into Wage Payment Systems in Ireland*, ESRI/European Foundation for the Improvement of Living and Working Conditions.

Moxon, G., (1951), *Functions of a Personnel Function*, Institute of Personnel Management.

Murray, S., (1984), *Employee Relations in Irish Private Sector Manufacturing Industry*, Industrial Development Authority.

NESC, (1984), *Building On Reality, (1985–1987)*, Government Publications Office.

Neumann, G., (1980), "The Predictability of Strikes: Evidence from the Stock Market", *Industrial and Labour Relations Review*, 33, July.

Newby, H., (1977), *The Deferential Worker*, Penguin.

O'Hagan, J., (1987), *The Economy of Ireland: Policy and Performance*, 5th Edition, Irish Management Institute.

O'Brien, J., (1989), "Pay Determination in Ireland", in *Industrial Relations in Ireland: Contemporary Issues and Developments*, University College Dublin.

O'Farrell, P.N. and Hitchens, D. (1990), *Small Firm Competitiveness and Performance*, Gill and Macmillan.

O'Farrell, P.N. and Hitchens, D., (1988), "The Relative Competitiveness and Performance of Small Manufacturing Companies in Scotland and the Mid-west of Ireland", *Regional Studies*, 22 (5).

Ost, E., (1990), "Team Based Pay: New Wave Incentives", *Sloan Management Review*, Spring.

Osterman, P., (1982), "Employment Structures within Firms", *British Journal of Industrial Relations*, November.

Osterman, P., (1984), "White Collar Labour Markets", in Osterman P., (ed.), *Internal Labour Markets*, MIT Press.

Osterman, P., (1987), "Choice of Employment Systems in Internal Labour Markets", *Industrial Relations Journal*, 26.

Parker, P., (1988), "IPM Conference — 21st/23rd October 1987", *Employee Relations*, Vol. 10, No. 4.

Peach, L., (1983), "Employee Relations in IBM", *Employee Relations* 5 (3).

Pearce, J., (1987), "Why Merit Pay Doesn't Work, Implications for Organisation Theory. in Balkin", D. and Gomez-Mejia L.(eds.), *New Perspectives on Compensation*, Prentice-Hall.

Peters, T. and Waterman, R., (1982), *In Search of Excellence*, Harper & Row.

Pettigrew, A., Hendry, C. and Sparrow, P., (1988), "The Forces that Trigger Training", *Personnel Management*, November.

Pfeffry J. and Cohen, Y., (1984), "Determinants of Internal Labour Markets in Organisations", *Administrative Science Quarterly*, 29.

Plumbley, P., (1985), *Recruitment and Selection*, London: Institute of Personnel Management.

Pollert, A., (1991), *Farewell to Flexibility?*, Blackwell.

Pollert, A., (1988), "The Flexible Firm: Fixation or Fact", *Work, Employment and Society*, Vol. 2, September.

Poole, M., (1984), *Theories of Trade Unionism*, Routledge and Kegan Paul.

Purcell, J., (1987), "Mapping Management Styles in Employee Relations", *Journal of Management Studies*, Vol. 24, No. 5.

Purcell, J., (1982), "Macho Managers and the New Industrial Relations", *Employee Relations*, Vol. 4, No. 1.

Rainnie, A., (1989), *Industrial Relations in Small Firms, Small isn't Beautiful*, Routledge.

Rainnie, A. and Scott, M., (1982), "Industrial Relations in the Small Firm", in Curran, J., Stanworth, J. and Watkins, D., (eds.), *The Survival of the Small Firm*, Volume 2, Gower.

Report of the Commission of Inquiry on Industrial Relations, (1981), Government Publications Office.

Reynolds Allen, K., (1991), "How Middle Managers View the Function", *Personnel Management*, June.

Robinson, O., (1984), "Part-time Employment & Industrial Relations Developments in the EEC", *Industrial Relations Journal*, Vol. 15, No. 4, Spring.

Roche, B., (1989), "State Strategies and the Politics of Industrial Relations in Ireland", in *Industrial Relations in Ireland: Contemporary Issues and Developments*, University College Dublin.

Roche, B., (1990a), "Trade Unions in Ireland in the 1980s", *European Industrial Relations Review*, No. 176.

Roche, B., (1990b), "Industrial Relations Research in Ireland and the Trade Union Interest", paper presented to the Irish Congress of Trades Unions Conference on Joint Research between Trade Unions, Universities, Third Level Colleges and Research Institutes, Dublin.

Roche, B., (1991), "The Future of Trade Unions — SIPTU Seminar Examines the Issues", *Industrial Relations News*, 25 April.

Roche, B., (1992), "Modelling Trade Union Growth and Decline in the Republic of Ireland", *Irish Business and Administrative Research*, Vol. 14.

Roche, B. and Larragy, J., (1989), "The Trend of Unionisation in the Irish Republic", in *Industrial Relations in Ireland: Contemporary Issues and Developments*, University College Dublin.

Roche, B. and Larragy, J., (1990), "Cyclical and Institutional Determinants of Annual Trade Union Growth and Decline in Ireland: Evidence from the DUES Data Series", *European Sociological Review*, No. 6.

Roche, W., (1992), "The Liberal Theory of Industrialism and the Development of Industrial Relations in Ireland", in Goldthorpe, J. and Whelan, C., *The Development of Industrial Society in Ireland*, Oxford University Press.

Roots, P., (1988), *Financial Incentives for Employees*, BSP Professional Books.

Ruane, F. and McGibney, A., (1991), "The Performance of Overseas Industry", in Foley A. and McAleese, D., *Overseas Industry in Ireland*, Gill and Macmillan.

Ruback, R. and Zimmerman, M., (1984), "Unionization and Profitability: Evidence from the Capital Market", *Journal of Political Economy*, 6, December.

Sanfilippo, F., Weigman, G. and Giblin, E., (1991), "A Compensation Strategy For the 1990s", *Human Resources Professional*, Vol. 4, No. 1, Fall.

Sargent, A., (1990), *Turning People On : The Motivation Challenge*, Institute of Personnel Management.

Schuler, R. and Walker, J., (1990), "Human Resource Strategy: Focusing on Issues and Actions", *Organisation Dynamics*, Summer.

Schuler, R., (1992), "Strategic Human Resource Management: Linking the People with the Strategic Needs of the Business", *Organisational Dynamics*, Summer.

Scott, M., Roberts, I., Holroyd, G. and Sawbridge, D., (1989), "Management and Industrial Relations in Small Firms", UK Department of Employment, Research Paper No. 70, HMSO

Shivanath, G., (1986), "Personnel Practitioners, Their Role and Status in Irish Industry", unpublished MBS thesis, University of Limerick.

Sisson, K., (1991), "Industrial Relations: Challenges and Opportunities", *Employee Relations*, Vol. 13, No. 6.

Smith, P. and Morton, G., (1993), "Union Exclusion and the Decollecti-
visation of Industrial Relations in Great Britain", *British Journal of
Industrial Relations*, Vol. 32, No. 1.

Smith, M., Gregg, M. and Robertson, I., (1988), *Selection & Assessment
— A New Appraisal*, Pitman.

Stanworth, J. and Gray, C., (eds.), (1991), *Bolton 20 Years On: The Small
Firm in the 1990s*, Paul Chapman.

Storey, D., (1982), *Entrepreneurs and the New Firm*, Croom Helm.

Storey, J., (1989), *New Perspectives on Human Resource Management*,
Routledge and Kegan Paul.

Storey, J., (1989), "Introduction: From Personnel Management to Human
Resource Management", in Storey, J., (ed.), *Developments in the
Management of Human Resources*, Blackwell.

Storey, J., (1992), *Developments in the Management of Human
Resources*, Blackwell.

Suttle, S., (1988), "Labour Market Flexibility", *Industrial Relations
News*, No. 38.

Thomas, S. and Kleiner, M., (1989), "Two-Tier Collective Bargaining
Arrangements and Shareholder Equity", unpublished manuscript,
University of Minnesota.

Thornicroft, K., (1991), "Promises Kept, Promises Broken: Reciprocity
and the Scanlon Plan", *Employee Relations*, Vol. 13, No. 5.

Tolbert, P. and Zucker, L., (1983), "Institutional Sources of Change in the
Formal Structure of Organisations, The Diffusion of Civil Service
Reform, 1880–1935", *Administrative Science Quarterly*, 28.

Toner, W., (1985), "The Unionisation and Productivity Debate: An
Employee Opinion Survey in Ireland", *British Journal of Industrial
Relations*, Vol. 23, No 2.

Toner, W., (1987), "Union or Non-union? Contemporary Employee
Relations Strategies in the Republic of Ireland", PhD, London School
of Economics.

Torrington, D., (1986), "Will Consultants Take Over the Personnel Function?", *Personnel Management*, March.

Torrington, D., (1988), "How Does Human Resource Management
Change the Personnel Function?", *Personnel Review*, Vol. 17, No. 6.

Torrington, D. and Hall, L., (1987), *Personnel Management: A New
Approach*, Prentice Hall.

Tyson, S. and Fell, A., (1986), *Evaluating The Personnel Function*,
Hutchinson.

Tyson, S., (1987), "The Management of the Personnel Function", *Journal
of Management Studies*, September.

Wallace, J., (1982), *Industrial Relations in Limerick City and Environs*, University of Limerick.

Walton, R., (1985), "From Control to Commitment in the Workplace", Harvard Business Review, March/April.

Watson, H. et al., (1990), *Executive Search & The European Recruitment Market*, Economist Publications.

Webster, B., (1990), "Beyond the Mechanistics of HRD", *Personnel Management*, Vol. 22, No. 3, March.

Whitaker, A., (1986), "Managerial Strategy and Industrial Relations: A Case Study of Plant Relocation", *Journal of Management Studies*, Vol. 23, No. 6.

Zalusky, J., (1991), "Labor Seeks Security Not Bonuses", *Personnel*, January.